NATO

IN SEARCH OF A VISION

NATO

IN SEARCH OF A VISION

GÜLNUR AYBET
and
REBECCA R. MOORE
Editors

FOREWORD BY LAWRENCE FREEDMAN

Georgetown University Press
Washington, D.C.

Georgetown University Press, Washington, D.C. www.press.georgetown.edu

Library of Congress Cataloging-in-Publication Data

Aybet, Gülnur.
    NATO in search of a vision / Gülnur Aybet and Rebecca R. Moore; foreword by
Lawrence Freedman.
    p. cm.
Includes bibliographical references and index.
ISBN 978-1-58901-630-9 (pbk. : alk. paper)
    1. North Atlantic Treaty Organization. 2. North Atlantic Treaty Organization—
Membership. 3. Security, International. 4. National security—Europe. 5. World
politics—21st century. I. Moore, Rebecca R. II. Title.
UA646.3.A935   2010
355′.031091821—dc22

                                                        2009024822

15 14 13 12 11 10   9 8 7 6 5 4 3 2
First printing

Printed in the United States of America

For our parents

CONTENTS

FOREWORD

This timely collection of essays comes out as NATO enters its seventh decade, asking itself, as it has done for much of its existence, how to adapt to ensure a useful future. The questions are almost as old as the Alliance. What changes is the context.

I recall my very first "whither NATO" conference, which I attended while a research student at Oxford in early 1974. This was a time when the U.S. and U.K. governments had been enfeebled by internal political developments and were facing "stagflation" as high energy prices triggered both inflation and recession. There was a deep sense of new power centers emerging in the Middle East (because of oil) and East Asia (because of industrial productivity). The Soviet Union was perceived to be getting militarily stronger, manipulating the West in the name of arms control and détente while looking to build up new strongholds in the developing world. I remember being fascinated as a senior British diplomat sought to reassure the representatives from other NATO member countries that the old leftists in the new Labour Party government would make no difference to Alliance commitments, and then being taken aside by another British diplomat to explain that I should be more welcoming of the Greek and Portuguese military dictatorships as members of NATO, even though they were unhelpful in terms of the rhetoric about the "free world." Within weeks the Portuguese regime was overthrown, and by the end of the year the Greek Colonels were out as well. With the accession of post-Franco Spain, NATO really did look more like an Alliance of democratic nations (although I also recall listening in astonishment as the U.S. secretary of defense described the Portuguese revolution as being a "blow to the free world").

I mention all this not just to show that there is nothing new in stories of NATO's disarray, nor even to note how misplaced most of the fears of the 1970s turned out to be. To the vulnerability of NATO's southern flank, the flabbiness of Western democracy, the inexorable rise of the Organization of the Petroleum Exporting Countries, and Soviet inroads into the developing world were added fears of a "standing start" attack by the Warsaw Pact members and talk of fancy Soviet nuclear strikes against U.S. intercontinental ballistic missiles that would render the United States unable to respond. My point is that contrary to so much contemporary commentary, there was never a period of a contented and coherent Cold War–era NATO when everything was clear-cut and stable, which meant that as long as the Alliance carried on as before with a mixture of détente and defense and balanced forces, plus occasional references to nuclear deterrence, the Warsaw Pact states would not try anything foolish and governments could concentrate on peaceful pursuits. NATO's history during the Cold War was one of regular disputes— over colonialism; German rearmament; nuclear strategy and flexible response; burden sharing; the relevance of conflicts outside Europe, especially in the Middle East; and how to deal with political stirrings in Eastern Europe.

By 1989 NATO had developed an identity and value that went beyond the Cold War logic that had created it. Instead of falling apart, as was regularly predicted, it went from strength to strength, particularly as it found key roles in addressing Europe's new security concerns, expanding in order to provide an institutional framework for the postcommunist states (before the European Union was able to cope), and then getting increasingly involved in the conflicts surrounding the breakup of the former Yugoslavia, culminating in the Kosovo war of 1999. In retrospect we can see that it began to get ahead of itself, taking on operations in Afghanistan without being fully aware of the nature of the commitment and its capacity to cope, and then being too casual about the potential implications of its expansion to Ukraine and Georgia, given Russia's evident irritation that its security concerns were being neglected.

NATO may now be tempted into a period of consolidation before it makes any more bold moves. But events may not allow this. Until the Afghanistan situation is resolved, it is hard to see how NATO can be sure of itself, whereas those states that have recently escaped from the Russian sphere of influence want the Alliance to make its first priority ensuring that they are not drawn back in.

It is in the nature of these issues facing NATO that they are more likely to be managed than resolved, which is why the debates surrounding the efforts to develop a new Strategic Concept may be more useful and illuminating than the concept itself. There is nothing wrong with creative tension between different notions of alliance and assessments of contemporary security challenges. There may be little point, for example, in trying to set down strict guidelines on the circumstances in which nuclear weapons will be used, because the idea is that they should never be used. There can be a strong presumption that they can only deter nuclear attacks by others, and it is hard to make the case that nuclear use should be prepared for any other contingencies. Nonetheless, any hostile power will not be able to ignore the thought that any major war with Alliance countries could set in motion a chain of events that could result in inadvertent nuclear use. Equally, it is hard to be too definitive about a renewed focus on the geopolitics of Europe at the expense of expeditionary warfare when upheavals in, for example, North Africa might suddenly require urgent attention.

What is always useful is to remember the great advantage that NATO brings to its members as a longtime Alliance. When trying to prevent a conflict or preparing for one that appears unavoidable, the first priority is to acquire allies. Yet these are normally the worst circumstances in which to put together a coalition. The fact that the Alliance is already in place, with established command structures and operating procedures, is an enormous plus. One of the explanations for the character of NATO's perpetual strategic debate and self-examination is that it starts at a point that might in other circumstances be the intended destination. The concern is always to prevent deconstruction rather than how to begin construction.

For policymakers and for students of NATO who are seeking to get beyond the headlines of disarray but are aware of the challenges ahead in a changing international environment, *NATO in Search of a Vision* provides an excellent guide. The editors have brought together some of the top names in the field to address the most pressing issues facing the Alliance with high-quality analyses and seriousness of purpose.

Lawrence Freedman
King's College, London

ACKNOWLEDGMENTS

Our sincere thanks go to Richard Brown, director of Georgetown University Press, for the support and trust he placed in our project from its inception. We are also deeply indebted to our acquisitions editor at the press, Don Jacobs, who kept us on track with sound advice and valuable suggestions that improved the text considerably. We thank all our contributors for sharing their expertise with us and for making this an even better volume than we initially envisaged. We would also like to thank the anonymous reviewers who enriched the text with their valuable suggestions.

A special thanks is due to Chantal de Jonge Oudraat for offering useful insights and identifying areas for improvement while serving as our discussant during a panel devoted to the book at the International Studies Association conference in New York in 2009. We are grateful as well to the International Staff at NATO Headquarters for responding so generously to our requests for interviews and to the Woodrow Wilson International Center for Scholars for providing such a conducive and scholarly environment in which to work during the project's final stages. Finally, we can say that this volume, which was conceived and edited from both sides of the Atlantic and which has benefited from the knowledge and wisdom of both European and American scholars and policymakers, truly is an exercise in transatlantic dialogue.

INTRODUCTION

Missions in Search of a Vision

Gülnur Aybet and Rebecca R. Moore

A$_S$ THE NORTH ATLANTIC TREATY ORGANIZATION, NATO, enters its seventh decade, it finds itself busier than at any time in its history. Not only is the Alliance involved in an array of military missions, widely ranging in scope and geographical area from Afghanistan to Sudan; NATO also stands at the center of a host of regional and global partnerships now increasingly focused on equipping it to address the new global challenges that it confronts in the post–Cold War, post–September 11, 2001, world. Yet despite NATO's wider engagement in these global missions and partnerships, it remains troubled by the absence of a grand strategic vision to guide its activities into the twenty-first century.

NATO demonstrated a newfound sense of political purpose in the early 1990s, first by reaching out to its former adversaries in Central and Eastern Europe and then by adopting a collective security role, beginning with its "out of area" operations in Bosnia and Kosovo. However, since the terrorist attacks on the United States on September 11, 2001, these roles have been overtaken by the intensification of NATO's mission-driven evolution and transformation, including its adoption of global military missions from the Balkans to Afghanistan. To some degree, this is a consequence of the demands placed on NATO as the only existing institution with an integrated military structure. This mission-driven focus, however, has eclipsed the importance of the Alliance's normative origins and the role of the liberal democratic values embedded in the preamble to the original North Atlantic Treaty in defining both NATO's identity and larger political purpose. In short, rather than looking to the values at its core to determine its missions, since the late 1990s NATO has permitted itself to be defined by its missions.

1

This trend is troubling, because NATO has always been something more than the sum of its members and its capabilities. Although its main function was to provide a system of collective defense to integrate and pacify Western Europe in the immediate post–World War II period, it also formed the core of a larger project that involved the creation and preservation of a new post-war order. But this was not entirely NATO's mission alone; nor was it taken up only by its member states. Rather, NATO represented a broader security community and a concept of the West not necessarily confined even to Europe. The idea of NATO as a values-based community was also critical to its evolution during the 1990s and the project of building a new European security order. That project was predicated on an assumption that the tools necessary to build a Europe that was "whole, free, and at peace" were as much political as military in nature. Indeed, NATO would ultimately pursue its vision through the creation of new values-based partnerships and institutions, including the Partnership for Peace and the Euro-Atlantic Partnership Council, and, ultimately, its enlargement. The success of its partnership initiatives during the 1990s subsequently led it to seek partnerships beyond the borders of Europe in the form of the Mediterranean Dialogue and the Istanbul Cooperation Initiative.

However, despite NATO's successes in contributing to the integration and democratization of the states of Central and Eastern Europe, the vision that guided its transformation during the 1990s now confronts multiple challenges. One of these challenges arrived on September 11 in the form of international terrorism—a threat that transcended the traditional understanding of security as deriving from the military capability of states. The al-Qaeda attacks on the United States also prompted the first-ever invocation of Article 5 of the North Atlantic Treaty (which is NATO's collective defense clause)—an ironic development, given the Cold War–era presumption that Western Europe depended on the United States in matters of security and defense.

September 11 thus revealed the fundamentally altered nature of NATO's strategic environment—an environment now populated by a variety of increasingly global and less predictable threats, ranging from the proliferation of weapons of mass destruction to failed states to the rise of global terrorism. As several Washington-based think tanks concluded in a joint report on NATO's future issued in February 2009, "the global has become local," and the well-being of the Alliance's member states will be "increasingly influenced by flows of people, money and weapons, good and services, technology, toxins and terror, drugs and disease." The report further suggested that "the networked nature of modern societies" now requires "reconsideration of what, exactly, needs protecting in today's world," a discussion that is vital to adapting NATO's collective defense mission to its new strategic environment.[1]

The September 11 terrorist attacks, however, also clearly revealed that NATO was ill prepared militarily for the security challenges its members now confronted, thereby prompting the United States to push during NATO's 2002 Prague Summit for a new focus on military transformation, which would include "new capabilities" and "new partners" as well as "new members."[2] The focus on capabilities, specifically, led to the adoption of NATO's Prague Capabilities Commitment, which identified priority categories for which improved military capabilities were required. Additionally, NATO authorized the development of a new, rapidly deployable NATO Response Force.

However, NATO's Prague Summit was ultimately about more than new capabilities. The George W. Bush administration in the United States was also determined to use the summit to focus NATO's attention beyond Europe. As the former U.S. ambassador to NATO, Nicholas Burns, explained, the Bush administration sought to "pivot the new NATO from its prior inward focus on threats within Europe to a new outward spotlight on the recent challenges to peace in the arc of countries from South and Central Asia to the Middle East and North Africa."[3] Less than a year after the summit, on April 16, 2003, NATO agreed to assume command responsibility for the International Security Assistance Force in Afghanistan. In late May 2003, NATO also agreed to provide logistical support to Poland, so that it might assume command responsibility for a peacekeeping sector in central Iraq. These decisions appeared to move the Alliance beyond the out-of-area debates that had divided the United States and Europe during the 1990s toward an understanding that threats would now need to be addressed from a functional rather than geographical perspective. As NATO's then–secretary-general, Lord Robertson, explained in late 2002, NATO's new security environment no longer gave its members "the luxury of fighting theoretical battles about what is 'in' and what is 'out of area.'" Rather, he stressed, NATO would have to be prepared "to act wherever our security and the safety of our people demand action."[4]

As suggested above, the attention devoted at NATO's Prague Summit to the need for new capabilities as well as NATO's new ventures outside Europe reflected important steps in its continuing transformation, but they did not reflect the articulation of a new, larger strategic vision—beyond the creation of a Europe, whole, free, and at peace—that would assist NATO's members in determining how, when, and where any new capabilities should be used or its relationships with other actors, such as the European Union and the United Nations. Rather, NATO's new out-of-area missions were largely tactical ventures, stemming from a recognition that these situations would benefit from its capabilities. Indeed, NATO still functions under its 1999 Strategic Concept, which predated the events of September 11 and, as its members recognized at their 2009 Summit in Strasbourg-Kehl, must now be replaced. Although the process of completing the integration of the rest of Europe into Euro-Atlantic structures has continued with NATO's admission of Albania and Croatia to membership in 2009, that vision is no longer sufficient to sustain the Alliance in a dramatically transformed strategic environment.

At the same time, however, NATO must grapple with the fact that Russia, with its military intervention in Georgia in the summer of 2008, has directly challenged the hitherto-unstoppable eastward expansion of the Euro-Atlantic community, and thereby the 1990s project of expanding a Western system of normative values with like-minded governments bonded to each other through the power of international institutions. Russia's intervention, and its subsequent recognition of the breakaway Georgian republics of South Ossetia and Abkhazia, which NATO condemned, have thus created a dilemma for the West in dealing with the ever-growing discrepancy between the realpolitik of regional geopolitics and the expansionary nature of a global system of values and norms based on Western-led principles of democracy, human rights, and free markets—the last of which has also been seriously challenged by the global financial crisis. As the foreign ministers of NATO's member states recognized in December 2008, though dialogue and cooperation through the NATO–Russia Council . . . remained important to addressing "common security threats and challenges . . . in a partnership based on common values, the lack of a shared commitment to those values must naturally cause the relationship and the scope for cooperative action to suffer."[5]

Yet it is also clear that Russia's actions have revealed a division within NATO over the balance between maintaining a cooperative relationship with Russia and the project of enlarging the Euro-Atlantic community. Indeed, this rift was already evident during NATO's 2008 Bucharest Summit, at which Germany and France, among other member states, refused to support the United States' bid to extend immediate invitations to Georgia and Ukraine to join NATO's Membership Action Plan, due largely to concerns about antagonizing a Russia on which Europe has become increasingly energy dependent. Russia's intervention in Georgia several months later, however, led to the establishment of a NATO–Georgia Commission and then a compromise several months later at the December 2008 meeting of the NATO members' foreign ministers, whereby it was agreed that Georgia and Ukraine would develop annual national programs aimed at advancing the reforms essential for NATO membership within the context of the existing NATO–Ukraine and NATO–Georgia commissions.[6] The agreement essentially deferred the decisions of how and when Georgia and Ukraine would become NATO members, but Germany reportedly remained unhappy with the terms of the compromise.[7]

NATO's internal divisions are also not limited to its relations with Russia. As is well known, NATO faces enormous challenges in Afghanistan, which some commentators now view as the key test of its continuing relevance. Although the United States has appealed repeatedly for NATO's European members to commit more troops to the International Security Assistance Force (ISAF) mission, there have been few significant increases in troop contributions. Moreover, at least some of NATO's European members continue to impose caveats on the location of their troop deployments that are aimed at reducing the chances that these forces will actually be involved in combat. These caveats have challenged NATO's solidarity by raising questions about whether the burdens of the ISAF mission are being fairly shared among its members. At the same time, a number of non-NATO, non-European states—such as Australia, New Zealand, Japan, and South Korea—have made significant contributions to the ISAF mission in the form of troop deployments or other forms of logistical support. Although NATO has welcomed this assistance and demonstrated a desire to enhance its cooperation with what have generally come to be known as its "global partners," the extent to which it should institutionalize this cooperation has also become a source of disagreement among its members.

Indeed, the fact that NATO has gone out of area in terms of both its military missions and its partnerships should not be seen as suggesting that a consensus has emerged within NATO as to just how "global" it should become. Some of its members, in fact, continue to resist giving it a truly global political and military role in favor of a more minimalist interpretation of its function. One concern these members have raised is that NATO's out-of-area missions have distracted it from its core function—the collective defense of its members' territories. The challenge for those members favoring a more global role is to reconcile its new missions with its traditional collective defense role. At the same time, however, those advocating a narrower role must explain what collective defense means in the context of a new strategic environment where regional threats can quickly become global.

These and a variety of other issues discussed in this volume will no doubt figure in NATO's drafting of its new Strategic Concept, although reaching a consensus will likely prove difficult. Indeed, one of the common themes that emerges from the chapters that follow is a recognition that some NATO members have avoided a concentrated discussion of many of these issues on the assumption that the Alliance works better in practice than it does in theory. This volume, however, suggests that NATO is increasingly hobbled by its ad hoc approach in the absence of a larger strategic vision. The process of drafting a new Strategic Concept represents an opportunity for it to shape a new, common transatlantic vision—one anchored in the normative principles so crucial to its successes during the Cold War and immediate post–Cold War eras but also designed to guide its continuing evolution from Cold War Alliance toward an increasingly complex political-military institution equipped to anticipate and address increasingly global and less predictable threats and challenges.

Structure of the Work

The contributors to this volume examine the key issues that will undoubtedly shape NATO's vision, while addressing the means whereby it can tackle the immediate and real challenges of the post–September 11 world. Hence the chapters in this volume not only provide an assessment of NATO's evolution thus far but also an analysis of where it must go if it is to remain relevant in the twenty-first century.

In chapter 1 Jamie Shea offers a NATO insider's perspective on the challenges and opportunities that the Alliance confronts in drafting a Strategic Concept for the twenty-first century. He devotes particular attention to two seemingly contradictory priorities: NATO's need to be an organizer of expeditionary missions beyond the territories of its members (including the Balkans and Afghanistan) while reassuring many of its member states that it is taking its Article 5 collective defense obligations seriously. He also discusses NATO's current operation in Afghanistan and analyzes the lessons to be learned as the Alliance adapts to being a contributor to stabilization and nation-building tasks.

In chapter 2 Gülnur Aybet suggests that the nature of NATO's 1991 and 1999 Strategic Concepts has contributed to its post–Cold War role, which has been driven largely by its military missions rather than a grand strategy or common transatlantic vision. This is because during this period, NATO acted as a "provider" within a larger Western grand strategy, which had a two-pronged purpose—first, exporting the norms and values of its security community to the former Warsaw Pact member states; and second, creating a system of collective security. This grand strategy is now outdated in the post–September 11 world. Aybet explains why NATO now needs a new comprehensive grand strategy and not simply an updating of its 1999 Strategic Concept. She argues that the development of this new Strategic Concept must begin with NATO's core values and principles and outline the kinds of tasks necessary to fulfill these values and principles in a new strategic environment, including the necessity for NATO to serve as a transatlantic forum for the discussion of global security issues beyond its ongoing missions.

In chapter 3 Ryan Hendrickson offers a comparative assessment of the role of NATO's secretaries-general in shaping a common strategic vision for the Alliance. He concludes that its post–Cold War secretaries-general have played an increasingly important institutional role in shaping its strategic direction. The chapter includes an examination of the more expansive institutional role played by Jaap de Hoop Scheffer as secretary-general, which reflects NATO's continuing evolution.

In chapter 4 Friis Arne Petersen, Hans Binnendijk, Charles Barry, and Peter Nielsen focus on the development of NATO's Comprehensive Approach to civil–military cooperation. They argue that the question is no longer whether NATO needs such an approach but rather how to define its content. And they thus explore how Europe and the United States can work together on joint training, sharing lessons learned, and generating best practices in this area, not only to ensure that military forces and civilians in the field share a common approach but also to harmonize the oversight, objectives, and resources of every country and institution engaged.

In chapter 5 Martin Smith considers possible future trajectories for NATO–Russia relations with reference to the course of the relationship thus far. In particular, he explores the breakdown of relations during the 1999 Kosovo crisis and the crisis that resulted from Russia's intervention in Georgia in 2008. On the basis of the subsequent reconstitution of NATO–Russia relations following the Kosovo crisis, he concludes that the prospects for both the survival and revival of NATO–Russia relations are surprisingly good.

In chapter 6 Sean Kay explores the impact on the NATO–Russia relationship of NATO's decision to endorse the development of European missile defense programs for deployment in Poland and the Czech Republic. He examines the primary rationales for these systems and concludes that NATO is incurring high costs in one set of security relationships with Russia to address a separate threat that is as yet undefined or undeveloped. He thus recommends a major revision of NATO's approach to missile defense and offers an alternative approach.

In chapter 7 Roger Kanet addresses four interrelated questions that are linked to NATO's expansion eastward to incorporate former Soviet client states and, later, states that emerged from the dissolution of the Soviet Union itself. First, he examines the degree to which NATO's eastward expansion has contributed to the deterioration in Russia's relations with the West. Second, he discusses the deterrent effect of Russia's opposition to Georgia and Ukraine's NATO accession on NATO's further expansion eastward. Third, he considers the likely impact of NATO's new central European and Baltic members on its future policy toward Russia, given their heightened level of security concern in the aftermath of the Georgian crisis. Fourth, given the serious existing tensions between both the United States and some of its key European Allies, which are also NATO members, and between these same Allies and the new members of NATO and the European Union, he discusses the likely impact of the NATO–Russia relationship on the future of transatlantic relations and the nature of NATO itself.

In chapter 8 Gabriele Cascone focuses on NATO's efforts to integrate the states of the Western Balkans nearly two decades after the breakup of Yugoslavia. He examines NATO's enlargement process and mechanisms, the main requirements and country-specific requirements demanded of NATO aspirants, the connection between this process and concurrent processes from other organizations (chiefly the EU), the results achieved so far, and prospects for the future. He also examines some of NATO's unfinished business in the region, chiefly its relationship with Serbia and the possible development of links and cooperative programs with Kosovo.

In chapter 9 Jeffrey Simon examines two social and economic factors that are likely to influence the development of the transatlantic relationship—the shift from large European conscript armed forces to smaller all-volunteer forces, and diverging transatlantic views on the military's role in providing defense and security. He also explores the future impact on NATO of four aspects of demography: the increasing pressures on the cohort available for European defense establishments, the United States' and Europe's diverging immigration patterns and changing social composition, diverging aging populations and its economic implications, and the changing global population mix and resulting political and economic impact. He concludes that these six diverging factors are likely to have a significant effect on Washington's and Brussels' future views of NATO's importance, its future role, and the transatlantic relationship.

In chapter 10 Rebecca Moore examines the impact of NATO's partnerships, both regional and global, on its continuing evolution and transformation. She observes that, as NATO's partnerships have multiplied, the growing diversity of their members has served to generate difficult questions about the partnerships' structures and purposes. The debate over NATO's so-called global partners, in particular, has raised the issue of whether NATO should move away from the traditional model of regionally based partnerships and toward a more functionalist approach. She concludes that this debate is about much more than the structure of NATO's partnerships. At a much more fundamental level, it is a debate over NATO's very purpose and identity.

The conclusion, by Gülnur Aybet and Rebecca Moore, evaluates the issues explored in the book's ten chapters in light of two dilemmas facing NATO today: the reemergence of regional geopolitics, and the need for NATO to find a common transatlantic vision that is based on the normative values of its inception rather than the mission-driven raison d'être that has prevailed during the post–Cold War era. These dilemmas signify the turning point that NATO has reached, and many of the challenges it now faces are laid out in the issue-specific focus of each chapter. The essential choice that NATO must now confront is whether to focus more on territorial collective defense or on global missions, which are both humanitarian and peace-building operations but nevertheless impinge on the security of it member states, given the transglobal nature of threats emanating from international terrorism and the potential proliferation of weapons of mass destruction to failed states.

Although these intra-NATO debates are presented as choices, NATO's options might be more limited than some suggest. The Alliance is essentially a collective defense organization, and its core mission is to provide territorial defense for its members. At the same time, security is now defined by a plethora of global factors, to the extent that global missions are not just a continuation of NATO's collective security function, which was developed in the early 1990s, but also have a direct impact on the security of its member states. That said, as several of the contributors to this volume acknowledge, it is going to be increasingly difficult for NATO to undertake missions out of its area, in places like Afghanistan, unless it effectively synchronizes its functional efforts with those of other organizations such as the European Union and the United Nations.

Notes

1. See the report of the Washington NATO Project: Daniel Hamilton, Charles Barry, Hans Binnendijk, Stephen Flanagan, Julianne Smith, and James Townsend, *Alliance Reborn: An Atlantic Compact for the 21st Century* (Washington, DC: Atlantic Council of the United States, Center for Strategic and International Studies, Center for Technology and National Security Policy at the National Defense University, and

Center for Transatlantic Relations at the Paul H. Nitze School of Advanced International Studies of Johns Hopkins University, 2009), www.acus.org/files/publica tion_pdfs/65/NATO-AllianceReborn.pdf, 6. The Washington NATO Project was launched by the four U.S. think tanks that published this report to "spark debate before and after NATO's sixtieth-anniversary summit in April 2009."

2. Marc Grossman, "21st Century NATO: New Capabilities, New Members, New Relationships," *U.S. Foreign Policy Agenda* 7 (U.S. Department of State), no. 1 (March 2002): 8.

3. R. Nicholas Burns, "The New NATO: Healing the Rift," speech to the Konrad Adenauer Foundation, May 27, 2003.

4. Lord Robertson, "NATO: A Vision for 2012," speech at a conference sponsored by the German Marshall Fund of the United States, Brussels, October 3, 2002, www.nato.int/docu/speech/2002/s021003a.htm.

5. NATO, "Final Communiqué, Meeting of the North Atlantic Council at the Level of Foreign Ministers Held at NATO Headquarters," Brussels, Press Release (2008) 153, December 3, 2008, www.nato.int/docu/pr2008/p08–153e.html.

6. Ibid.

7. Steven Erlanger, "NATO Duel Centers on Georgia and Ukraine," *New York Times*, December 1, 2008.

CHAPTER 1

NATO at Sixty—and Beyond

Jamie Shea

For SEVERAL DECADES, NATO has represented something of a paradox: An Alliance that is generally seen as being permanently in crisis reaches yet another milestone of longevity. Twenty years have passed since the Berlin Wall came down and a Soviet analyst, Giorgy Arbatov, famously jibed that the Soviet Union had dealt NATO a death blow by taking away its enemy. On the contrary, the Alliance has been enlarged, become globalized, and become involved in more activities in more parts of the world than its founding fathers could ever have envisioned. At NATO's Summit in April 2009 in Strasbourg-Kehl, its leaders welcomed two new members, Albania and Croatia; noted that after an absence of nearly half a century, France would return to its integrated military structure; and felt sufficiently confident about its long-term future to initiate the preparation of a new Strategic Concept. The hundreds of seminars and thousands of scholarly articles, op-eds, and editorials that are devoted each year to agonizing over NATO's problems stand in puzzling contrast to its ability to just soldier on and add yet another decade and summit celebration to its already impressive life span.

This chapter explores the historical evolution of NATO's "acquis atlantique" and how it can be preserved and moved forward in an era of multiple challenges. Though NATO needs to address the immediate challenges it faces related to the proliferation of nuclear weapons, its relations with Russia, and its ongoing mission in Afghanistan, it also needs to develop a common vision for the future—including a common threat assessment that achieves a balance between the requirements of Article 4 (political consultations) and Article 5 (collective defense) of the Washington Treaty.

Forging a Consensus from Crises: The Cold War Experience

Certainly, all historians of NATO understand that there has never been anything easy or automatic about its evolution. Its successive transformations have often been preceded by bitter internal debates. It sometimes seems to need to go through a period of disarray as a precondition for later reemerging stronger and more purposeful. For instance, in the 1940s, its American founding fathers hotly contested whether a Western Europe falling under the strategic shadow of the Soviet Union needed a short-term economic shot in the arm or a long-term military pact. It took more than a year to persuade a skeptical Congress, where even convinced internationalists were worried about Europe's long-term dependence on the United States, to accept the permanent commitment to Europe that the North Atlantic Treaty implied. Even then the Senate would not accept an automatic obligation to use force as part of the treaty's mutual assistance clause, Article 5, which accordingly had to be watered down. And the Harry Truman administration still found it very difficult to provide its new European Allies with military equipment because Congress feared that such supplies would only weaken the Europeans' willingness to increase their own defense budgets. However, at every critical moment when the treaty seemed to be doomed, Joseph Stalin, somewhat providentially, engineered an East/West crisis that temporarily cowed its critics and helped to keep the proposal for a transatlantic pact alive. The Berlin Blockade and the Prague coup d'état in 1948 combined with the Soviet first atomic bomb test in 1949 to persuade the Truman administration and Congress that the Marshall Plan's economic aid would not bear fruit if the United States was not first and foremost ready to underwrite the military security of Western Europe.

The second great crisis occurred in the early 1950s, when the outbreak of the Korean War finally put the "O" into NATO—in other words, it forced the still-reluctant United States to convert the paper guarantees of the Washington Treaty into an actual organization—with a peacetime headquarters, a command structure, a secretary-general, a U.S.-chosen but European-located supreme Allied commander, and, inevitably, civilian as well as military bureaucracies. The nineteenth-century Italian nationalist Massimo d'Azeglio once proclaimed that he had to first make Italy in order to make Italians. NATO went the other way round; it first created the Allies and only some years later created a functioning Alliance. The paradox was that this emerging NATO structure—originally located in Paris at the Place du Trocadéro and in Fontainebleau, in the heart of France, which would later become the NATO dissident—was the creation of a war in Asia and not in Europe. Had that Asian war not broken out in Korea, the U.S. secretary of state, Dean Acheson, and the Truman administration would have found it much harder to break their promise to never send U.S. forces to Europe, notwithstanding the creation of NATO.

Other famous crises characterized NATO's next decades, each time threatening to undermine an institution that always depended more on the "entente cordiale" among its members than on the size and strength of its organization. The first crisis occurred already in the 1950s, when the United States pushed the French into proposing the European Defense Community (EDC) as the way to place German troops at NATO's disposal and to facilitate America's concentration on the war in Korea. John Foster Dulles, the U.S. secretary of state, threatened the Europeans with an "agonizing reappraisal" of the U.S. commitment if they voted down the EDC. In the event, the French National Assembly did precisely this in August 1954; but instead of weakening NATO, the failure of the EDC project positively strengthened it. The Germans were brought into NATO in 1955, the United States increased its forces in Europe by more than a division and then brought in thousands of tactical nuclear weapons, the British agreed to station an Army of the Rhine in northern West Germany, and the prospect of a purely European defense identity replacing NATO in the long run disappeared for several generations. Heeding the lessons of the EDC, European statesmen relaunched the European project in Messina a year later with the idea of economic integration and a common market (the European Economic Community) rather than a common European army directed by a single supranational European authority, as provided by the failed EDC Treaty.[1]

The 1960s witnessed another major rift within NATO, when it had to respond to France's attempt to either gain a seat at its top table (Charles de Gaulle's great-power "Directoire") or leave it altogether. The French decision to withdraw from NATO's integrated military structure in 1966 was all the more painful because it exposed two other fault lines in the Alliance at that time: a disagreement between the United States and Europe over the desire of Robert McNamara, the U.S. defense secretary, to reduce the role of nuclear weapons in NATO's strategy (Europeans feared this might make their continent "safe" for a conventional war); and the unhappiness of the small Alliance member states at their lack of a voice and role in NATO's discussions, particularly in exploring détente with the Soviet Union.

De Gaulle's decision to partially withdraw from NATO in 1966 cleared the way for the Harmel Report of 1967, which for the first time gave NATO a political role in seeking security with the East through negotiation, confidence building, and arms control as much as through deterrence, military exercises, and the occasional nuclear modernization program.[2] The Harmel exercise, by creating more space in the Alliance for political consultations, also gave its smaller members a voice and a sense of belonging that a set of military arrangements alone had previously denied them. But it could also be argued that France's partial withdrawal, by burying the notion of the Directoire, was just as important in upgrading the role of the small Allies. They could offer political insights and show solidarity even if they could not offer many troops.

Another crisis-driven nadir was reached in the late 1970s, when NATO's members were obliged to reluctantly give up détente—a comfortable if ultimately unproductive policy—in order to face up to a more intimidating Soviet Union. NATO's dual-track decision of 1979 proposed to deploy nuclear weapons carried by Cruise and Pershing missiles in Europe in response to the Soviet deployment of SS20 missiles. At the same time, the Alliance offered to negotiate, through U.S.–Soviet arms control talks, a reduction in the levels of these weapons on both sides—although no NATO planner at the time would ever have dreamed of the ultimate outcome of the zero-zero option enshrined in the later Intermediate-Range Nuclear Force (INF) Treaty of December 1987.

At the time of the dual-track decision in 1979, NATO's opponents believed all too readily that the offer of arms control talks was nothing but a fig leaf to disguise the United States' firm intention to modernize NATO's nuclear arsenal in Europe. The Soviet Union had begun first with its SS20 missile deployments, had taken advantage of détente to back a number of its allies in Africa, and, for the first time since 1945, had sent its forces outside its Cold War boundaries to invade a neutral state, Afghanistan, thereby dealing a death blow to détente and the ratification of the Second Strategic Arms Limitations Talks (SALT) treaty by the U.S. Congress. Yet for the peace movements in NATO's member countries, the Cruise and Pershing missiles were more the cause of the return to Cold War conditions in Europe than the symptom of increased tensions. The next few years were to rock the Alliance as Western European governments had to contend with massive antinuclear protests and the defection of many left-wing European parties away from the prevailing political consensus on defense strategies toward the East. The "INF saga," as it came to be known, cost Chancellor Helmut Schmidt control over his own Social Democratic Party in West Germany. And the other NATO members' governments also wobbled as the year for the deployment of the missiles—1983—approached.[3]

Once again, however, crisis brought unexpected benefits. After years of anticipating more and more détente against the backdrop of a permanent military status quo, NATO had demonstrated that it could return to 1950s-style vigilance if necessary. France, which supported the INF deployments by West Germany and others, showed, as it had done at the time of the construction of the Berlin Wall in August 1961 and the Cuban missile crisis in October 1962, that in a time of crisis it would instinctively draw back to NATO's center ground. The Alliance's governments finally decided to respond publicly to the arguments of the peace movements and to the abundant Soviet propaganda. The actual deployment of some Cruise missiles in the United Kingdom, Germany, and Italy in late 1983 produced a "fait accompli," which led the peace movements to fade away remarkably quickly. President Ronald Reagan's "zero-zero" option, which many had dismissed as a propaganda stunt to make a realistic arms control result less likely, ultimately turned out to be the basis for the INF Treaty. The NATO members' governments, by pulling together at a difficult time, achieved the double benefit of strengthening military containment and totally removing hundreds of very unpopular, controversial nuclear weapons. The anticommunist right and the pacifist left emerged equally satisfied. What was significant about the INF Treaty was not so much its unprecedented arms reductions but its extensive verification provisions, including onsite inspections. If the Soviet Union was willing to accept these intrusive verification and transparency measures, then surely the suspicions and distrust that had fed the Cold War must be waning. Viewed from this perspective, NATO's INF crisis in the early 1980s was one of the most productive in its entire history. Yet, and not for the first time, it was based on a paradox: The acceptance of escalation was the key to a peaceful outcome. If the Alliance was not prepared to face up to its adversaries head-on, it could never hope to persuade them to cooperate. The specter of Afghanistan was perhaps already present in the difficult debate over the INF strategy in the early 1980s.

NATO's New Missions and the Balkan Crisis of the 1990s

As we draw closer to the present, we see the same pattern of NATO's "crisis of the decade." In the 1990s there were in fact two crisis points: one caused by the "catastrophic success" of the end of communism in the USSR in 1990–91, when the challenge to NATO came from the overfulfillment of its objectives rather than failure or stagnation; and the second in the form of the collapse of Yugoslavia in 1991–92, when NATO had to decide whether to move "out of area or out of business" (as U.S. senator Richard Lugar famously put it) and use its forces not to defend its members' territories but to impose peace on their peripheries.[4] In hindsight, and somewhat ironically, the conflict in Yugoslavia was more important for NATO's post–Cold War evolution that the collapse of the Warsaw Pact and the Soviet Union. As a political-military organization, whose forte is to use military power to bring about peaceful international outcomes, NATO needs military challenges. Otherwise what purpose would its military capabilities and political-military culture serve?

At one level, the fall of the Berlin Wall twenty years ago was a fitting vindication of NATO and a retroactive endorsement of most of what it had undertaken and stood for. It could then have gone out on a high note, or at least been downsized to something significantly smaller than what we have today. No doubt the Treaty of Washington would have survived (who in today's circumstances would wish to give up a U.S. security guarantee?); but NATO might well have contracted to something more closely resembling its structure in the early 1950s, before the full impact of the Korean War began to be felt. A permanent peace in Europe after 1989 would have given NATO a role in partnership activities, security sector reform, and exercises and training as the old adversaries of the Warsaw Pact grew economically and politically closer to Western Europe. But how long could NATO have claimed a front rank in the world's system of international institutions on the basis of managing a secure peace rather than of dealing with crises and intractable conflicts? Those who invest in NATO's stock are not devotees of Emmanuel Kant's "perpetual peace" or of what some believe is the increasing obsolescence of military force as the dominant element in crisis management and conflict resolution.

The Balkan crisis of the 1990s was perhaps the most bitter and protracted in all of NATO's history. Many of the usual ingredients were present. The United States and the European nations differed over strategy—the United States wishing to use air power against the Bosnian Serbs or alternatively Belgrade and to take sides in the conflict, but the Europeans opting for even-handedness and a UN peacekeeping force on the ground. Some viewed the conflict in Bosnia as a civil war based on ancient feuds and hatreds that had to be allowed to burn themselves out before international peacemaking had a chance of succeeding beyond the short-lived cease-fire agreements. Others perceived a Kuwait-style instance of international aggression, an attempt to change borders and populations by force, which had to be militarily resisted to prevent setting terrible precedents and killing any hope for a post-1989 "New World Order." Some put their faith in negotiation backed by vague threats to use force; others were convinced that NATO had to use force first to restore its tarnished credibility and lay the basis for real negotiations, undergirded by the credible prospect of a major NATO intervention.

NATO's old dividing lines were thus supplemented by new ones—about its role in the post–Cold War world. Would it move from "being" (deterrence) to "acting" (intervention)? Thus far, it had been good at preventing conflicts; would it be as successful at fighting them? Would its new out-of-area role be essentially a timid and secondary one, in support of leading actors such as the United Nations or the Organization for Security and Cooperation in Europe, or would it be able to prepare politically to take on the primary roles of first responder and chief enforcer, with all their implied risks and responsibilities for winning the peace? During the Cold War, the comfort of deterrence was that it was unlikely to be tested, allowing NATO to maximize its strengths and minimize its weaknesses. As Napoleon often stressed, "On s'engage et puis on voit." Action has a way of making a mockery of the best-laid plans. It tends to do the opposite of deterrence—expose weaknesses and minimize strengths. Nuclear deterrence may never have worked very convincingly in theory, but it turned out to work very well in practice. Conversely, and on paper at least, NATO seemed massively superior to the Serbs and its Balkan opponents; but would superiority on paper easily translate into NATO victories on the battlefield? The Kosovo air campaign of 1999, lasting seventy-eight days, showed that such assumptions were highly vulnerable to real events.

This said, the Balkan crisis once again turned out to be a blessing for NATO. The Alliance was good for the Balkans, but the Balkans were perhaps even more beneficial for it. They were the proving ground where the Alliance could adapt to its major new post–Cold War role: organizing peace support operations beyond its members' territories and learning to specialize not only in the techniques of conflict termination (naval embargoes, no-fly zones, and air campaigns) but also of peace implementation (ground forces turning "mission creep" into a full spectrum of tasks beyond more patrolling—from disarming militias to the reconstruction of roads and railways). As NATO was learning these things, it manifestly did make many mistakes—not anticipating the collapse of Yugoslavia and being totally absent from the initial international crisis prevention efforts; not intervening early enough, as when Dubrovnik was shelled by the Bosnia Serbs in the spring of 1991; not having confidence for too long in the only real asset at its disposal, the use of its multinational military force to stop a conflict; and perhaps most damagingly, agreeing to "dual key" arrangements, whereby it subcontracted its air assets and ultimately its credibility to the United Nations, which had a very different approach to peacemaking strategy in Bosnia.

Despite all these mistakes, however, to paraphrase Winston Churchill, having done all the wrong things, NATO ultimately did all the right ones. Thus, when Kosovo imploded in March 1998, NATO had learned its lessons—its threats to use force were made credible and were much more tightly linked to its international crisis management and negotiation strategy; it had the benefit of a focused United States and Europe; it made a much more concerted effort to analyze the dynamics of the conflict and to reach a common analysis; and finally it showed a willingness to escalate through the use of a ground offensive which, contrary to Bosnia, made it much more difficult for Slobodan Milošević and Belgrade to determine where the limits of the Alliance's determination and readiness to use force actually lay.

"Bosnia alive or NATO dead," the U.S. columnist William Safire had written in 1994.[5] For a long time NATO seemed to be losing its way in the Balkan conflicts—even to be losing for a while to Milošević during the Kosovo air campaign of 1999. Yet it emerged from these conflicts with a new role and with its prestige immeasurably enhanced. Not only had the Europeans painfully emerged from their post–Cold War "peace dividend" euphoria or "strategic vacation," but the United States had also become prepared to revise its doctrine of overwhelming force in clearly defined conflicts and accept a new military role in peace support and stabilization operations. The U.S. secretary of state, Condoleezza Rice, might later have expressed her skepticism about using the 101st Airborne Division to "escort kids to school," but NATO had nonetheless emerged with a new purpose and a new transformation agenda. In contrast to the former situation, France had participated in the Kosovo air campaign as the second-largest contributor, and Germany had crossed the Rubicon in sending its forces into combat action for the first time since 1945. What could hold NATO back in the future?

This historical recapitulation clearly shows that NATO is either good at escaping from crises or uncannily skillful in using them to good effect. History also demonstrates that as an organization, it is better able to resolve its difficulties through action, and the bottom-up pressure of events, rather than through theoretical discussions or new treaty-drafting exercises. In this respect, it is very different from the European Union, which is based more on the top-down, constitutional approach. If something works in practice, who cares whether it works in theory? Yet the purpose of this historical overview is to bring out a more fundamental point. In each decade of NATO's existence, an external or internal crisis (ultimately, they tend to be one and the same) has placed it at a turning point—and after a period of drift and uncertainty, and of looking for cheap, quick-fix solutions to its problems, its leaders have had to decide whether to renew and re-resource it or allow it to drift into obsolescence. Thus NATO has always reached a fork in the road requiring strong political leaders who can make the decisions needed to guide it in adapting to new circumstances and move it from a phase of introspection and self-doubt into one of clarity and a sense of shared purpose. As ever in the past, such decisions do not make themselves. Ultimately, then, its leaders must use the Alliance. They cannot hide behind it.

Multiple Challenges, One Vision

Today, NATO marks another anniversary decade beset by formidable challenges and problems—how to rise to the challenge in Afghanistan to avoid the first strategic defeat in its history; how to salvage its post–Cold War cooperative relationship with Russia and prevent Russia from becoming a new factor of division between the Allies; how to extricate its troops from the Balkans, where they have already stayed longer than anyone would have predicted in 1999; and how to define its role in a world of multiple security challenges that have no obvious military solutions and where it seems to provide part but no longer all the answers. NATO's forte has always been coming to grips with strategic complexity and learning how to integrate all the facets of an issue into a single strategy. But this time around, will it be overwhelmed by these complexities?

In truth, as NATO reaches sixty years of age, it must confront two related challenges that are both somewhat paradoxical. In the first place, its "good" news is that it has no shortage of things to do. The world is a dangerous place. There will always be states and nonstate actors that challenge the basis of international order. Even small-scale threats, such as rampant piracy in the Gulf of Aden, and natural disasters, such as an earthquake in Kashmir, require a multinational military response that NATO is still well able to provide. And of course more serious threats, such as the proliferation of nuclear weapons in the wake of the Iranian and North Korean reprocessing and missile programs, also loom on the horizon. NATO should be actively discussing these threats and palliatives such as missile defense well before Europe once again becomes vulnerable to catastrophic attack. Yet the abundance of challenges with which NATO can help in principle does not mean that its member countries are actually willing to use it as their preferred instrument to discuss these challenges and arrive at common responses. Too often these days, it seems to be involved in an issue or a region only after it has deployed troops there. Too often, and despite deploying thousands of its forces and even becoming more exposed than other international organizations in a particular conflict zone, it is not sufficiently engaged in the international diplomacy or strategy aimed at achieving a political settlement.

The first challenge for NATO's leaders in adapting the Alliance to meet the potential crises of the twenty-first century is therefore to broaden its strategic consultations to include any issue, in whatever region, that affects the security of any member or all the Allies and to better use the North Atlantic Council not just to exchange information or oversee its current operations but also to coordinate transatlantic policy in dealing with such issues. NATO cannot be simply a troop provider or a "taxi company" that provides peace support capabilities at the request or under the mandate of other organizations. Moreover, it cannot be reduced to only its operations or whatever it does militarily. The security challenges of the twenty-first century are so multiple, interconnected, and potentially destructive that a strategy of reacting only after the event will not work. Anticipation, preventive diplomacy, and a prioritization of efforts according to where the threats are most pressing will become increasingly crucial to a viable security strategy.

Quite simply, NATO must expand its political horizons and use the North Atlantic Council for much more than discussing issues that are immediately linked to the prospect of its taking military action. Thus both Americans and Europeans need to invest more in the council as a consultation and policy coordination forum and cease trying to do this work bilaterally outside NATO's structures. Conversely, if the Allies have not been collectively involved in the elaboration of a policy or decision, it will be increasingly difficult for them to implement it with their military forces. A pattern of selective implementation on an à la carte basis, undermining the principles of solidarity and equitable burden sharing, is too often the consequence, as we see today in Afghanistan. In this respect, it is ironic that as NATO has sent its forces to more and more parts of the world, its political horizons have in fact narrowed. But now is the time to put the political before the military, and to put strategy before action. A situation like that whereby NATO deployed forces in Afghanistan in August 2003 but only produced a comprehensive political-military strategy for that nation at its 2008 Bucharest Summit should not occur again.

NATO's second fundamental problem lies not in the unique assets that it still possesses but in the lack of trust that many Allies today feel about whether it will meet their security needs and expectations. "Will NATO really support me in Afghanistan?" ask some. "Will NATO really uphold its Article 5 treaty commitment to the defense of my territorial integrity?" ask others. "Is NATO devoting enough time and attention to the particular challenges I face in my region—whether the High North, the Black Sea, or the Mediterranean—even though these may be far from the priorities of the other Allies?" is another often-heard refrain inside NATO Headquarters. If NATO is felt to be a jack of all trades by many of its members, they may underinvest in its capabilities and operations in order to keep something back for their strictly national purposes. NATO is consequently threatened by a vicious circle, in which declining national engagements could over time make it less effective, thereby accelerating more of the very disengagement that is so detrimental to it, because it relies on mostly voluntary national contributions to carry out all its operations, training, or partnership programs. Thus, at a recent conference on NATO's future sponsored by the Ditchley Foundation in the United Kingdom, the high-level discussion centered largely on this question: "Is Afghanistan a cause of the decline of NATO, or is the decline of NATO a reason for the lack of progress in stabilizing Afghanistan?"[6]

As stated above, NATO retains unique assets—an integrated military structure, first-class planning staffs and deployable headquarters, a military transformation program, common capabilities, the ability to plug into its operations a wide spectrum of partners from as far afield as Australia and New Zealand, and a well-oiled political-military consultation structure. Yet if its stakeholders, and especially its larger member states, come to feel that they are being asked to contribute to it collectively more than they obtain from it individually—in terms of having their security needs and expectations fully met—they will be tempted to do the minimum for it, underinvest in it, and progressively hollow it out.

Past success is therefore no guarantee of, or even guide to, future performance. As NATO reaches sixty and looks ahead to its next decade, how can it escape from the vicious circle of increasing ambitions for it and demands upon it, matched by decreasing solidarity and national contributions? In short, how can it escape the fate of the League of Nations and so many other once-promising multilateral security organizations—strong on principle but weak on collective follow-up—that marked the history of the last century?

The answer lies in a two-phased response. The first is for NATO to deal quickly with the three most pressing and divisive issues that it already faces in its sixtieth-anniversary year. The second is to give itself the time and political space to think in depth about its basic, underlying choices before developing a new Strategic Concept for the twenty-first century.

To begin with, NATO must extract from each of its twenty-eight member states an endorsement of its existing "acquis atlantique." In recent months, many of its debates have had a reductionist, either/or quality. Those committed to Afghanistan have tended to downplay the importance of reassuring the Baltic states about the robustness of their Article 5 territorial guarantee. Vice versa, to visit the Baltic states for a NATO security conference these days is to often hear protracted debates about Russia and Article 5 or cyberdefense, with barely a mention of Afghanistan, Africa, the Mediterranean, or the other areas of interest. Those who advocate NATO's enlargement to Ukraine or Georgia are frequently pitched in an artificial either/or debate against those who favor more dialogue and cooperation with Russia. The most corrosive element in any alliance is when its members begin to specialize politically; in other words, they show interest only in their own immediate issues and priorities and refuse to engage constructively in those of fellow allies. Camps or factions begin to appear that spend more time confronting each other than charting a common course for the organization. The common denominator exemplified in such famous slogans of the past as "one team, one mission" and "in together, out together" begins to fray.

NATO arrived at its current "acquis atlantique" painfully, as we have seen from the historical overview given above. Consequently, it could not be a credible security organization these days if it returned to the old Europe-centric alliance of the Cold War era focused exclusively on collective defense. That is not where the most immediate and dangerous threats lie. The satisfaction of its smaller members would be short-lived once its larger members, which are inevitably focused on the global picture, began to lose interest. In the twenty-first century, initiatives promoting transformation abroad will be increasingly necessary for its members to enjoy peace and stability at home—just as its military forces trained and equipped for expeditionary missions in Afghanistan and the surrounding region would also be the ones best suited for the rapid reinforcement of its borders in an Article 5 crisis. NATO must prepare for both types of operations—for its internal consensus as well as for its relevance as a multilateral security provider. And thus it needs to have many real and necessary debates. The best thing that it can do is to avoid squandering precious time and effort in a false and futile discussion about the priority accorded to Article 5 over expeditionary operations. Success in Afghanistan will make it far less likely that major attacks in Europe or against Europe will arise in the future. In short, NATO's future deterrent value is tied as much to success in its present endeavors as to its preparation for future contingencies.

Whether or not one believes that NATO's future depends solely upon the success of its International Security Assistance Force (ISAF) mission in Afghanistan, clearly its overwhelming priority in 2009 and the near future must be to obtain better results from the massive effort in personnel and money that it has made there since 2003. Nothing succeeds like success, but this is several years off in Afghanistan, given that the country is in a far worse state of destruction and dilapidation than anything the Alliance ever encountered in the Balkans—it needs to be built, rather than rebuilt, and virtually from scratch. As NATO already learned from intervening in the 1990s in the former Yugoslavia, it can only achieve a real and lasting impact when its leaders realize that there is no cheap, quick-fix solution and they resolve to commit the resources needed to do the job properly. An early conclusion is that nothing happens without security and that it is difficult to pursue both security and reconstruction simultaneously in the hope that the one will have a positive impact on the other. In truth, as ISAF's experience has shown, efforts to ensure security must be countrywide and felt very much at the local level before any major and lasting reconstruction can go ahead. The local Afghans tend to prefer to sit on the fence and wait to see who will emerge as the clear winner. Although it will be unpalatable for those Allies that have branded their contribution to ISAF essentially in terms of reconstruction and development to acknowledge that the operation is increasingly concentrating on counterinsurgency and preventing the Taliban from infiltrating from Pakistan, there really seems to be little choice if Kabul and the international community are to preserve all the progress of recent years in education, democracy building, women's rights, and infrastructure refurbishment. Those nationalist Taliban elements that are not beholden to al-Qaeda will not give up the fight unless they are convinced that they cannot succeed and the Afghan government is able to negotiate from a position of strength.

No one can contest that Afghanistan needs a civilian surge to help with governance, police reform, alternative livelihoods to poppy production, and the like. Ultimate success, as elsewhere, will depend on the military focus on peace building progressively giving way to civilian reconstruction and Afghan ownership of residual security tasks. But we are obviously still far from this stage, and moving prematurely to a civilian surge at the expense of deploying more U.S. and NATO troops would be prejudicial to NATO's ultimate success. At this stage, it would not be fair to say that troop levels are adequate or that a civilian contribution would have, proportionally, the equivalent value of an additional combat battalion, medivac helicopter, or operational mentoring and liaison team that trains the Afghan National Army. Counterinsurgency experts frequently point out that NATO has far fewer forces in Afghanistan per resident of the nation than it ever had in the Balkans (international aid per capita is also a fraction of the Balkans level). Moreover, around a hundred "caveats" or operational restrictions imposed by contributing nations limit the uses to which the troops that are sent can be put, further fueling debates about burden sharing and prompting the U.S. secretary of defense, Robert Gates, to warn of a "two-tier Alliance." At a time when the Barack Obama administration is reviewing the overall NATO strategy in Afghanistan and considering whether to increase U.S. troop levels by some 30,000 in 2009 alone, it will be difficult for the European Allies not to match this effort through additional force contributions of their own. The problem, in this regard, is that many European states, such as the United Kingdom, France, and Poland, already sizably increased their forces in 2008 under the George W. Bush administration, thereby not leaving them with much room to maneuver in 2009.

The problem in the long run for NATO is not, however, essentially one of military deployment, no matter how useful it would be for its members to lift their caveats, find more enablers such as helicopters and engineering units, and reorganize ISAF to be more a theater-wide task force and less an amalgam of national units concentrated on their provincial bases of operations. The real problem is that success in Afghanistan is largely outside NATO's control, even if it runs a textbook military operation. Achieving security, especially in the south, will only be feasible if the other major institutions—such as the United Nations, the European Union, and the World Bank—accord Afghanistan the same priority as NATO currently does and are ready and able to push ahead with governance and reconstruction as soon as NATO has stabilized the security environment. In the past it has proved easier for these other institutions to obtain contributions from NATO (e.g., for the UN in Kashmir, or for the EU in Bosnia) than vice versa.

The "Comprehensive Approach" of major institutions and civilian and military players working closely together is now NATO's official doctrine for all its non–Article 5 missions, but contrary to its past experience with transformation, this has proved easier to postulate in theory than to implement in practice. Organizations prefer to coordinate rather than to be coordinated. The Afghan aid effort has been described by Richard Holbrooke as the most wasteful, duplicated, and uncoordinated effort he has witnessed in a lifetime of dealing with internal conflicts.[7] Moreover, the military and civilian cultures are still far apart, making on-the-ground coordination difficult. Over time, the experience of Afghanistan will undoubtedly lead the United States and other Allies to invest more in civilian reconstruction expertise and rapid response civilian capabilities able to operate for long periods in dangerous areas. But this will take time as well as resources, leaving the Comprehensive Approach as a work in progress as far as the ISAF mission in Afghanistan is concerned. One of the most useful things that President Obama can do for NATO is not only to increase U.S. forces in southern and eastern Afghanistan but also to use some of his international political capital to persuade Afghanistan and Pakistan to cooperate more closely on cross-border security and the UN, EU, World Bank, and other actors to put Afghanistan higher up on their priority list. This said, the willingness of the Allies to come together on Afghanistan in 2009 and to develop an effective counterinsurgency strategy together with Pakistan will go some way toward calming the internal situation within the Alliance.

Of equal importance will be the willingness of NATO's member nations to contribute extra forces on a temporary basis to secure the Afghan elections in August 2009, which are needed not only to lock in the democratic gains of 2003–4 but also to reinvigorate the political process in Afghanistan. Additional funds and equipment as well as trainers are also needed if NATO is to meet its goal of forming a robust Afghan National Army able to take over major security responsibilities within six years. Naturally it is not easy for the Allies to countenance extra spending on two fronts at the same time—for more NATO troops as well as a larger Afghan National Army Trust Fund and training program. But, as so often in the past, the willingness to spend more for a short period is the key to achieving savings and force reductions in the medium term.

The way to progress in Afghanistan will be a long and winding road, but the urgent need is for the Allies to break the sense of deadlock and stalemate in the fight against the Taliban in the south, even if, as General David Petraeus has pointed out, the security situation may get worse before it gets better. The publics of NATO's member nations will not stay the course unless they sense that it has turned the strategic corner against the Taliban. A clear, publicly articulated strategy based on realistic and attainable objectives and a transparent political framework to reconcile Afghans will be key to this objective. The United States in particular will need to hear more from the Europeans that they are in Afghanistan because preventing the reemergence of al-Qaeda's training camps is also in their fundamental security interest. Too frequently the Europeans imply that they are in Afghanistan first and foremost to prove their loyalty to NATO and America. Solidarity is a fine thing, but NATO operations that are based primarily on a sense of mutual obligation (and a "you scratch my back and I'll scratch yours" attitude) rather than on shared threats and security interests are unlikely to be successful.

NATO's third and final immediate challenge is how to deal with Russia. It would be wrong to base the Alliance's future credibility on the achievement of a cooperative, relaxed relationship with Russia. It takes two to tango, and Russia in its current nationalistic and assertive mood, and with its opposition to core NATO policies such as enlargement, may not desire a truly cooperative relationship, no matter how sincerely and often Brussels extends the hand of friendship to Moscow. "Cooperative containment," as one analyst has put it, may be the only realistic option. NATO may well find, however, that the current global financial crisis and economic downturn will reduce

Russia's swagger as its budget contracts rapidly in the wake of declining oil and gas prices. In time Moscow may hopefully come to see that it needs the NATO Allies as much as it has believed in recent years that they need it—for transit routes to Afghanistan, to secure their energy supplies, to fight terrorism, and to put pressure on Iran to curb its reprocessing activities. Future NATO–Russia accommodation may therefore still be possible and thus rekindle the hopes of all those who dreamed of a strategic partnership after the Cold War. Yet a number of contentious issues may well delay such an understanding for some time—including arguments over missile defense in Europe, Kosovo's independence, NATO's assistance to Ukraine and Georgia, and Russian president Dmitry Medvedev's ideas for a new Europe Security Treaty, which seem calculated to reduce NATO's autonomy and role. For some time, then, a NATO–Russia partnership will be an aspiration rather than a fact.

This said, NATO's urgent priority is not to allow Russia to divide it. Russia is an increasing factor—Banquo's ghost at the banquet—in many NATO debates: enlargement, missile defense, Afghanistan, energy security, cyberdefense, and arms control policy, to name only the most obvious. If NATO's member states are divided on their approach to Russia, it will be consequently difficult for them to make progress on many of these core twenty-first-century security tasks. Thus a crucial challenge in 2009 and the near future is for its member states to either agree to disagree on Russia and forge a consensus on tactical issues or, better still, agree to a framework for handling Russia in discussions with Moscow in the NATO–Russia Council. Avoiding exaggerated rhetoric about "common values" and "partnership" where it is not justified (and does not make such things come true simply by being invoked so often) would be a starting point. Defining common interests would be the next step, especially in areas where Russia shows a real readiness to work with NATO. The third step would be for NATO to establish a better order of priorities for working with Russia, together with a clear definition of its red lines, so that Russia does not play some Allies off against others.

In a context where Russia may be simultaneously NATO's partner and competitor, the Alliance's unity will be, as it was in the past, the precondition for success in dealing with Russia, as will a willingness to negotiate outcomes rather than assume that dialogue in itself will produce a meeting of minds. What would help NATO would be for its members to agree on a common analysis of where Russia is today and the exact content of its strategic, foreign policy, and military objectives. As long as every NATO member has a different national analysis of what Russia is and where it is going—some seeing a badly treated or humiliated but still-pluralist country, others a resurgent and assertive power—forging a common NATO position will be difficult; but avoiding an intellectual effort to reach a shared analysis is not an option if NATO is to function optimally.

Moreover, NATO needs to become more self-confident about dealing with Russia—it does not need to be the *demandeur* where Russia is concerned. In this respect, for prime example, Russia has shown as much interest in restarting the NATO–Russia dialogue since the conflict in Georgia in August 2008 as has NATO. And a number of other pressing issues should keep the NATO–Russia Council busy well into the future—the looming arms control agenda, with the need to define successors to the SALT/Strategic Arms Reduction Treaty nuclear arms accords; the future of the Second Conventional Armed Forces in Europe Treaty on conventional weapons; further confidence-building measures as Russia sends its aircraft and ships farther afield; and the future of the Non-Proliferation Treaty regime, as Russia switches from wanting to pressure the United States to becoming aware of the dangers to Russia itself from nuclear-armed states on its borders.

In the near future, then, NATO would be best advised to immediately relieve these three pressure points described above—how to preserve the acquis atlantique, alleviate the conflict in Afghanistan, and renew its relationships with Russia—before it embarks on the even more fundamental exercise of drafting its new Strategic Concept. Once it has met these three pressing challenges, it will be in a better collective frame of mind to take a hard and fresh look at its underlying issues and choices. The issues it faces are complex, and it should give itself the necessary time to think them through. By contrast, if it succumbed to the temptation to go for a quick fix and hastily revamped its current Strategic Concept that dates back to 1999, it would hardly be likely to produce a document that would help it move forward and stand the test of time.

What, then, are the big issues that NATO will need to debate when it starts work on its new Strategic Concept? Specialists at security conferences generally come up with a well-known shopping list of challenges that range from defining NATO's added value in tackling the new threats from proliferation, terrorism, and energy cut-offs to pushing ahead with NATO's military transformation through more common capabilities and funding and by completing its Response Force. But for this author at least, a truly worthwhile Strategic Concept exercise needs to go a level deeper and dispassionately examine the philosophical and doctrinal issues underlying the Alliance's current malaise.

One such issue concerns the "utility of force," to borrow a term from General Rupert Smith. What distinguishes NATO is its capacity to use force multilaterally in ways that achieve its political objectives at an acceptable cost. Without this capacity, it would not have had the influence or impact on world affairs—whether in the Fulda Gap, the Balkans, or Afghanistan—that it fairly claims. Nearly all its uses of force before Afghanistan were still in the "war without tears" category. The "Revolution in Military Affairs" of the 1990s promised zero casualty conflicts (at least on the NATO side), essentially through the use of air power. Ground troops were not needed until a peace was at hand. During the decade following the Dayton Peace Accords, NATO's member countries sent hundreds of thousands of soldiers to Bosnia and Kosovo. Not one has so far been killed as the result of hostile action. Training or road accidents have constituted greater dangers. Due to this efficient use of force, NATO's stock as an international conflict solver has risen considerably.

But Afghanistan marks the end of this period of "war without tears." It resembles far more the colonial conflicts of an earlier era, with nearly 1,100 Allied soldiers having been killed in action at the time of writing. Already Kosovo gave NATO a warning of the problem to come. Thousands of high-technology missiles were fired at Serb forces, but only fourteen tanks were destroyed. The actual damage to the Serb armed forces was slight. Force helped to persuade the Serbs to withdraw, but it could not succeed by itself. And now, during a time of financial crisis in the Western world, public opinion may become increasingly skeptical of the value of pouring billions of dollars and euros into NATO defense budgets and equipment modernization programs if military force appears to obtain only modest or even diminishing results in pacifying distant conflicts. If official and public confidence in the utility of the military instrument declines, so too will NATO's stock.

NATO needs to reflect carefully on this issue and learn the hard but right lessons from the Afghanistan conflict. This reflection will need to embrace tactics, counterinsurgency doctrine, the role of special forces, intelligence-gathering technologies, and the cultural as well as military preparation of forces deploying on missions. In addition, ways to improve capabilities for training local security forces quickly and effectively must be considered. NATO talks a good deal about transformation as an end in itself; it needs to talk far more about the right kind of transformation and play a more influential role in determining its member states' force-restructuring and equipment modernization programs.

A second point that also deserves to be carefully considered is NATO's increasing dependence on others to achieve its security objectives. On all previous occasions when it drafted a Strategic Concept, its objectives could essentially be reached solely through the work of its own members. Partners were a useful but nonessential adjunct in these endeavors. Today, in contrast, virtually everything NATO does requires the ability to leverage the involvement and contribution of others. Its partners today contribute about 15 percent of the troops on its missions as well as vital military bases and lines of communication. Even when dealing with new challenges such as energy security, critical infrastructure protection, narcotics in Afghanistan, cyberdefense, and security-sector reform, its ability to add value depends on a seamless web of interaction with those other players that also have roles in these areas. To give but one example: NATO's naval actions against piracy in the Gulf of Aden require coordination with the vessels of many nations; with the African Union in Somalia; with the World Food Program transporting food aid to Somalia; and with the United Nations, whose efforts to strengthen international law on detaining and prosecuting pirates help NATO to give its naval commanders clearer and more robust rules of engagement. As Lord Paddy Ashdown, the former NATO high representative in Bosnia, likes to summarize the situation in "Ashdown's Law No. 1": "The best things that you can do are what you do with others."

What are the consequences for NATO of its growing dependence on what others do or do not do? In the first place, it needs to have closer working relations with the United Nations and the European Union. The signing of a joint declaration between NATO and the UN in September 2008 was certainly a major step forward. However, NATO–EU relations still do not reflect the reality of two institutions that share twenty-one common members, the same values, and largely overlapping security strategies, not to mention engagement in the same places—Africa, Afghanistan, the Balkans, and the Gulf of Aden. The objective of NATO's leaders in the years ahead will be to bring NATO and the EU together, rationalizing their respective military forces, headquarters, and command structures; and using their comparative advantages according to the nature of the intervention—all precisely because they realize that anything short of a NATO–EU strategic partnership would be a squandering of scarce resources. The long-awaited political breakthrough in NATO–EU relations is likely to happen much sooner than seemed possible just a year or so ago.

This said, NATO's improved institutional relationships and closer relations with its partner countries beyond their involvement in its military operations are only one dimension of the challenge. Its diplomacy has traditionally been internal—to keep its own members in line. Henceforth its diplomacy will be increasingly external—all about the ability to connect with other actors across geographic and cultural boundaries, about the skillful use of strategic communication to explain its aims and policies to distrustful publics, and about redefining its role in many instances from an organization leading others to one ready and able to support others. Its current discreet role in helping the African Union and its Standby Force with training, logistics, and transport is a pointer to new kinds of future activities.

The third issue with which NATO must come to grips concerns homeland defense. Too often this issue is reduced to Article 5 territorial defense, and particularly to the question of how to reassure the Alliance's easternmost members, particularly the Baltic states and Poland, that it is willing and able to protect them against a resurgent Russia. They would like to see it become more visible in their territories and in their region in the form of more formal military contingency planning, exercises, and air defense measures. Poland and the Czech Republic, which have agreed to host U.S. missile defense radar installations and interceptors, often give the impression that this is a quid pro quo for more U.S. assistance to their armed forces and their territorial defense. Article 5 remains NATO's core purpose, around which all its other activities hang, so it can hardly ignore any sense of insecurity among a significant group of its members. At the same time it must be mindful of its commitment, made before its enlargement, to the Soviet Union and thereafter Russia that it would not station combat forces or nuclear weapons on the territories of its new member states. Article 5 assurance must not be done in a way that upsets the strategic balance in Europe. Nor must it be to the detriment of NATO's capacity to generate and equip forces for its Afghan mission, given that the greatest current threat to Allied security is on the Afghan-Pakistan border.

What NATO must avoid at all costs is a bifurcated defense planning system whereby some of its member states invest in deployable, quick response expeditionary capabilities, while others recreate Cold War–style static defense forces based on heavy armor and mobilizable reserves. Such a development would hamper still further its capacity to carry out demanding peace support operations in places such as Afghanistan, let alone a number of lesser but simultaneous missions. It has often been pointed out that deployable forces able to travel 6,000 kilometers on operations can also travel 600 kilometers from Western Europe to the Baltic states or eastern Poland—and that because NATO has based its concept of territorial defense not on forward defense but on the ability to rapidly reinforce, taking advantage of longer warning times in the post-Soviet era, the emphasis on versatile, easily transportable forces is all the more evident. As was explained above in addressing the balance between in-area and out-of-area missions, whereas expeditionary forces are as capable of peacekeeping as of war fighting, the converse is rarely true.

Nevertheless, and with the above-noted observations in mind, NATO needs to address the security anxieties of its new members, albeit in a manner that causes the least disruption to its ongoing process of transformation. Desktop contingency planning, preferably in secret, Headquarters exercises, and visibility activities such as naval visits could all be part of the solution, along with the installation of nonmilitary facilities on the territories of the new members states similar to the Baltic Defense College in Tartu, Estonia, and the NATO Cyberdefense Center of Excellence in the same country. The critical factor is not to overreact to a risk situation that NATO's military planners continue to estimate as low, notwithstanding the political anxieties that have been generated by the conflict in Georgia and Russia's drift toward authoritarianism. To reiterate a point made above, the last thing that NATO needs at the moment is division into two distinct camps—the one wanting to focus only on Europe, the other only outside Europe. The Allies badly need to agree on a threat assessment, ranking in order of concern the many challenges they face, as the driver of their defense planning and resource allocation. These ranked threats should then determine the geography of NATO's strategic engagement, rather than the other way round.

With all this said, however, territorial security these days goes well beyond the classical defense of borders against major state actors. In the short to medium terms, the populations of NATO's member states are more likely to be endangered by terrorist attacks (including the use of chemical or biological weapons), by cyberattacks, or by the proliferation of weapons of mass destruction that could once again hold NATO territory hostage. Moreover, the reduction or even wholesale cutoff of Russian gas supplies through Ukraine on two occasions over the past three years has arguably done more to cause Europe's populations misery in the middle of harsh winters than any classical military threat. These unconventional or asymmetrical threats are especially problematic for NATO because they can be approached from many angles—economic, regulatory, judicial—as well as military. In many instances the police and the intelligence services are more useful and more likely to be the first responders than armed forces.

Yet it would be wrong and even prejudicial to NATO's future if it were to abandon these challenges and hand them over to the EU or to national emergency response and civil defense agencies. In many areas, NATO has added value. For instance, its maritime task forces have been in the Mediterranean since 2001 (Operation Active Endeavor) to check on merchant shipping that could be used for terrorist purposes. Another maritime task force has oper-ated off the Gulf of Aden to prevent piracy, given the 25 percent of Europe's trade and energy that transits through the Suez Canal every day. Missile defense is another field where the reliance on U.S. technology and the essen-tial military nature of the program—not to mention the costs—would suggest a leading role for NATO. Equally, the Alliance has formed units to respond in the event of biological or chemical attacks as well as laboratory facilities for the analysis of chemical and biological agents. To the extent that these assets can be effectively plugged in to national or EU-wide emergency response plans, they can provide a useful backup in crisis situations. Given the role that the EU is increasingly playing in combating terrorism and cy-bercrime and in ensuring energy security through the storage of reserves and by connecting Europe's distribution networks, NATO's role in this area will largely depend on the quality of its interaction with the EU. Both institutions need to avoid duplication and develop better synergies to more closely link their comparative advantages.

The last fundamental question for NATO goes to the very heart of its raison d'être in the modern world. Is it an organization that basically con-ducts operations, coming into its own only when it has deployed troops to a given crisis area, or does it conduct operations and also do something else? In recent years political leaders, such as the German chancellors Gerhard Schröder and Angela Merkel, have used the annual Munich Security Confer-ence to lament that NATO is no longer the central forum for the transatlan-tic strategic dialogue. But, as we saw above in discussing the "acquis atlantique," it will be difficult for NATO to assume—or reassume—this role if it limits itself to operations and does not engage in the major security debates of our age. Currently there is little or no debate in the North Atlantic Council on the Middle East, on Iran, or on the future of the Non-Prolifera-tion Treaty and of nuclear arms control. Complex peace support operations, such as Afghanistan, can easily take up the vast bulk of the NATO ambassa-dors' average working day.

This said, NATO's future security environment may well be influenced as much by global climate change or Iran acquiring weapons of mass destruction as by events in Afghanistan. The most urgent issue is not the only one that is important now—or even the most important one in the long run. This is not to suggest that NATO should drop its current focus on Afghanistan and take up every issue that can be linked to a direct—or indirect—security threat. But it needs to do a better job of scanning the strategic horizon and of formu-lating ideas and policies to mitigate risks before they assume threatening mili-tary dimensions, forcing it into a reactive and belated catch-up posture. The realistic prospect of an early NATO military response should not become the prerequisite for the willingness of its member countries to debate an issue in the North Atlantic Council. Rather, these should be the criteria: Is this issue of such overriding concern to a particular member that it risks becoming a general concern; does this issue have the potential to disrupt our way of life and durably undermine our security, especially in terms of the physical safety of our citizens; and is this issue likely to be mitigated by a common transatlantic approach, even if it is articulated outside NATO itself?

If NATO is perceived as being largely absent from the top of the security issue agenda that its member states' governments and publics are discussing everyday, it will be viewed as less relevant. Too often, its public diplomacy must try to raise the level of awareness and interest in issues that it has selected for its activities rather than demonstrate how it has connected with the issues that are already uppermost in the public's mind. This is not to say that it should only follow the popular "fear of the moment"; but in a complex multi-issue and multidimensional security world, it cannot put all its eggs in one basket—or in one single "make or break" operation.

From all the above, it is clear that NATO, contrary to the situation of individuals reaching the ripe age of sixty, cannot look forward to peace and quiet, nor to an early clarity about its future. Because it must never rest on its laurels and always needs to adapt to a world where change is the only constant, it is condemned—or cursed, if one prefers—to continually reinvent itself search time and time again and to go in for the intra-European and transatlantic solidarity that will alone enable it to solve its security challenges. Its "acquis atlantique" can be preserved only through constant adaptation and its application of political will and leadership. Given the major challenges NATO faces in the twenty-first-century world, some skeptical observers may be tempted to proclaim that, this time round, it will not pass the test of transition. But, given its record of pulling together in extremis, would one really want to bet on that?

Notes

1. For an account of the EDC, see Gülnur Aybet, *The Dynamics of European Security Cooperation 1945–1991* (London: Palgrave, 2001), 69–92.

2. NATO, *The Future Tasks of the Alliance ("The Harmel Report")* (Brussels: NATO, 1967).

3. For an account of the INF saga, see Strobe Talbott, *Deadly Gambits* (New York: Alfred A. Knopf, 1984), and for an account of the limited impact of pacifist movements during the Euromissile crisis, see Josef Joffe, "Peace and Populism," *International Security*, Spring 1987.

4. Richard Lugar, "Redefining NATO's Mission: WMD Terrorism," *Washington Quarterly* 25, no. 3 (Summer 2002): 7–13.

5. William Safire, "The UN Entraps Clinton," *New York Times*, August 30, 1993.

6. Conference on the Future of NATO, Ditchley, England, October 23–25, 2008.

7. Author conversations with high-level officials.

CHAPTER 2

The NATO Strategic Concept Revisited

GRAND STRATEGY AND EMERGING ISSUES

Gülnur Aybet

SINCE THE INCEPTION of its Strategic Concept of 1991 and the revised version of 1999, NATO's post–Cold War role has been largely driven by its missions and less so by a grand strategy. This chapter explains what a grand strategy is and how NATO, in the early post–Cold War era, had the relatively comfortable task of being part of a grand strategy of the wider "Western security community," which incorporated not only NATO but also the European Union and the Organization for Security and Cooperation in Europe.[1]

The first grand strategy of the post–Cold War era was the extension of the Western security community's liberal norms to the postcommunist space in Central and Eastern Europe. The second grand strategy was the Western security community's leadership in championing an international system of collective security. This involved military interventions for humanitarian reasons and to uphold international law. Therefore NATO on both counts was able to utilize its technocratic expertise as a trainer in defense reform and as a peace enforcer to fulfill a wider grand strategy that was not entirely its own. In this sense, the Strategic Concepts of 1991 and 1999 did not spell out a grand strategy for the Alliance but reiterated its core functions as well as acknowledged the necessary changes in its defense posture from forward defense to more rapid, mobile units ready to meet new security challenges and emerging threats.

In fact one could have lived with the 1999 Strategic Concept for a while had it not been for the turning point of the September 11, 2001, terrorist attacks on the United States, which inevitably brought collective defense back to the center of NATO's agenda. Only this time, the military requirement was not for a territorially based collective defense but a "borderless" one. This has inevitably made the evolution of NATO's post–Cold War role "mission driven," from addressing regional instability in the Balkans to the threat of failed states in Afghanistan. Though the template of NATO's 2002 Prague Summit work plan fine-tuned the vagueness of the 1999 Strategic Concept toward focusing specifically on the Alliance's capabilities and its capacity to deal with international terrorism, this has also emphasized its mission-driven nature.

Today, NATO has become an Alliance with a plethora of global missions but without a common vision. This discrepancy between its "missions" and "vision" is at the core of how it needs to reevaluate its common values and interests. This chapter explores why NATO is in need of a new Strategic Concept and why this cannot simply be an updating of the 1999 document but requires a perspective of grand strategy, pulling together the normative strands of NATO's core values and principles, and outlining what kinds of tasks it should take on to better fulfill these values and principles in a changing security environment.

Grand Strategies in the Early Post–Cold War Era

"Grand strategy" refers to the security and nonsecurity goals of the state and the means that are employed, both military and nonmilitary, to pursue these goals.[2] I take the grand strategy of the Western security community as the goal of preserving a liberal international order, based on the norms of democracy and free markets. This was a mission to preserve a certain way of life. The means to achieve this goal were military power projection and the use of international institutions to legitimize the security community's norms. In this sense NATO has been but one aspect of a wider Western grand strategy, albeit a central one. In fact because the grand strategy of the Western security community has been driven by the United States since the end of World War II, one can argue that like the U.S. grand strategy since World War II, it has also been based on preponderance.[3] Now that this is increasingly questionable as a grand strategy for the West, it is hard to envisage how preserving a certain way of life can be achieved through military power projection alone, whether it be for the purposes of collective defense or collective security. In this sense, the early post–Cold War years were still a continuation of this post–World War II grand strategy of preponderance.

In the early post–Cold War era NATO did not have a need to rethink its grand strategy because in fact it was one of the institutions central to a broader Western grand strategy at the end of the Cold War. Therefore it was part and parcel of a package deal of exporting the Western security community's liberal norms of democratic governance, free market economics, and human rights to the emerging vacuum of the postcommunist space in its immediate neighborhood. This was a convenient task for the Alliance as it carved out a new role for itself after the main purpose for its existence—the Soviet threat—had evaporated. It was convenient because it incorporated NATO's two essential attributes: its technocratic know-how of military alliance matters, including training and defense reform; and its normative power as the core institution of a security community of values.[4]

This situation meant that NATO had the right qualifications to reach out to the Central and Eastern European states and absorb them into its Euro-Atlantic structures. In fact it was fulfilling a grand strategy by exercising a rather technocratic task: that of extending its expertise as an integrated military alliance of democracies to countries in need of reform in that particular area. Of course, its unique attribute of collective defense, the direct security guarantee if any member should come under attack, and the inevitably attractive link this creates to the United States was something that the Central and Eastern European states could not have attained through accession to any other organization, such as the European Union.

However, beyond the provision of collective defense, NATO by simply being NATO was part of this wider grander strategy of exporting the Western security community to the former communist countries of Central and Eastern Europe and through partnerships even beyond that region. This also involved restructuring the Organization for Security and Cooperation in Europe into a body with multiple organs, ranging from early warning in crisis prevention to election monitoring. The EU's outreach, with a view toward its first enlargement since the mid-1980s, was also part of this agenda. In this sense NATO was part of this emerging architecture of so-called interlocking institutions. Therefore nobody asked NATO to develop its own grand strategy, which probably explains why its 1991 Strategic Concept was rather a dull document, reiterating the changes that had already taken place in Europe, reaffirming its core functions, and suggesting preparedness for anything in a world that saw emerging threats as "multidirectional."[5] The fact that the 1991 Strategic Concept was announced on the heels of the official end of the Cold War indicates that it was seen as part of the jubilation of heralding in a new era, and this in a sense was so profound that the actual substance of the document mattered less.

That was the first grand strategy of the post–Cold War era. By the time the second Strategic Concept was announced at NATO's 1999 Washington Summit, the second grand strategy had become apparent. Thus the Western security community had not only expanded its norms to the postcommunist countries in Central and Eastern Europe, but by now it was also militarily intervening to put things right whenever there was a human catastrophe. The wars in the Balkans put NATO at center stage in this new grand strategy, which heralded the Western security community as the guardian and implementer of a new international system of collective security. This had already become evident with the Gulf War of 1991, where a Western-led coalition of the willing, armed with the blessing of a UN Security Council resolution, had carried out the first collective security operation of the post–Cold War era. Although NATO was not involved as an organization, it was nevertheless the "nuts and bolts" of NATO that were utilized.[6] Thus NATO, as the only participating organization with an integrated military structure, became the centerpiece of this new grand strategy. Again, by carrying out military tasks based on its expertise of years of training as an integrated military structure, NATO was once more fulfilling the tasks of a grand strategy.

The Story of Strategic Concepts Past

NATO's Strategic Concepts have predominantly been military documents, and therefore have been classified and out of the public sphere. This has also contributed to the technocratic confinement of NATO's expertise. The 1991 Strategic Concept changed all that. It was the first Strategic Concept to be made public. Therefore, since 1991 NATO's Strategic Concepts have no longer been exclusively for its military guidance and implementation, but because they spell out its political as well as military missions, they are in fact also tools for public diplomacy. Previously, the Cold War–era, classified Strategic Concepts documents addressed political compromises between the Alliance's nuclear and conventional postures and perceived incremental changes in the Soviet threat.

NATO's first Strategic Concept, which was known as DC 1 and was issued in December 1949, addressed the division of labor among the Allies and the formulation of an integrated defense plan, as demanded by the Mutual Defense Assistance Act passed by the U.S. Congress in October 1949. The plan was approved by the North Atlantic Council in January 1950.[7] By the end of the year, NATO's integrated military structure was established with the creation of the Office of the Supreme Allied Commander in Europe and the Supreme Headquarters of the Allied Powers in Europe—in other words, putting the "O" in NATO.

NATO's second Strategic Concept sought to address the shortcomings of its conventional forces in the wake of the outbreak of the Korean War, the Soviet advancement in nuclear technology, and the Soviet Army's preparedness to launch an invasion of Western Europe. As the Soviet threat became more imminent, NATO's three regional commands—the Allied Forces Central Command, Allied Forces South, and Allied Forces North—were established, along with its two naval commands, the Supreme Allied Command Atlantic and the Office of the Allied Commander in Chief, Channel. NATO's integrated military structure that would prove to be so useful in its post–Cold War missions had emerged. The most significant milestone in Allied force planning during this period was the Lisbon force goals of 1952, which ambitiously called for a mixture of active and reserve forces.

This was followed by NATO's third Strategic Concept, massive retaliation, which was adopted in 1957. Massive retaliation reflected the Dwight Eisenhower administration's emphasis on nuclear weapons for European defense, following the militarization of containment and cutting down on the costs through reliance on nuclear deterrence—or, as was the common phrase of the day, "a bigger bang for the buck." It was also the time when NATO's theater nuclear weapons were introduced in Europe. The idea behind this strategy was that the inadequate NATO conventional forces coupled with the theater nuclear weapons would act as a "tripwire" or a "pause" before the launch of a massive strategic nuclear strike from the United States. This established the so-called nuclear umbrella of extended deterrence over Europe. NATO's reliance on extended deterrence and U.S. strategic nuclear weapons was also because of the United States' heavy involvement in Vietnam and its inability to send reinforcements in a crisis. It was also during this time that NATO's conventional posture of forward defense was gradually becoming established. Some improvement in conventional capabilities was made despite the strategy's focus on nuclear deterrence.

This was followed with the adoption of NATO's next Strategic Concept, flexible response, in 1967, which in many ways was a compromise document to heal the emerging rifts within the Alliance in the 1960s as well as a military document addressing the increased Soviet nuclear capabilities of the same period. The then–U.S. secretary of defense, Robert McNamara, initially wanted to increase the Alliance's conventional forces as a response to the problem of overreliance on the United States' strategic nuclear retaliation against a Soviet conventional attack. The European Allies had their concerns that would weaken the so-called nuclear umbrella or the United States' strategic nuclear guarantee, which covered Europe in an eventual attack from the Soviet Union—be it nuclear or conventional. The political rift that ensued was not to be underestimated, for it led to the withdrawal of France from NATO's integrated military structure in 1966.

At the end, the 1967 Strategic Concept of flexible response was an appropriate mix of conventional and nuclear forces, with enhanced conventional capabilities and a more specific role for theater nuclear forces. This was established through the "mutually supporting tiers," which were direct defense (i.e., forward defense by conventional forces), deliberate escalation (the employment of theater nuclear forces), and general nuclear response (the use of strategic nuclear forces, e.g., intercontinental ballistic missiles and submarine-launched ballistic missiles). Therefore, unlike the 1957 Strategic Concept of massive retaliation, weaker conventional forces and theater nuclear forces were no longer simply thought of as a tripwire to set off a massive strategic nuclear response but as mutually reinforcing layers of escalation.[8] The 1967 Strategic Concept of flexible response was the last of the classified military Strategic Concepts. However, it was accompanied by a public document, which clarified NATO's political goals, which thus complemented its new strategy. This was the Harmel Report of 1967, which set NATO's policy toward the Soviet bloc for the next twenty-three years.[9] That policy advocated a mix of dialogue and firm preparedness for defense with an appropriate mix of conventional and nuclear forces. This dual approach enabled NATO to welcome détente while maintaining a robust collective defense.

By the time the Cold War was over, NATO announced its first public Strategic Concept. This 1991 New Strategic Concept not only reiterated the changes that had taken place, such as the end of the Cold War and the reunification of Germany, but also laid down general policy goals for NATO to deal with the issues that lay ahead. Drafted in a time of transition, the document was inevitably going to be vague. However, references were made to the spread of weapons of mass destruction and to terrorism, and an emphasis was placed on possibly extending NATO's "out of area" role with a reference to Article 4 of the Washington Treaty. Under the New Strategic Concept, NATO reorganized its military command structure and carried out massive reductions in its forces in accordance with the Conventional Forces in Europe Treaty. It was also during this period that NATO successfully launched its various outreach activities to the former Warsaw Pact countries to the East. These initiatives included the North Atlantic Cooperation Council, which was later replaced by the Euro-Atlantic Partnership Council in 1997, and the Partnership for Peace initiative, which was launched in 1994. During this time NATO also commenced its involvement in peace-building activities in the Balkans, first in Bosnia and then in Kosovo.

However, one could argue that the various missions and initiatives NATO undertook under the auspices of the 1991 Strategic Concept were not due so much to the guidance provided by that document as to NATO's evolution in a reactive way to the changing security situations in its immediate neighborhood. The 1991 Strategic Concept did not address NATO's shortcomings vis-à-vis meeting its new security challenges, such as "lift capability" and rapid deployment, to enable it to deploy forces to distant places at times of crisis. In fact this persisted as a problem up to and beyond its 2002 Prague Summit.

NATO's 1999 Strategic Concept, adopted at its 1999 Washington Summit, updated the 1991 document, taking into account further changes in the security environment. During the preparation for the drafting of the 1999 Strategic Concept, NATO was dominated by debates focusing on the nature of its Article 5 (of the Washington Treaty) and non–Article 5 type interventions, as in Bosnia and Kosovo, and its increasing out-of-area profile, along with the legitimacy of its United Nations–mandated operations.[10] Its 1999 Strategic Concept did outline five fundamental security tasks: security, consultation, deterrence and defense, crisis management, and partnership. It also called for an enhanced preparedness for crisis response operations outside the traditional Article 5 tasks, due to the "wider" nature of the threats that the Alliance could face, thus implying a link between Articles 5 and 4: "Alliance security interests can be affected by other risks of a wider nature, including acts of terrorism, sabotage and organized crime, and by the disruption of the flow of vital resources."[11] However, both the 1991 and 1999 Strategic Concepts are by and large reactive documents, incrementally addressing the key issues of debate at the North Atlantic Cooperation Council during the time when they were drafted. Their forward-looking aspects are vague at best, and the documents do not address a wider grand strategy. Thus the urgency to revise them has become inevitable since the terrorist attacks of September 11, 2001, which put NATO's core function of collective defense back on the forefront of its agenda.

Borderless Collective Defense

After September 11 and the United States' and then NATO's subsequent engagement in Afghanistan, NATO's military engagement was no longer confined to a part of a wider Western system of collective security. NATO's Balkan interventions of the 1990s had been part of a wider Western grand strategy of collective security in the post–Cold War era. But for NATO, its Balkan missions had reflected its desire to uphold the very norms that the "Western international community" was promoting to the postcommunist geographical space. This meant that, through its military interventions, NATO was also fighting off "bad examples." After all, the Western Alliance could not be seen to be preaching the liberal discourse of democracy, human rights, and free markets while helplessly watching a humanitarian catastrophe unfold on Western Europe's doorstep. Therefore, because the interest to intervene was no longer solely confined to geostrategic logic or resources but also extended to the ownership of international norms, conflicts such as the breakup of Yugoslavia could "serve as bad examples gradually undermining the rules of conduct of the (West) European security community."[12] But after September 11, NATO was no longer merely fighting off "bad examples" but actually fighting a new enemy. Therefore, Afghanistan became the frontier for this new "borderless collective defense."

This reversal from collective security to collective defense also confirmed the outdatedness of the 1999 Strategic Concept, because it had "envisioned operations outside the Euro-Atlantic as taking place under Article 4, not Article 5."[13] However, collective defense during the Cold War was tied to territorial contiguity. It was the territories of NATO's member states that had to be protected—and Afghanistan is as remote as one can get from these territories. Yet it is not a 1990s collective security–type, out-of-area operation either. In this sense, NATO's involvement in Afghanistan did not commence as a humanitarian intervention in the early 1990s "Balkan" sense but as a downright, straightforward Article 5–type operation to safeguard the security of its member states. Of course, as Jamie Shea points out in chapter 1 of this volume, there are different perspectives on whether Afghanistan is a straightforward Article 5–type collective defense operation or more of an Article 4, peace-building type of mission. Many would argue that Article 4 is the main driver of the Afghanistan mission today. It is in fact Afghanistan that has opened the debate about prioritizing between redirecting more sources to territorial defense or redirecting additional sources to out-of-area operations like Afghanistan. Therefore the concept of borderless collective defense cannot be said to be shared on an equal basis by all NATO members. This is evident in the national caveats that are being imposed, which prevent the troops of some nations from being deployed in areas where they are likely to be in combat.

However broad its interpretation across NATO, there are operational reasons and requisites as to how this new form of collective defense ought to be implemented. Because it is not confined to territorial defense, it requires a much broader projection of stability to defend against new, non-state-centric threats such as terrorism, weapons of mass destruction, and instability emanating from failed states. It emanates from what Ronald Asmus and Richard Holbrooke refer to as the common threats facing Europe and the United States, which are concentrated in an "arc of crisis that stretches from Northern Africa through the wider Middle East to Afghanistan and Pakistan to Central Asia."[14] Therefore, for the sake of arguments favoring territorial contiguity in defense, in this sense, "Afghanistan is no further from NATO capitals than Sarajevo."[15]

The operationalization of this new borderless collective defense also means that NATO not only has to think about security in a conceptually different way but also has to plan its operations to fit this new thinking. This includes stabilization missions far away from its traditional defense perimeter, which also brings together political, military, and economic tools. Afghanistan also shows that these missions are becoming more complex, more distant, and more dangerous. The Balkans were essentially peaceful by the time NATO's troops went in. In Afghanistan, by contrast, counterinsurgency has become a serious challenge for NATO. Instead of one mission, there are in reality several missions—peacekeeping and postconflict reconstruction in the north, combat and counterinsurgency operations in the south.

The main thrusts of NATO's transformation since its 2002 Prague Summit has been how it works with its global partners, how it uses its economic and political tools alongside military ones, and how it manages to deploy and maintain missions long distances from its Headquarters. In this sense, its partnerships with countries such as Australia and Japan are crucial in achieving these missions, and Afghanistan has also shown that institutional synergy between NATO and other intergovernmental and nongovernmental organizations has become as crucial as the cooperation between NATO and its partner states.

Between NATO's 2002 Prague Summit and 2004 Istanbul Summit, the Alliance edged slowly forward with its transformation, following in a piecemeal fashion the detailed Prague template. Reaching out to its partner states in combating terrorism was another aspect of the Prague template. The Istanbul Summit was more preoccupied with building upon existing partnerships and forging new ones in the Gulf and Mediterranean regions. Therefore, between Prague and Istanbul, the Alliance in fact had plenty to chew upon with regard to specific missions and operations. This meant that at least during this time—with the preoccupation of managing "damage limitation" after the transatlantic fallout over Iraq in 2003, and the day-to-day implementation of the Prague and Istanbul templates—there was no urgent need to revisit the question of the now-elusive grand strategy. Throughout this time, the question of a grand strategy and how NATO ought to evolve was addressed outside its circles. Some analysts even went so far as to suggest replacing it with a global "Alliance of Democracies."[16] But any long-term vision about its purposes and goals was not addressed within it.

At NATO's 2006 Riga Summit, it adopted the "Comprehensive Political Guidance" (CPG), a halfway house between a new Strategic Concept and reiterating the full range of missions and tasks that it now faced. In fact the CPG stressed the importance of Article 5–type territorial defense as well as NATO's developing global missions, like Afghanistan, outside the Euro-Atlantic area. In this sense the CPG endorsed the "broad approach" taken by the 1999 Strategic Concept. But just like the various communiqués before and after it—such as the 2006 defense ministerial communiqué, which approved guidance for NATO to conduct two major and six smaller operations simultaneously—the CPG was also a reactive document. However, it is evident that a new Strategic Concept is now necessary not just to answer the question of grand strategy, which seems to be lost in NATO's plethora of missions, but also to address the emerging "two-tier Alliance" between those of its members that favor a territorial collective defense and those that favor further support for its missions beyond the Euro-Atlantic area as essential for both Articles 4 and 5. Though there is general agreement about NATO's ongoing missions on paper, there seems to be an ever-dwindling political consensus on the purposes of these missions and on what it ought to be prioritizing in the twenty-first century.

A New Strategic Concept: Bridging the Missions and Vision

NATO's past Strategic Concepts were driven by military and defense issues. But the challenges it is facing today are no longer confined to the military sphere. Security now requires a new approach to political engagement with countries like Iran that do not necessarily share the norms and values of Euro-Atlantic structures, new partnerships beyond the Euro-Atlantic area to tackle security threats that emanate beyond NATO's borders, a pragmatic common-interest-based relationship with Russia, and political engagement and military preparedness to deal with disruptions of energy supplies.

At the heart of this new security environment is the imperative for NATO to have a clarified vision of common transatlantic norms and values and a better working relationship with other institutions, especially the European Union. This is why NATO's new Strategic Concept can no longer simply reiterate and fine-tune its functions in reaction to the changing security environment, while, as it fulfills these functions, it acts as a component of a wider Western grand strategy. That approach worked when the Western security community had a clear agenda set by specific tasks, such as the Alliance's enlargement to Central and Eastern Europe and peace building in the Balkans. But now NATO must rewrite the grand strategy itself as its political vision and military missions become inextricably linked. It can no longer be part of a grand strategy by confining itself to a role of narrow technocratic expertise.

Combining the political and military for an overall vision is not a new approach for NATO. Its Harmel Report of 1967, which advocated military preparedness and dialogue, was part of a dual approach that was announced at the same time as its Strategic Concept of flexible response.[17] Interestingly, this 1967 dual approach followed on the heels of an intra-NATO crisis culminating in France's departure from its integrated military structure. Now, as it is welcoming France back into this structure forty-three years later, it is once more marking the occasion, contemplating yet another dual approach of a broad vision for political engagement accompanied by a Strategic Concept for implementing it.

However, NATO's experience in dual approaches is by no means confined to the Harmel Report and the 1967 Strategic Concept of flexible response. In 1979 NATO launched the dual-track decision to deploy intermediate-range Cruise and Pershing nuclear missiles in Europe and simultaneously open arms control negotiations on the same class of weapons with the Soviet Union. This kind of experience is at the heart of the present debate within Alliance circles when it comes to dealing with nuclear proliferation and in particular Iran. Should NATO only provide the hardware by providing missile defense in Europe, or should it also engage in a politically active transatlantic dialogue with Iran? It would seem that the German view of late is that the Alliance ought to be proactive, engaging in disarmament and arms control and not just providing the hardware.[18] If it has done so in the past, it can do so again.[19]

NATO's last Strategic Concept of 1999 was found to be quite out of date in the immediate aftermath of September 11 because it had concentrated on the Euro-Atlantic area and enlargement issues and was no longer relevant to the requirement of the borderless collective defense, which required deployment to distant places. Since then, NATO has dealt with updating its outdated Strategic Concept through a series of communiqués coming out of subsequent summits. The first major post–September 11 summit, in Prague in 2002, tried to fine-tune the shortcomings of the 1999 Strategic Concept by addressing the immediate issues of military capabilities and the "transatlantic capabilities gap," which became evident as borderless collective defense was needed in the aftermath of September 11. The Prague Summit communiqué tried to deal with this by establishing a new Allied Command Transformation, a new NATO Rapid Response Force, and the launching of the Prague Capabilities Commitment, designed to replace the Defense Capabilities Initiative launched in Washington in 1999, which had failed to meet its targets. The 2004 Istanbul Summit dealt with partnership outreaches to tackle the challenges of global terrorism, and the 2006 Riga Summit focused on the next round of enlargements. Since the 1999 Washington Summit, these updates in the shape of communiqués have been quite responsive to the issues of the day. But as Richard Kugler and Hans Binnendijk point out, without a new Strategic Concept, NATO "will be left relying on periodic summit communiqués and related documents for its guidance, but for all their importance these documents lack the authoritativeness of Strategic Concepts."[20]

Therefore, if a new NATO Strategic Concept is inevitable after the 2009 Strasbourg-Kehl Summit, what shape should it take? Binnendijk and Kugler have recommended the adoption of a "transatlantic compact" consisting of three baskets: strategic missions, which Europe and the United States ought to perform; procedures and processes, with EU–NATO cooperation to implement them; and improved capabilities. They envisage that the transatlantic partnership ought to have four key strategic missions: homeland security, preparation against threats of cutoffs to energy supply, NATO and EU enlargement, and expeditionary missions to the Greater Middle East and adjoining regions.[21] If anything, one of the more urgent things the "strategic missions" ought to address is the balance between Article 5 and non–Article 5–type operations. This is particularly important because some of NATO's Central and Eastern European members would like to see more concrete commitments to Article 5–type operations; some have even talked about the reestablishment of the old Cold War–era regional commands, and others would like to see old-style contingency planning and exercises. This quest for a more "visible" Article 5 commitment is evident with the speedy ratification of the missile defense agreement between Poland, the Czech Republic, and the United States immediately after the Georgian crisis.[22]

The return of geopolitics to NATO's own region has inevitably increased the urgency for a more pronounced role for Article 5. However, visible reassurances over Article 5 in the NATO area can also trigger a "security dilemma" with Russia. This will inevitably affect the now-repairing rift in

Russia–NATO relations in the wake of the Georgian crisis, especially given Russia's agreement to contribute to supporting logistics supply for NATO's operations in Afghanistan. Here, despite intransigent differences on the future status of Georgia and South Ossetia, there is ground for common interests that NATO and Russia can work on together, as Martin Smith explores in chapter 5. After all, it is not in Russia's interest to see a failed state in Afghanistan, so close to its own doorstep.

The need to balance Article 5 and Article 4 to some extent has already been addressed with the Declaration on Alliance Solidarity adopted at the Strasbourg-Kehl Summit in April 2009. However, the reassurance of words without deeds can have its limits, if it is the only means for building Alliance cohesion. But this issue cannot be tackled until there is a common transatlantic vision of the future NATO mission in Afghanistan. The debate that dominated much of the Munich Security Conference in February 2009 was between those members of the Alliance that advocated fewer troops but an increase in civilian peace-building activities and those that argued that these activities will be impossible to carry out without securing a stable and peaceful environment. Therefore, before any compact can be signed, NATO must get this "more troops" or "no troops" debate right when it comes to Afghanistan.

However, Ronald Asmus is more hopeful when he suggests that the recent transatlantic rift was not caused by fundamental differences in threat perceptions of strategic cultures but by bad policies on both sides of the Atlantic.[23] If this is the case, bad policies can be mended. However, a crucial challenge for NATO will be reengaging Russia in a pragmatic approach, not a "value-based" one, while reassuring its Central and Eastern European and Baltic member states over Article 5 vis-à-vis their concerns about Russia. This leaves us with the catch-22 situation. On the one hand, the drafting of a Strategic Concept could be a healthy exercise to forge Alliance consensus. But on the other hand, it could be equally divisive, as it opens further rifts in the Alliance. It is a matter of choice as to whether the *process* itself will be enough to muster the much-needed consensus, or, in David Yost and Lionel Ponsard's words, "a Strategic Concept reflects consensus; it does not create it."[24]

Like the Harmel Report, it is envisaged that a "transatlantic compact" would also be a boost to NATO's public diplomacy. In fact its public diplomacy has diminished considerably since Kosovo. As Basil Liddell Hart would put it, any grand strategy must involve public support: "the moral resources—for to foster the people's willing spirit is often as important as to possess the more concrete forms of power."[25] The impact of the transatlantic rift over Iraq in 2003 has left a profound mark on the future legitimacy of any Western-led military intervention, and in restoring those "moral forces," this is going to be the hardest challenge. When Dieter Mahncke was writing in 1993 about how "bad examples" could hurt the norms of the Western security community, it seems that preserving the values and norms of the community was seen to be important, in comparison with the mission-driven 2000s.[26] Although there is a lack of common vision on how to perpetuate common values on both sides of the Atlantic, achieving this vision seems to be less imperative than in the early 1990s. Perhaps, as Michael Mandelbaum puts it, this is because international terrorism does not really pose an existential threat to the Western liberal system inherited from the Cold War, because there is no viable alternative to it.[27]

Whatever the reasons for deferring the process of revisiting the development of a common transatlantic strategic vision, it is evident that it cannot be put off much longer. The challenges that NATO is facing today are far more complex than the ones it faced at the time of the Harmel Report. However, that report's basic structure is still at the heart of the issues it now faces: how to have an appropriate mix of dialogue and preparedness for defense. Its role in balancing its tasks of political engagement with its preparedness in terms of capabilities and hardware is as essential today as it was then. Therefore, it needs fine-tuning and clear guidelines on its strategic missions and how to implement them—for a transatlantic engagement with Iran, preparedness with missile defense, capabilities to engage in out-of-area missions, and reassurance to its member states over Article 5 without jeopardizing relations with what could be a more cooperative Russia. At the end of the day, the common norms and values at the heart of NATO have not gone away. But they need to be reiterated and placed in the context of the new challenges that it faces today.

Notes

1. The "Western security community" is the transatlantic community of states that evolved from an accumulation of defense and security cooperation during the Cold War. However, beyond the technical/military level, there was also a broader cultural aspect to this cooperation that spanned more than military cooperation between NATO member states. This transatlantic community, as such, was not just NATO, although it was built around the existence of NATO and the East/West divide. The components of this "Western security community" were bound together by economic, social, and cultural links as well as military ones. In this sense, the "culture" of the Western security community went beyond NATO, because it embodied the preservation of a certain "way of life." See Gülnur Aybet, *A European*

Security Architecture after the Cold War: Questions of Legitimacy (London: Macmillan, 2000).

2. In this sense, I employ a wider definition than Robert Art, who concentrates on military means alone. See Robert J. Art, "A Defensible Defense: America's Grand Strategy after the Cold War," *International Security* 15, no. 4 (Spring 1991): 5–53.

3. See Christopher Layne, "From Preponderance to Offshore Balancing: America's Future Grand Strategy," *International Security* 22, no. 1 (Summer 1997): 86–124.

4. See Karl Deutsch, *Political Community and the North Atlantic Area* (Princeton, NJ: Princeton University Press, 1957).

5. NATO, "The Alliance's Strategic Concept Agreed by the Heads of State and Government," November 1991, 8.

6. For a detailed explanation of the use of NATO's "nuts and bolts," see Jonathan T. Howe, "NATO and the Gulf Crisis," *Survival*, May–June 1991; and William H. Taft IV, "European Security: Lessons Learned from the Gulf War," *NATO Review*, June 1991.

7. International Studies Group, Brookings Institution, *Major Problems of United States Foreign Policy, 1950–1951* (Menasha, WI: George Banta, 1950).

8. See Gülnur Aybet, *The Dynamics of European Security Cooperation, 1991–1945* (London: Palgrave, 2001). See also Richard L. Kugler and Hans Binnendijk, *Toward a New NATO Strategic Concept and Transatlantic Compact* (Washington, DC: Center for Technology and National Security Policy, National Defense University, 2008).

9. NATO, *The Future Tasks of the Alliance ("The Harmel Report")* (Brussels: NATO, 1967).

10. For more details on these debates following the Operation Allied Force and the preparation for the Washington Summit, see Gülnur Aybet, *NATO's Developing Role in Collective Security*, SAM Paper 4/99 (Ankara: Ministry of Foreign Affairs Center for Strategic Research, 1999), www.sam.gov.tr/perceptions/sampapers/NATOs DevelopingRole.pdf.

11. NATO, "The Alliance's Strategic Concept, Approved by the Heads of State and Government Participating in the Meeting of the North Atlantic Council in Washington," April 23 and 24, 1999.

12. Dieter Mahncke, *Parameters of European Security*, Chaillot Paper 10 (Paris: WEU Institute for Security Studies,1993), 10.

13. Kugler and Binnendijk, *Toward a New NATO Strategic Concept*, 25.

14. Ronald D. Asmus and Richard C. Holbrooke, *Re-Inventing NATO*, Riga Paper (Riga: German Marshall Fund of the United States, 2006), www.gmfus.org/publica tions/article.cfm?parent_type = P&id = 233.

15. Philip Wilkinson, "NATO in Afghanistan," *The World Today*, November 2006.

16. Ivo H. Daalder and James Lindsay, "An Alliance of Democracies: One Way or the Highway," *Financial Times*, November 6, 2004; Ivo Daalder and James Goldgeier, "NATO: For Global Security, Expand the Alliance," *International Herald Tribune*, October 12, 2006.

17. NATO, *Future Tasks of the Alliance*.

18. Angela Merkel, chancellor, Federal Republic of Germany, "Germany's Foreign and Security Policy in the Face of Global Challenges," speech at Munich Security Conference, February 4, 2009.

19. Interview with a member of International Staff, NATO Headquarters, February 11, 2009.

20. Kugler and Binnendijk, *Toward a New NATO Strategic Concept*, 25.

21. Ibid., 33.

22. Interview with an official of the NATO International Staff, February 11, 2009.

23. Ronald D. Asmus, "New Purposes, New Plumbing, Rebuilding the Atlantic Alliance," *The American Interest*, November–December 2008, 2.

24. David Yost and Lionel Ponsard, "Is It Time to Update NATO's Strategic Concept?" *NATO Review*, Autumn 2005.

25. Basil Liddell Hart, *Strategy*, 2nd rev. ed. (New York: New American Library, 1974), 322.

26. Mahncke, *Parameters of European Security*.

27. Michael Mandelbaum, *The Ideas That Conquered the World* (New York: Public-Affairs, 2003), 12.

CHAPTER 3

NATO's Secretaries-General

ORGANIZATIONAL LEADERSHIP IN SHAPING ALLIANCE STRATEGY

Ryan C. Hendrickson

NATO'S SECRETARY-GENERAL, the Alliance's civilian political leader, is one organizational facet of its evolution that has received considerably less scrutiny than many other elements of its past and ongoing transformations. Although some historians have begun to give increased attention to the roles played by NATO's Cold War secretaries-general and military leaders, major research gaps remain regarding the roles these individuals play in shaping the Alliance's strategy. As NATO continues to evolve and develop new Strategic Concepts, it is useful to consider the extent to which NATO's secretary-general shapes and influences its strategic vision.

This chapter provides a comparative assessment of the evolution and institutional role played by NATO's secretaries-general. The analytical focus is on how each leader viewed the parameters of his institutional role(s) regarding his individual interest in shaping NATO's broader strategic vision. Much of this assessment centers on how this leadership position has evolved since its creation in 1952, and the chapter concludes with an examination of the current secretary-general, Jaap de Hoop Scheffer, whose more expansive institutional role reflects the Alliance's ongoing evolution. The findings presented here indicate that the secretary-general increasingly plays a key institutional role in shaping the Alliance's strategic vision, especially in the post–Cold War era, which is clearly evident over the course of de Hoop Scheffer's leadership tenure. The chapter begins with a short discussion of the creation of this office, and follows with assessments of the Cold War and post–Cold War secretaries-general.

The Creation of NATO's Secretary-General

At its creation in 1949, NATO was little more than its North Atlantic Treaty and ad hoc meetings of the foreign ministers of its Allied member states. Article 9 of the treaty allowed for the creation of a council, which eventually developed into the North Atlantic Council (NAC) in 1952; yet for NATO's first year in existence, it had very little real "organization." The Korean War, however, proved to be a catalyst for greater institutionalization, and, most important, produced the Office of NATO's Supreme Allied Commander, Europe (SACEUR).[1] The first SACEUR, the American general Dwight D. Eisenhower, was brought in by the Harry Truman administration to assist in the coordination and integration of the Allies' military forces after World War II. Throughout the rest of the Cold War, the SACEUR, who was and remains an American by tradition, was the Alliance's dominant institutional leader.[2]

By 1952, however, it became increasingly clear that additional civilian political leadership was needed to enhance consultation and communication among the Allies. The United States envisioned a secretary-general with a staff of specialists, who would oversee meetings of the NAC and have the ability to place issues onto its agenda. The British viewed the holder of this position more conservatively—as an institutional leader with a small staff and very limited authority. In its final version, the Americans and British compromised, so that the new secretary-general would be permitted to have a considerable staff but only very limited authority within the NAC. The United Kingdom was also granted the first secretary-general, Hastings Ismay, whose leadership and personal views on NATO's broader strategic vision had a critical impact on the Alliance.[3]

NATO's Cold War–Era Secretaries-General

Upon NATO's creation, its secretary-general faced considerable constraints in steering the Alliance. Nonetheless, each leader has sought to exercise some influence, albeit to varying degrees, on NATO's broader strategy.

Hastings Ismay

In the first years after his position was created, Lord Hastings Lionel Ismay, NATO's first secretary-general, remained institutionally weak; not until 1955 was he permitted to officially chair NAC meetings. He also did not speak in

NAC sessions unless an ally specifically requested to hear his views. This modus operandi likely helps explain why he preferred short NAC meetings, in which he provided primarily concluding and summary points at the end. It was his own view that if, as secretary-general, he had attempted to be more assertive in the NAC, he would have jeopardized his already-limited political stature among the Allies. When he did wish to present his own perspectives within the NAC, he would call upon a national diplomat to present on his behalf. He viewed his own role as a facilitator who could enhance communication among the Allies rather than as a policy entrepreneur who should drive or forcefully advocate certain policy directions. Therefore, he preferred quiet diplomacy and was not publicly confrontational with Allied diplomats. In this respect, he played a very limited policymaking role, and instead worked to coordinate views among the Allies.

At the same time, Ismay did want NATO to broaden its strategic vision to include military planning and coordination with other democracies. This view was most clearly evident in his desire to see NATO coordinate, in some capacity, with members of the 1952 ANZUS Treaty, which consisted of Australia, New Zealand, and the United States. With some political backing from a number of the European Allies, he lobbied now–U.S. president Eisenhower to accept this broader role for the Alliance. His efforts, however, had little impact on the American position, and thus when the Southeast Asia Treaty Organization (SEATO) was created, he lobbied much less aggressively, ostensibly as recognition of his own leadership limitations and the sustained American opposition to the expansion of NATO's role.

Ismay also envisioned a more aggressive diplomatic role for NATO when he called upon the NAC, at the height of his own institutional influence, to engage diplomatically in the Turkish–Greek clash over Cyprus in 1956. With opposition from Turkey and the United Kingdom, his efforts generated little positive response from NATO's other members, much like his efforts on the ANZUS treaty and SEATO. Thus, for most of his tenure in office, he refrained from aggressively lobbying NATO's members. On those occasions when he did advance a new strategic vision for NATO, his efforts generated little policy response. Though he is well regarded for his organizational efforts to institutionalize the Alliance, he had little impact on its broader strategic vision.

Paul-Henri Spaak

The Belgian Paul-Henri Spaak became NATO's second secretary-general in the aftermath of the Suez Canal crisis—just as NATO produced the "Three

Wise Men's" Report, which called upon its member states to enhance and strengthen consultation.[4] This report also argued for a strengthened secretary-general, who could better foster this consultation objective. Although this recommendation did not necessarily call for a fundamental revision of NATO's broader strategy, it certainly set the stage for NATO to become a more "political" organization that would openly discuss and debate issues of concern. Such a view fit precisely with Spaak's vision of how NATO's members should interact, and thus as secretary-general he fostered a new environment within the NAC. Not only would he encourage debate but, unlike Ismay, he would frequently interject his own views on what he felt was the appropriate policy course of action. In this respect, he is credited with having a lasting impact on the organizational norms within NATO, by allowing the NAC to become a larger forum for discussion and consultation among the member states.[5]

Given Spaak's very different leadership approach within the NAC, it is not surprising that he did not shy away from publicly advocating his own views on the appropriate strategic direction for NATO. He is most famous for encouraging it to consider playing a global economic role, especially in Africa and Asia. It was his view that it needed to cultivate diplomatic relationships through foreign aid and assistance programs to states in the developing world, partly to counterbalance against any Soviet efforts to do much the same thing.[6]

Initially, some NATO members responded favorably, but Spaak's efforts were soon curtailed by the United States, which preferred to have the Organization for Economic Cooperation and Development (OECD), rather than NATO, play this role. Although Spaak was always willing to look for compromise and did offer a revised version of his economic vision for NATO, he was not able to convince the United States or a number of the European states to interject NATO into this kind of economic role.[7] Nonetheless, it is clear that he was independently trying to reshape NATO's strategic vision, which constituted a new organizational role for the secretary-general.

By his own admission, Spaak also failed to find a compromise between France and the United States on a number of issues.[8] Most important, French president Charles de Gaulle called for NATO to have a decision-making "triumvirate"—consisting of France, the United Kingdom, and the United States, the Alliance's three nuclear powers—whereby NATO itself would have nuclear capabilities and the triumvirate would play a role in deciding whether or not to use nuclear weapons. Such calls were the beginning of de Gaulle's deep dissatisfaction with France's role in NATO, which eventually culminated in the removal of France from NATO's integrated military planning and his demand for the removal of all NATO offices from Paris. Although Spaak made considerable efforts to work with France and sought to find compromises that both France and the United States could accept, his ideas were dismissed by both states.[9] In this case, his actions were comparatively different from his proposals for NATO to take on an economic role in the developing world; he was responding to a crisis among NATO's members rather than initiating a new strategic direction for them. Nonetheless, the result was another failure for him.

One additional event during Spaak's tenure provides further insight into his ability to shape NATO's strategic direction. In 1959, the U.S. secretary of state, Christian Herter, called upon NATO to develop a ten-year planning program. Spaak dutifully took up the task of consulting the Allies on this proposal, but he was quickly met with resistance. His inability to promote a consensus, let alone Allied consultation, led to his decision in December 1960 to announce his departure from the office. Again, the secretary-general had been unable to advance a new strategic direction for the Allies.[10]

Dirk Stikker

Much like Spaak, Dirk Stikker of the Netherlands, who served as NATO's secretary-general from 1961 to 1964, also failed to have a meaningful impact on its broader strategy, albeit for much different reasons. First, he became its leader under very difficult political circumstances, in which France initially opposed his nomination. French president de Gaulle later rescinded his opposition, but his wider problems with NATO plagued Stikker during his entire tenure. Although Stikker sought to be partially receptive to French calls for change within the Alliance, for the most part France did not work through him and, in many respects, treated him as an insignificant actor in international affairs.[11]

Unlike Spaak, Stikker was cautious and generally reserved, so he did not attempt to exercise his influence within the NAC. Rather, he sought to cultivate a close relationship with the United States, although he was not entirely successful in this endeavor. He often complained that he was not provided with enough information on recent political and military developments from the Americans, and thus he proposed the creation of a NATO official who would be permanently stationed in Washington to represent him and also serve as an information gatherer for the Alliance. This idea was rejected by the United States, but it showed the focus of his consultative efforts. He made frequent trips to the United Sates and developed a close working relationship with the American general Lauris Norstad, NATO's influential SACEUR.[12]

In contrast to his good relations with Norstad, Stikker did not consult closely with many NATO members, especially the smaller states, thereby prompting the creation of the ambassadors' Tuesday luncheons meetings, which were informal weekly gatherings of the NATO ambassadors where policies could be discussed in an off-the-record environment. Stikker was invited to attend these meetings, but he decided against joining the group.[13] This personal decision was likely another factor that may have contributed to his limited personal impact within the NAC. He also suffered from poor health during his time in office, which took him away from NATO Headquarters for weeks at a time and limited his ability to shape events.[14]

Stikker made two notable attempts to influence NATO's broader strategic vision, which appeared to be independent of its members. Early in his tenure, he argued on behalf of NATO, while having its own nuclear strategy as distinct from those of individual member states. Although his efforts, and his knowledge of military affairs more generally, were appreciated by NATO's military officials, this proposal went beyond what the United States was willing to support. He had more success in developing support among the Allies through what became known as the "Stikker exercise," discussions aimed at developing a set of circumstances whereby NATO could be called upon to utilize nuclear weapons. This effort reached its highest level of support at NATO's 1962 ministerial meetings in Athens. Stikker's leadership on this issue, which came with initial backing from U.S. secretary of defense Robert McNamara, was later opposed by France.[15] Otherwise, Stikker left few independent marks on NATO. His personal choices, which included his very cautious leadership approach and his unwillingness to engage in the less-formal consultative leadership activities, and his many absences from NATO due to his poor health, all likely limited his ability to have an independent impact on the Alliance. Nonetheless, even if he had chosen to lead NATO differently, it seems likely that France, and to a lesser extent the United States, would have opposed a strong secretary-general. Such conditions would have plagued any NATO leader at the time.

Manlio Brosio, Joseph Luns, and Peter Carrington

The three secretaries-general who followed Stikker all had very different personalities and leadership preferences; yet a common theme across each leader's tenure was a cautious leadership approach. Each leader during this era, from 1964 to 1988, viewed NATO's strategic mission in very limited terms: NATO was not going to go "out of area" but rather would remain focused on protecting the national sovereignty of its members from external threats. All three NATO leaders had strategic visions of the Alliance that generally remained embedded in its original purpose as a Cold War pact created to protect Europe from the Soviet Union.

Manlio Brosio, a former Italian defense minister and Italian ambassador to a number of NATO's member nations, served as secretary-general from 1964 to 1971. As NATO's political leader, he adopted a much different leadership style from Stikker. Brosio was well-liked by the Allies—both large and small—due in part to his impressive consultative skills. He was considered by many to be meticulous in his preparation for NAC sessions. When debate arose within the NAC, which happened less frequently than under previous leaders, he would call for a recess to see if a resolution or compromise could be identified before additional debate ensued. Unlike Spaak especially, Brosio discouraged open disagreements among the Allies and did not envision the office of the secretary-general as a forum for advancing his own policy preferences.[16]

As secretary-general, Brosio was accused of being extremely cautious for the duration of his leadership. One example of this caution occurred when de Gaulle announced France's withdrawal from NATO's integrated military command in 1966 and called for the removal of all NATO offices and deployments from France within one year. Instead of exercising leadership over the NAC himself during this time, Brosio allowed the Belgian ambassador to NATO, André de Staercke, to take the lead among NATO's members, noting that he remained secretary-general to *all* its members—including France. Brosio believed that it would be inappropriate for him to play a leadership role at a time when France had such deep qualms about NATO.[17]

Brosio did, however, help drive the process for the 1968 Harmel Report, which called upon NATO to adopt both defense- and détente-oriented policies toward the Soviet Union.[18] This new approach permitted NATO to adopt both military and diplomatic strategies in interacting with the Soviets, which definitely soothed transatlantic differences over how best to confront the Soviets.[19] Brosio is credited with managing this process effectively, even though he personally opposed the détente sought by many of NATO's European members. In this sense, he clearly contributed to a major change in NATO's strategic vision; his negotiating and consultative skills were an important element of the diplomatic process that generated consensus among the Allies for the Harmel Report, but the vision was one that he privately opposed.[20]

A former Dutch foreign minister, Joseph Luns, was NATO's longest-serving secretary-general, holding office from 1971 until 1984. He was primarily a force for keeping NATO's mission limited and conservative in nature, which was consistent with his own personal political beliefs as well as those of the United States. Like Stikker, Luns was quite favorable to the Americans' position on most issues, while many of NATO's European members criticized the United States for not engaging in meaningful consultation. In this regard, his personal favoritism toward the United States served to limit NATO's role to national defense. In support of the United States, but consistent with the position of nearly all secretaries-general, he also pushed for higher defense spending for all the Allies.[21] Yet in his final years as secretary-general, and especially by 1982, he was viewed by the United States as particularly uncreative and focused entirely on maintaining current established practices at NATO—just when others, especially the United States, were seeking more energetic leadership. In some respects, he had become an institution himself, whom some ambassadors themselves had no desire to challenge. This limited NATO's ability to evolve and adapt, and prompted the U.S. ambassador to encourage him to retire.[22]

Peter Carrington, who before his service at NATO was the United Kingdom's defense and foreign secretary, served as secretary-general from 1984 to 1988. During this period, a number of intra-Alliance challenges sparked fierce transatlantic debates. Contentious issues included debates over defense burden sharing, American missile defense strategies, and the Ronald Reagan administration's military actions in Libya. Carrington has been credited with handling these crises extremely well and assuring the Allies of their commonly shared values. He also worked well with members of Congress, who brought forth challenges aimed at encouraging the Europeans to increase their defense spending. He handled these problems adeptly and with grace.[23] The former U.S. ambassador to NATO David Abshire noted that Carrington had a "light touch" and was well skilled at presiding over the NAC, in part due to his good humor and his ability to deal effectively with different personalities. However, he was not viewed as entrepreneurial in the sense of advancing his own ideas among the Allies. He brought a pragmatic approach to leadership. He was not a "conceptualist" but rather a leader who steered the Allies toward a consensus, especially when diplomatic crises developed.[24]

Carrington viewed himself as "the servant of the institution," and he noted that as secretary-general he "cannot take initiatives, or give instructions to anybody actually to do anything." He also said that he "experienced undeniable moments of frustration" as NATO's political leader.[25] At the same time, he has been depicted as bored in the position of NATO secretary-general and as not particularly interested in its day-to-day leadership demands.[26]

Summing Up

Although much room remains for additional analysis of the Cold War–era secretaries-general, even the limited existing research offers evidence of some leadership trends. With the exception of Paul-Henri Spaak, NATO's secretaries-general have largely not been credited with advancing their own independent strategic vision(s) for the Alliance. Rather, they adopted leadership approaches that were quite conservative. In this sense, they were institutional players in maintaining NATO's limited strategic focus on the defense of Europe.

At the same time, due to the political conditions during this era, the potential for making an independent policy impact from this office—beyond the pressures to keep the strategic status quo—remained limited. Carrington himself noted the institutional limits in how far the secretary-general could actually *lead* NATO. During much of the Cold War, NATO's politically influential SACEURs provided much of its strategic direction and, in effect, diminished the influence of its secretary-general. In addition, NATO was—and still is—in effect governed by some member states, which often chose unilateral foreign policy directions without meaningful consultation with its other members. These unilateral tendencies, especially from the United States and France, have often marginalized NATO's place in national foreign policy decision-making processes. Moreover, the office of the secretary-general had limited "authority" from the start, and, despite the ostensible advancements provided in the "Three Wise Men's" Report in 1956 in favor of stronger political leadership, nearly all the existing scholarship on the Cold War–era secretaries-general emphasizes the limits, rather than the impact, of this office on NATO's strategic direction.

NATO's Post–Cold War Secretaries-General

The post–Cold War era ushered in profound changes in how NATO viewed its strategic role in the world. With the adoption of the Rome Summit principles and its "New Strategic Concept" in 1991, NATO introduced a much broader strategic vision for its security management, which permitted peacekeeping missions, conflict resolution, and crisis management operations.[27] In this new post–Cold War environment, the evidence suggests that individual secretaries-general were instrumental in helping to shape new strategic visions for the Alliance. Their ideas were not without early backing from some of the major Allies, especially the United States, but the presence of individual and entrepreneurial roles is nonetheless evident among the secretaries-general who helped foster support for new strategic directions among the Allies.

Manfred Wörner

Manfred Wörner became secretary-general with impressive military-defense credentials, having served as Germany's defense minister from 1984 until his selection as secretary-general. Historically, he is particularly significant because of the substantive policy impact he had as secretary-general. Unlike the majority of his predecessors, he viewed his role as serving as an independent agent within the Alliance *and* as the holder of an office that could function as an institutional catalyst for shaping NATO's broader strategic vision.

Within the NAC, Wörner had an especially powerful presence, which generated respect from the ambassadors and fostered his ability to encourage a consensus. Certainly, by 1993 and 1994, NATO senior officials and ambassadors regarded his approval as necessary before anything could pass through the NAC.[28] Even in the early years of his leadership at NATO, it was clear that he believed he had the credibility to advance his own independent views regarding an appropriate strategic vision for the Alliance.[29] Moreover, in contrast to Carrington, who was more of a policy mediator than policy entrepreneur, Wörner was especially skilled as a broad, strategic thinker, who would advance his own ideas regarding what was best for the Alliance.[30] Evidence of his personal influence and willingness to use his office as an agent for change is evident across at least three strategic issues that the Allies faced.

During Wörner's tenure, one of NATO's key strategic changes was the adoption of its Rome Summit agreement and New Strategic Concept in 1991, which permitted its member states to undertake non–Article 5 missions, and in many ways set the strategic foundation for much of what it does today. Like the United States at the time, Wörner was a strong advocate of this broader mission. In early discussions regarding the New Strategic Concept, the United States, Germany, the United Kingdom, and France worked together to craft the final document. When it became clear during the preparation for the Rome Summit that an agreement was to be reached by the NAC, Wörner recognized the French ambassador to NATO, Gabriel Robin, who then announced his government's support for the New Strategic Concept. In this regard, Wörner saw the need for this change, appreciated France's efforts to advance and reengage more comprehensively with the Alliance, and then worked within the Alliance to advance its passage.[31]

In addition to backing the New Strategic Concept, Wörner wanted NATO to reach out to former members of the Warsaw Pact and the former Soviet Union.[32] Through his own independent judgment and will, he used his office to reach out to these states and to begin the process of their integration into a democratic Europe. Though it was clear that the United States supported him in these endeavors, he alone chose to travel to and visit these embryonic democracies.[33] Similarly, he independently came to the decision to support NATO's enlargement in 1993, before the Bill Clinton administration had formally agreed upon a policy direction. By September 1993, he had become both a private and public advocate for expanding the Alliance. He brought these concerns to members of the Clinton administration and encouraged them to prioritize this issue.[34] Although the Clinton administration eventually settled on the Partnership for Peace plan in 1994—a smaller step (other than a membership invitation) in the process of reintegrating the military forces of Eastern Europe into NATO, in 1997—just three years after Wörner's death—the Alliance invited three new states to join its ranks, followed by invitations at the 2002 Prague Summit for seven additional states to join. More recently, the enlargement process moved forward at the Bucharest Summit in 2008, as Albania and Croatia received invitations to join NATO. Though Wörner should not be credited as a critical player in shaping whether or not expansion occurred, his influence clearly helped to build a foundation for the "Open Door Policy," which has become a cornerstone of NATO's strategic evolution in the post–Cold War era.

The violence in the Balkans also consumed much of Wörner's time and energy as secretary-general, and this is where his leadership and impact were especially evident. From the early stages of the conflict in Bosnia, he consistently and publicly made the case for NATO engagement and military action. He believed that the civil conflict in Bosnia was not only a moral tragedy but also an appropriate place for NATO to exercise its military influence. Part of his thinking on Bosnia was shaped by the miserable performance of the United Nations Protection Force (UNPROFOR), which was unable to prevent or curb additional violence in the region. He viewed the United Nations as underequipped to manage this task. In public addresses in the United States, he made institutional comparisons between NATO and the United Nations, noting that NATO was the only organization with the military capabilities necessary to bring about peace in the Balkans. He also openly challenged the Clinton administration to assume a more robust leadership role among the Allies. Such a direct challenge to the United States is not a typical strategy employed by the NATO secretary-general—and for the most part, one that has been avoided by all previous NATO leaders—but Wörner used both moral and strategic arguments to advocate for NATO military intervention, and he did so without damaging his personal credibility. His arguments were made publicly and even more aggressively in the private sessions with NATO's ambassadors at their Tuesday luncheons.[35]

Among Wörner's achievements as secretary-general and in Bosnia in particular, he is remembered for his presence at a key NAC meeting on April 22, 1994. During his last two years in office, he suffered from stomach cancer, which eventually took his life on August 13, 1994, while he was still in office. Throughout 1993 and 1994, he was often in and out of the hospital and thus was absent from NATO Headquarters for extended periods. But when the NAC hit a deadlock on whether or not to authorize additional military action at this April meeting, he rose from his sickbed in Aachen, Germany, and was driven to NATO Headquarters for a late night meeting, where he made a passionate case for NATO military action against the Bosnian Serbs. He was clearly quite ill at this meeting; he had his physician in attendance, he was equipped with an intravenous feeding tube visible near his shirt collar, and he exhibited significant weight loss due to his cancer treatments, but his pleas for military strikes against the Bosnian Serbs have been viewed by many as instrumental in pushing the NAC to support more aggressive military engagement in Bosnia.[36]

In sum, Secretary-General Wörner believed that, as an institution, NATO was in need of a major strategic change. In his leadership capacity, in both public and private forums, he advanced new strategic doctrines that went well beyond NATO's Cold War–era perception of its proper role. By some accounts, he brought about a cultural change at NATO Headquarters that ushered in a new energy for reform and adaptation to meet new and future security challenges.[37] In doing so, at a minimum, he helped set a policy foundation for NATO's enlargement, its use of force beyond its members' borders, and the placement of its forces in peacekeeping roles abroad in accordance with the Rome Summit principles. He demonstrated that a secretary-general can have an impact on both the definition and implementation of NATO's strategic vision.

Willy Claes

The Belgian Willy Claes had the difficult task of serving as Wörner's successor. Unlike Wörner, Claes has not been credited with playing a major role in defining a new strategic direction for NATO during his short time as secretary-general. He served only thirteen months—from September 1994 to October 1995. After serving as foreign minister as well as a cabinet official in a number of Belgian governments, he entered NATO at a time when many of its key strategic decisions had already been made, including the adoption of the New Strategic Concept and the establishment of the Partnership for Peace. Only four months into his leadership tenure, his name surfaced in a political bribery scandal, stemming from his earlier days in Belgian politics as a finance minister. He initially indicated that he had no part in the allegations, but only days later he had to recant and admit that he had been aware of the bribery issue at the time. Even before these allegations surfaced, he had adopted a cautious leadership style. Given his damaged leadership credibility, generally cautious approach to leadership, and the fact that new strategic decisions were already in place, he should not be considered a catalyst for new strategic policy initiatives.[38]

Nonetheless, in terms of implementing NATO's new 1991 Strategic Concept in Bosnia, Claes's influence was relevant in Operation Deliberate—NATO's three-week bombing campaign against the Bosnian Serbs. First, as a consensus builder, he was an effective leader in late July and early August 1995, in support of the Clinton administration's determination that some heightened form of coercive diplomacy was necessary to stem the violence in Bosnia. With this new commitment from the United States, Claes eschewed some of his more conservative leadership tactics and pushed NATO's members to adopt more aggressive policies toward the Bosnian Serbs.[39]

Another example of Claes's leadership influence came after the mortar attack on Sarajevo on August 28, 1995. After a brief investigation, it was determined that the Bosnian Serbs had conducted the attack and were again in violation of previous UN Security Council resolutions, thereby justifying NATO's military response. He could have called the NAC into session to discuss the mortar strike, but that ran the risk of inviting additional debate among the sixteen member states over what to do. Instead, he chose *not* to convene the NAC and allowed Operation Deliberate Force to begin. In so doing, he lent his support to the military strikes, which ushered in the most aggressive and sustained military operation in NATO's history. Similarly, when a cease-fire, which he opposed, was implemented only two days later, he reconvened the NAC to argue for a resumption of NATO's military strikes, which likely helped to shape the NAC's political environment that led to the continuation of NATO's air strikes on September 4, 1995.[40]

One final example of Claes's influence was evident in his decision not to consult with NATO's member states on the use of Tomahawk missiles near the city of Banja Luka on September 10, 1995. At the time, NATO's military officials understood that the use of Tomahawk missiles potentially represented an escalation of NATO military options, which had the potential to generate intra-Alliance opposition. In recognizing the potential political ramifications of using the tomahawks, SACEUR George Joulwan provided a thirty-six-hour notification to Claes, requesting NATO's political approval for their use. Rather than calling a meeting of the NAC, Claes approved of Joulwan's request, and chose to notify the ambassadors in writing, which meant that they would not receive the communication until after the strikes had occurred. In effect, he independently authorized the use of the Tomahawks, which some military analysts have viewed as critical in ending the conflict.[41]

With the successful conclusion of Operation Deliberate Force, Claes resigned from office in October 1995, well before many of the operational details of NATO's Implementation Force were adopted. Nonetheless, his impact on Operation Deliberate Force was clear and helped to usher NATO into a new era of out-of-area operations. Given the perceived success of this operation, his tactical political choices during the bombing served to shape what the Allies would in the future come to believe was strategically possible.

Javier Solana

On December 5, 1995, Spain's foreign minister, Javier Solana, became NATO's ninth secretary-general. Much like Claes's legacy, Solana's influence was felt primarily through his private leadership of NATO's member states. Unlike Wörner, Solana did not use his position as a bully pulpit to move the members in certain policy directions. His oversight of NAC sessions could also be characterized as laissez-faire, in that he allowed the members to discuss an array of policy options and permitted more free-flowing deliberations.[42] He also entered office when NATO's peacekeeping operation in Bosnia was nearly under way and the foundation for NATO's expansion had already been established. NATO's willingness to use force had also been established. However, he did demonstrate that the secretary-general can play a significant role in guiding NATO's members and thereby can have a major influence on the strategic direction they choose to adopt.

Solana's influence was especially evident at NATO's Madrid Summit in 1997, when its members invited three former Warsaw Pact members states to join. At the summit Solana became a key mediator, using the confidence he had established among the members to find a consensus on how to proceed despite different views on which applicant states should be granted membership invitations. In his private meetings with members' leaders, he identified the language that allowed them to move forward on NATO's expansion with the Czech Republic, Hungary, and Poland, while also noting the ongoing membership ambitions of the Baltic states, Romania, and Slovenia.[43]

Solana was also critically important in shaping many elements of NATO's Operation Allied Force. Once it became clear in 1998 that the UN Security Council was not going to grant its approval for military action against Slobodan Milošević for his continued human rights violations, Solana served as the central intra-Alliance mediator for finding the legal-diplomatic language NATO needed to use force without a UN Security Council Resolution. In consulting closely with the Allies, he found that they could agree that a "sufficient legal basis" existed for NATO's military action, which entailed his creative use of past UN Security Council Resolutions and a report from UN secretary-general Kofi Annan on the situation in Yugoslavia. Solana was crucial in crafting the legal agreement that allowed NATO to undertake the seventy-eight-day bombing campaign that came later in March 1999.[44]

In addition to establishing the legal foundation for NATO's military action in Kosovo, Solana was involved in the target selection process during Operation Allied Force. Through his consultations with the NAC, he eventually steered the Alliance toward military targets that increased the risks of civilian casualties, which was especially contentious among a number of NATO's European members. In addition, he privately advised the SACEUR, General Wesley Clark, on targets that would be acceptable to the Allies.[45] In this respect, like Willy Claes, Solana played a role in the Alliance's tactical military decisions. This role contrasts sharply with the approach taken by the Cold War–era secretaries-general, and it certainly demonstrates the degree to which the secretary-general can contribute to the manner in which NATO's strategic decisions are implemented.

George Robertson

Lord Robertson of Port Ellen was appointed NATO's tenth secretary-general on October 14, 1999. He came to NATO with impressive defense credentials, having served as the United Kingdom's minister of defense during Operation Allied Force. As defense minister, he had ushered in a number of defense reforms that modernized and reformed the U.K. military to allow for greater flexibility and more rapid deployment capabilities. When his name was forwarded as a candidate to become Solana's replacement, he quickly moved to the top of the agenda and was selected with very little controversy.

Robertson's leadership style as secretary-general was markedly different from Solana's. Robertson exuded personal confidence in his own ability to steer NATO in accordance with his goals. He envisioned an Alliance that needed to evolve to meet new threats beyond its borders, including terrorism, whose saliency increased after the September 11, 2001, terrorist attacks on the United States. Though it was the Canadian ambassador to NATO, David Wright, who initially proposed the invocation of NATO's Article 5 after al-Qaeda's strikes, Robertson became the central diplomatic envoy in building an Allied consensus for approving this step—a first in NATO's history.[46] It was not precisely clear what this decision would mean for the Allies or NATO as an organization at the time, but Robertson clearly favored and advocated NATO's engagement in this case, which later corresponded to his vigorous support for its role in fighting terrorism and defeating terrorists in any capacity possible.[47]

In this context, Robertson's own personal "strategic" legacy centers largely on his repeated calls for enhanced military capabilities for NATO. He repeatedly called upon NATO's members to devote more money and resources to their own national defense budgets, as well as to NATO itself. In private meetings with NATO's ambassadors and defense ministers, he would personally lobby them to spend more on defense, much like many of his predecessors. In public, however, he would use his office to challenge, if not chastise, NATO's European members for not spending enough on defense. In many of his public addresses, he repeated his mantra for more "capabilities, capabilities, capabilities," which he viewed as crucial if NATO was going to be able to meet future security challenges. Among his more memorable speeches—one which won him few friends in Europe—he remarked: "The truth is that Europe remains a military pygmy."[48]

Robertson's calls for increased defense spending, which were strongly supported by the United States, culminated at NATO's Prague Summit in November 2002. There, its member states agreed to the Prague Capabilities Commitment, which provided for new pledges of military modernization and improved military capabilities across all members.[49] On paper, Robertson's efforts had come to fruition, and at the time, they suggested a virtual revolution in Europe's commitment to defense modernization. In Prague, NATO also agreed to create a NATO Response Force (NRF), which would permit more rapid deployment during times of security crises. In reality, however, in the years that followed, European defense spending trends changed very little, a fact that Robertson himself recognized upon leaving office in 2003 when a number of the European NATO members, including his own United Kingdom, refused to increase their budgets for NATO. He referred to the

British budget decision as "pathetically mean."[50] Similarly, the NRF struggled to become functionally useful, as was evident when NATO experienced difficulties in responding rapidly to the humanitarian crisis in Pakistan in October 2005.[51]

Nonetheless, the Prague Summit was strategically important for NATO. As secretary-general, Robertson had initially discouraged discussion of NATO's expansion until a new American president came into office, but he soon became an ardent supporter of the largest expansion in the Alliance's history, when seven states were offered membership invitations in Prague. In addition, he advocated major institutional reforms, including a sizable reduction in the number of committees at NATO Headquarters, as well as a reduction in the number of military command structures.[52]

Beyond Robertson's calls for Allied improvements in capabilities and NATO's membership expansion, his advocacy for NATO's engagement in fighting terrorism corresponded with his belief that it should go "out of area" as necessary to counter new threats and terrorism. In this regard, he supported its efforts to assume command of the UN peacekeeping operation in Afghanistan in 2003, which was a natural progression for it in many respects. The NATO Allies had transferred operational leadership among themselves since the mission's inception, so bringing the mission under its organizational framework ensured a continuity of command. For much of the rest of his tenure as secretary-general, Robertson pushed (if not, begged) the Allies to contribute more resources to the operation and, more generally, to reform their military capabilities to allow for extended and more ambitious deployments.[53]

Despite all these efforts to influence NATO's strategic vision, it is Robertson's leadership role at NATO Headquarters in February 2003, following the United States' request for a NATO presence in Turkey in the preparation for Operation Iraqi Freedom, that will likely shape much of his legacy. In keeping with his view that NATO had out-of-area security roles to play, he gave essentially full backing to the United States' request that missile defenses should be provided to Turkey. This internal crisis at NATO resulted in an eventual agreement to assist Turkey, although he chose during the process to employ the "silence procedure," the invocation of NATO's Article 4, and the use of NATO's Defense Planning Committee, which includes all NATO Allies except France.

During these diplomatic negotiations, the Turkish ambassador to NATO, Ahmet Üzümcü, remained silent in the NAC, as did the U.S. ambassador to NATO, Nicholas Burns, and Robertson negotiated with the French, Germans, and finally the Belgians to reach an agreement. In effect, that agreement provided little more than what individual NATO member states had previously pledged to provide Turkey on a bilateral basis.[54] Though it is clear that the United States decided to push the other members publicly and aggressively to back its demands to assist Turkey, it is also clear that Robertson played a central role in this process by closely aligning himself with the United States in its attempt to stretch NATO in a new strategic direction. Though he ultimately succeeded in gaining consensus on this issue, his own diplomatic choices and tactics helped exacerbate deep and existing political divisions within NATO, and they clearly highlighted the different strategic views within the Alliance regarding American foreign policy toward Iraq.

Jaap de Hoop Scheffer

Jaap de Hoop Scheffer inherited a wounded NATO when he became its eleventh secretary-general on January 5, 2004. Over the course of his leadership tenure, de Hoop Scheffer pushed NATO's members in a number of new strategic directions, leading it into uncharted political territory. His legacy as secretary-general is likely to be influenced strongly by his efforts to emphasize the primacy of NATO's mission in Afghanistan. This view was evident at his first press conference as secretary-general in 2004 and stressed repeatedly through 2009, including in the form of an op-ed essay published in the *Washington Post* in January 2009 in which he called upon NATO's members to devote more resources to its mission in Afghanistan.[55]

During his time in office, de Hoop Scheffer was also of critical importance to negotiations leading to the expansion of NATO's presence into Southern and Eastern Afghanistan. He also supported combat operations in these regions as appropriate for the Alliance. Much like Lord Robertson, he consistently called upon the Allies to provide more military resources to the mission. Although he was often careful to compliment the NATO Allies for their contributions, he was also critical of the national caveats that individual member countries placed upon their own ground forces, creating restrictions on engagement and leading to very different kinds of military commitments from the Allies. This belief that NATO should be engaged in Afghanistan and should be fighting the Taliban was in many ways the guiding strategic emphasis shaping his entire tenure.[56]

Apart from the emphasis he placed on Afghanistan, and his commitment to carrying out the NATO peacekeeping operation in Kosovo, de Hoop Scheffer proved to be quite hesitant in advocating additional deployments of NATO troops to other missions. Despite the massive humanitarian crisis in Sudan and the African Union's calls for assistance from NATO, he did not publicly advocate for NATO's engagement beyond its conservative commitment to provide only air transportation assistance to the African Union in 2005. With regard to its ground troops in Sudan, he was unambiguous: "NATO troops on the ground . . . that will not happen."[57]

Similarly, NATO's small operation in Iraq, which eventually involved only ninety troops, most of whom are American or Dutch, provides additional perspectives on de Hoop Scheffer's leadership. In his first year in office, he publicly made the case for NATO's strategic interest in the success of the American operation in Iraq, and indicated his desire to see NATO provide military advisers to the Iraqi government.[58] In the days leading up to NATO's Istanbul Summit in 2004, he also called upon the wider international community to assist with Iraq.[59] Evidence also suggests that when NATO's members began to debate precisely how it could assist Iraq in the summer of 2004 and the political divide between the United States and France resurfaced at NATO Headquarters, he was instrumental in finding a compromise that allowed the Dutch military to deploy an assessment team to Iraq, which would then report back to NATO to determine what sort of assistance it could provide.[60] Yet once an agreement on NATO's presence had been finalized later that year, he did not lobby again for any major role for it in Iraq; his focus remained on Afghanistan.

De Hoop Scheffer's global travel schedule was also quite different from that of any previous NATO secretary-general. His travels and public addresses outside the borders of NATO's members—in many cases "a first" for a secretary-general—led him to Israel, Japan, Australia, New Zealand, and South Korea, among other states. He then utilized these global forums to advance NATO's strategic mission to combat terrorism, which in his view went far beyond the borders of its member states and required international cooperation. He also called upon other states and international organizations to assist the Alliance in defeating terrorism.[61] These efforts certainly squared with the agreement at NATO's 2004 Istanbul Summit to heighten its cooperation with the Mediterranean Dialogue states, as well as the creation of the Istanbul Cooperation Initiative, which resulted in new bilateral contacts between NATO and individual members of the Gulf Cooperation Council, which includes Bahrain, Kuwait, Oman, Qatar, Saudi Arabia, and the United Arab Emirates. These efforts reflected another important element of de Hoop Scheffer's strategic vision for NATO—namely, his desire for wider diplomatic contacts and enhanced relationships for the Alliance and its members.

Another area of concern for de Hoop Scheffer stemmed from his view that multiple aspects of defense spending—both within NATO as an institution and in its members' budgets—were in need of considerable reform. Like his predecessors, he consistently pushed for higher defense budgets for all NATO members, but he also lobbied for additional defense spending reforms and new procedures, so that the members would work together jointly to determine how national spending priorities could be coordinated to more effectively meet the whole Alliance's needs. In addition, he called for "common funding" policies within NATO to cover the operational costs of its missions in progress.[62] These proposals, much like Robertson's calls for enhanced capabilities, did not receive a favorable response from the Allies, which meant that NATO would continue to face serious financial and diplomatic challenges in Afghanistan. Spending reforms remained a wider strategic concern for de Hoop Scheffer during his entire tenure.

Most recently, at NATO's Strasbourg-Kehl Summit, de Hoop Scheffer was mostly directly involved in the writing of the "Declaration on Alliance Security," which was approved by the Allies and again calls for improved military capabilities and budgetary reforms, so that NATO will be able to face a wider set of security challenges and become a "leaner and more cost-effective organization." In addition, this document calls upon the Allies to begin the process of creating a "New Strategic Concept" that will be incorporated at NATO's next summit. To what extent NATO will evolve from now until then is uncertain, but it is clear that de Hoop Scheffer helped set the foundation for the forthcoming diplomatic dialogue on the future of NATO's strategic vision.[63]

In sum, de Hoop Scheffer's strategic emphasis from day one was NATO's mission in Afghanistan. Indeed, many of his additional efforts as secretary-general in many ways revolved around this mission or fed into the success of this mission, including his desire to foster new partnerships around the globe, his calls for higher defense budgets, and his lobbying for internal budgetary reforms within NATO, all of which he saw as critical to its efforts to combat terrorism and respond rapidly to new security threats and challenges.

Conclusion

NATO's Cold War–era secretaries-general, apart from the exception of Paul-Henri Spaak, were generally conservative in their strategic perspectives for the Alliance. From Hastings Ismay to Peter Carrington, the NATO secretaries-general worked to find a consensus where possible, but in most cases they did not serve as policy entrepreneurs in advancing new strategic visions for the Alliance. Rather, because these leaders were embedded in the Cold War environment, they worked to maintain NATO's focus on the defense of its members. Thus, these institutional leaders have not been depicted as entre-preneurial in trying to fundamentally change or reshape NATO's strategic role in the world. Though the leadership styles of these individuals varied widely, their conservative visions of NATO's security missions were generally similar.

In the post–Cold War era, however, Manfred Wörner stands out as a sec-retary-general who had a significant impact in shaping NATO's broader stra-tegic role in the world. His influence in the NAC, coupled with his views on the appropriate strategic direction for NATO's evolution in the Soviet Union's absence, were especially noteworthy. Rather than serving simply as a messenger for the Allies, he was a true policy entrepreneur who attempted to shape and helped define a new strategic direction for NATO.

Willy Claes and especially Javier Solana were also instrumental in *imple-menting* critical aspects of new strategic roles for NATO that were introduced during their tenures. Solana's success in gaining consensus for military action in Kosovo without a UN Security Council resolution stands out among the diplomatic initiatives that paved the way for fundamentally new missions for the Allies after the Soviet Union's collapse. Lord Robertson also brought his strong personality and presence to NATO Headquarters, which certainly was felt during the Article 4 crisis in February 2003, but he also helped promote new Strategic Concepts at the Prague Summit, some of which have come to fruition, whereas others—especially the Prague Capabilities Commitment—have had only a marginal impact on the Allies. Jaap de Hoop Scheffer's strate-gic vision was, in many respects, an extension of the ideas promoted by Robertson, which included a wider presence for NATO in Afghanistan, more global partners for NATO's members in the war on terrorism, and improved military capabilities for these members. Though the secretary-general does not work in a political vacuum, independent of the interests of NATO's members—especially those of the United States—it is clear that he can and often does play an independent and central role in the process of shaping the Alliance's definition of a new strategic direction. As NATO's Strategic Concepts expand and broaden, much as they did under de Hoop Scheffer, so too does the role of its secretary-general in crafting new strategic principles.

Notes

1. See Lawrence S. Kaplan, *The United States and NATO: The Formative Years* (Lexington: University Press of Kentucky, 1984); and Sean Kay, *NATO and the Future of European Security* (Lanham, MD: Rowman & Littlefield, 1998). See also John C.

Milloy, *The North Atlantic Treaty Organization 1948–1957* (Montreal: McGill–Queen's University Press, 2006), chaps. 1 and 2.

2. Robert S. Jordan, ed., *Generals in International Politics: NATO's Supreme Allied Commander, Europe* (Lexington: University Press of Kentucky, 1987); and Robert S. Jordan, *Norstad: Cold War NATO Supreme Commander* (New York: St. Martin's Press, 2000).

3. Hastings Lionel Ismay, *The Memoires of General Lord Ismay* (New York: Viking Press, 1960), 458; Kaplan, *United States and NATO*, 169.

4. NATO, *Report of the Committee of Three on Non-Military Cooperation in NATO* (Brussels: NATO Information Service, 1956).

5. See Robert S. Jordan with Michael W. Bloome, *Political Leadership in NATO* (Boulder, CO: Westview Press, 1979), 68. See also Paul-Henri Spaak, *The Continuing Battle: Memoirs of a European 1936–1966*, trans. Henry Fox (Boston: Little, Brown, 1971), 266, 269.

6. Jordan, *Political Leadership in NATO*, 72.

7. Ibid., 75–76.

8. Spaak, *Continuing Battle*, 268.

9. Jordan, *Political Leadership in NATO*, 88–91.

10. Ibid.

11. Jordan, *Political Leadership in NATO*, 113, 130. See also Dirk Stikker, *Men of Responsibility* (New York: Harper & Row, 1965), 352–56.

12. Jordan, *Political Leadership in NATO*, 117–26, 141.

13. Ibid., 127.

14. Ibid., 118.

15. Ibid., 139, 145.

16. Ryan C. Hendrickson, *Diplomacy and War at NATO: The Secretary-General and Military Action after the Cold War* (Columbia: University of Missouri Press, 2006), 24.

17. Harlan Cleveland, *NATO: The Transatlantic Bargain* (New York: Harper & Row, 1970), 106; Jordan, *Political Leadership in NATO*, 196–200.

18. NATO, *The Future Tasks of the Alliance ("The Harmel Report")* (Brussels: NATO, 1967).

19. Stanley R. Sloan, *NATO, the European Union, and the Atlantic Alliance* (Lanham, MD: Rowman & Littlefield, 2003), 51.

20. Hendrickson, *Diplomacy and War at NATO*, 25–26.

21. Ibid., 33–34.

22. Telephone interview with David Abshire, former U.S. ambassador to NATO, November 26, 2008, Champaign, IL. In a telephone interview, William Taft IV, former U.S. ambassador to NATO and deputy secretary of defense, December 1, 2008, Charleston, IL, similarly noted that some of the allies found Luns to be intimidating and domineering.

23. Hendrickson, *Diplomacy and War at NATO*, 34–37.

24. Abshire, interview. Carrington also refers to himself as a "pragmatist," in his memoirs: Lord Carrington, *Reflecting on Things Past* (London: William Collins, 1988), 373.

25. Carrington, *Reflecting on Things Past*, 380.

26. See Michael Rühle, "Preface: Manfred Wörner's Legacy and NATO," in *Civil–Military Relations in Post Communist States: Central and Eastern Europe in Transition*, ed. Anton Bebler (Westport, CT: Praeger, 1997); Hendrickson, *Diplomacy and War at NATO*, 37.

27. Rome Summit Declaration, "The Alliance's New Strategic Concept," November 7–8, 1991, www.nato.int/docu/comm/49–95/c911107a.htm. See also Rebecca R. Moore, *NATO's New Mission: Projecting Stability in a Post–Cold War World* (Santa Barbara, CA: Praeger Security International, 2007), 19–21.

28. Hendrickson, *Diplomacy and War at NATO*, 58.

29. Taft interview.

30. Abshire interview.

31. Taft interview.

32. Hendrickson, *Diplomacy and War at NATO*, 46.

33. Taft interview.

34. Ronald D. Asmus, *Opening NATO's Door: How the Alliance Remade Itself for a New Era* (New York: Columbia University Press, 2002), 40–49.

35. Hendrickson, *Diplomacy and War at NATO*, 52–57.

36. Ibid., 58–60.

37. Ibid., 56.

38. Ibid., 70–71.

39. Ibid., 76–88.

40. Richard Holbrooke, *To End a War* (New York: Random House, 1998), 99, 120. Colonel Robert C. Owen, "Summary," in *Deliberate Force: A Case Study in Effective Air Campaigning*, ed. Colonel Robert C. Owen (Maxwell Air Force Base: Air University Press, 2000), 499.

41. For a summary of the research on these events and the body of literature that suggests the importance of the Tomahawk strikes, see Hendrickson, *Diplomacy and War at NATO*, 83–85.

42. Ibid., 98. One very public exception to his otherwise reserved role in public was his criticism of the Czech Republic and its ambassador to NATO, Karel Kovanda, for voicing its open disagreement with aspects of the diplomatic peace initiatives provided by NATO during Operation Allied Force. See William Drozdiak, "NATO's Newcomers Are Shaken by Airstrikes; Czechs, Hungarians Express Greatest Dismay," *Washington Post*, April 12, 1999.

43. Asmus, *Opening NATO's Door*, 247–48.

44. Catherine Guicherd, "International Law and the War in Kosovo," *Survival* 41, no. 2 (1999): 19–34; Hendrickson, *Diplomacy and War at NATO*, 101.

45. Hendrickson, *Diplomacy and War at NATO*, 106–8, 110–13.

46. Ibid., 119–21.

47. George Robertson, "NATO after September 11," January 31, 2002, www.nato.int/docu/speech/2002/s020131a.htm.

48. George Robertson, "The Transatlantic Link," January 21, 2002, www.nato.int/docu/speech/2002/s020121a.htm.

49. NATO Press Release, "Prague Summit Declaration," November 21, 2002, www.nato.int/docu/pr/2002/p02–127e.htm.

50. Quoted by Judy Dempsey, "Head of NATO Has Parting Shot at 'Mean' Members," *Financial Times*, December 4, 2003.

51. Daniel Dombey, "Problems Still Plague Earthquake Relief Effort as Death Toll Mounts in Pakistan, Hitches Are Being Identified in the NATO Response Force," *Financial Times*, November 3, 2005.

52. Judy Dempsey, "An Alliance in Search of a Role," *Financial Times*, April 10, 2002; Ryan C. Hendrickson, "NATO's Open-Door Policy and the Next Round of Enlargement," *Parameters* 30 (Winter 2000–2001): 53–66.

53. E.g., see George Robertson, "NATO: The Challenges Ahead," October 27, 2003, www.nato.int/docu/speech/2003/s0310027d.htm.

54. Hendrickson, *Diplomacy and War at NATO*, 131–37.

55. Jaap de Hoop Scheffer, "Afghanistan: We Can Do Better," *Washington Post*, January 18, 2009.

56. E.g., see Roger Cohen, "The Long Haul in Afghanistan," *New York Times on the Web*, February 28, 2008. See also Ryan C. Hendrickson, "NATO Secretary General: A Changing Job Description?" *NATO Review*, March, 2009, www.nato.int/docu/review/2009/0902/090202/EN/index.htm.

57. National Public Radio, "Interview: Jaap de Hoop Scheffer Discusses Current NATO Missions," *All Things Considered*, June 1, 2005.

58. Elaine Sciolino, "NATO Chief Offers a Bleak Analysis: Iraq and Afghanistan Both Seen at Risk," *New York Times*, July 3, 2004.

59. Jaap de Hoop Scheffer, "Looking to Iraq, Afghanistan and Beyond; NATO Summit," *International Herald Tribune*, June 22, 2004.

60. Leon Bruneau, "Compromise Proposed on NATO Deadlock over Iraq Training," Agence France-Presse, July 30, 2004.

61. Among his many addresses outside NATO states, see, e.g., Jaap de Hoop Scheffer, "Speech at Victoria University Institute of Policy Studies and New Zealand Institute of International Affairs," March 31, 2005, www.nato.int/docu/speech/2005/s050331a.htm.

62. Quoted by Judy Dempsey, "Budget Cuts Worry NATO Chief," *International Herald Tribune* April 18, 2005. See also James Blitz and Stephen Fidler, "NATO Chiefs Step Up Push for Nations to Pool Resources," *Financial Times*, October 22, 2007; and Judy Dempsey, "NATO Chief Says Huge Shake-Up Is Needed," *Financial Times*, May 27, 2004.

63. NATO Press Release, "Declaration on Alliance Security," April 4, 2009, www.nato.int/cps/en/natolive/news_52838.htm?mode = pressrelease; telephone interview, senior NATO official, April 8, 2009, Charleston, IL.

CHAPTER 4

Implementing NATO's Comprehensive Approach to Complex Operations

Friis Arne Petersen, Hans Binnendijk,
Charles Barry, and Peter Lehmann Nielsen

LIKE MANY ORGANIZATIONS involved in complex missions in recent years, NATO has been rethinking the balance between its military and non-military instruments. It has learned important lessons in difficult operations such as Afghanistan and Kosovo, and (albeit largely outside the NATO framework) in Iraq. The conceptual basis of this effort is NATO's Comprehensive Approach, which seeks to make closer cooperation among civilian and military responses an integral part of Alliance operations. Developing a coherent and relevant approach to this complicated problem is now at the forefront of the major challenges facing the Alliance today.

In fact, the elaboration of the Comprehensive Approach has been on NATO's agenda for several years and will be a key component of its new Strategic Concept. The issue is no longer whether NATO needs such an approach—something that before the 2006 Riga Summit was hotly debated—but rather the difficult business of defining its scope and content, and ensuring effective implementation. The more visible political debate over NATO's crucial mission in Afghanistan has focused on mobilizing additional military forces, based on the premise that stabilization and reconstruction cannot be effective without a minimum of security. But today there is also broad agreement that success cannot be achieved with military power alone. Cooperation with civilian actors cobbled together on an ad hoc basis in the field is not sustainable in the long run.

The Origin of NATO's Comprehensive Approach

There is ample experience to show that managing conflict requires the application of all elements of national and international power—political, diplomatic, economic, financial, informational, social, and commercial, as well as military. Recognizing this challenge, NATO has taken the first steps toward developing the Comprehensive Approach initiative that would enable the collaborative engagement of all requisite civilian and military elements of international power to end hostilities, restore order, commence reconstruction, and begin to address a conflict's root causes. NATO can provide the military element called for by the Comprehensive Approach and NATO's member states can provide many of the civilian elements. Additionally, many other national, international, and nongovernmental actors can contribute even greater legions of essential civilian resources.

Important gains have been made toward making NATO's Comprehensive Approach a reality, including the development of an Action Plan for its implementation. Yet the scope of NATO's Comprehensive Approach is still too narrowly defined, and overall progress in turning words into deeds has been slowed by unrelated political obstacles. Everyone agrees that the Alliance needs to do better in this field, particularly in the context of Afghanistan, but there remain institutional and political barriers to moving forward in a significant way. First, NATO members are still grappling with how to organize their national-level civil–military coordination efforts. Many countries have undertaken significant independent efforts in this field, particularly based on experiences and lessons learned from Iraq and Afghanistan. However, most national-level initiatives to achieve the necessary cooperation between military and civilian actors are still at an early stage of development. What is already known is that fundamental change in bureaucratic cultures is needed on all sides. A new awareness must be instilled favoring cross-agency cooperation, information sharing, early engagement, longer-term solutions, and process experimentation. These characteristics are essential for a comprehensive approach to take hold and thrive, but they represent difficult changes. They will require a long-term commitment and a shared belief in the necessity of a comprehensive approach to solving complex operations.

Second, the same challenges exist on the international level—and what is complicated to achieve nationally is already proving even more difficult internationally. NATO's members must agree to reform a host of its long-standing internal structures and procedures, many of which were established with a view toward purely military efforts in defense of its members' territories. NATO must also find ways to synchronize its efforts with many external partners, including other international organizations working simultaneously in crisis regions to bring about stabilization and reconstruction.

Among institutions, the unresolved division of labor and the method of cooperation between NATO and the European Union are perhaps the most salient obstacles to progress in developing the Alliance's Comprehensive Approach. As long as institutional uncertainties remain about which roles and responsibilities should be assigned to NATO vis-à-vis the EU and other relevant international organizations, it will be difficult to mobilize the necessary engagement in and support for a reconfiguration of the Alliance to create an effective civil–military framework. This should not, however, be an excuse for inaction as NATO turns sixty years of age and looks ahead. The decision to draft a new Strategic Concept for NATO, the EU's progress in defining and strengthening its common security and defense policy, France's reintegration into NATO's military structure, and the Barack Obama administration's emphasis on a new approach in Afghanistan and on strengthened cooperation with Europe all provide a positive context for forging a new Atlantic compact for the twenty-first century that includes a collective international approach to conflict resolution—one with substantive, cooperative institutional roles for NATO and the EU at its core. A new Strategic Concept will incorporate the Comprehensive Approach as a major underpinning of future plans and operations. Both NATO and the EU have the opportunity to define the vision and mechanisms for the Comprehensive Approach in the coming years, if the political will can be found.

Much work remains before mature civilian–military mechanisms can augment and facilitate cooperation across all agencies in a given crisis. However, the imperative that military efforts in the field must be complemented throughout any operation by nonmilitary means is already clear. Appropriate international agencies or NATO itself must bring to bear in a coordinated way the expert civilian competencies of nations and international organizations. In the Balkans and Afghanistan, NATO engaged belatedly with other actors through ad hoc, situational arrangements rather than as the result of prior common planning. Not knowing in advance what roles and which participants will eventually come into play exacerbates already-difficult coordination and results in longer, more costly conflict resolution in terms of lives, treasure, and ultimate effectiveness. Civilian and military teammates cannot meet for the first time on the front lines of a crisis and cooperate effectively. NATO must plan and train better with its partners to protect its forces, alleviate civilian suffering, and bring missions to a successful conclusion as soon as possible.

The time has come for a new approach, for an "Alliance Reborn," so that NATO can address tasks for the future just as successfully as it has done in the past.[1] The adage that "NATO works in practice better than in theory" has become a too-convenient excuse for not reaching much-needed, comprehensive agreements on civil–military cooperation, from the topmost political levels down to face-to-face relationships in the field. More than enough operational experience has been gained to indicate that it is past time to replace expedient constructs with systemic, institutionalized procedures for cooperation on tasks that, as is widely agreed, must be accomplished quickly and effectively. The last remaining core task of NATO's transformation is to link its military capabilities effectively with the indispensable nonmilitary elements of power essential to successful conflict resolution. Failure to finish this work hampers and at times frustrates success in the field by operational personnel, civilians, and military across all organizations who are simply trying to get the job done.

Denmark's Role Leading to the Riga Initiative for NATO's Comprehensive Approach

Denmark has been at the forefront of crisis response and crisis management operations both inside NATO and through the United Nations, the EU, and the Organization for Security and Cooperation in Europe (OSCE). From their engagements, it was apparent that better cooperation and earlier coordination would improve how the international community responded, if only organizations could overcome their deeply rooted habits of independent action, institutional bias, and often mutual misunderstanding of each other's roles. In seeking a solution, the Danes took the initiative to help start a process within NATO. The goal was neither to make NATO the centerpiece of cooperation nor a coordinator among international actors. Instead, the vision was to seek positive change in all organizational cultures over time, beginning by making NATO a partner that is more ready to work with other organizations.

The government of Denmark, with the support of like-minded NATO members, took the initiative in late 2004 to put the concept of the Comprehensive Approach on the Alliance's agenda, initially under the heading Concerted Planning and Action (CPA). At that time, it was clear that even though NATO had no capabilities for a purely civilian crisis response, the Alliance had in fact already taken a number of pragmatic steps in this area, such as appointing a senior civilian representative in Afghanistan. However, there remains no defined frame of reference or codification of existing practices on the civilian side, especially regarding NATO's collaboration with other actors in the field.

In June 2005, Denmark convened a seminar to kick-start the discussion within the Alliance. Political disagreements on the broader aspects of NATO's future role led to skepticism from some countries on the idea of the CPA, so much time was spent in the first phase spelling out what the initiative was *not*. It was stressed that the aim was not to develop new, independent NATO capabilities but to improve its existing capabilities as well as strengthen its ability to engage in cooperation with—not control of—other actors and to improve mission planning in these areas.

In the spring of 2006, Denmark and six other NATO members—Canada, the Czech Republic, Hungary, the Netherlands, Norway, and Slovakia—circulated a paper within the Alliance describing some of the basic ideas underpinning the CPA approach and what they were trying to achieve in the Alliance. The United States later joined the initiative through an eight-nation letter in September 2006, further clarifying the ideas behind what had by then become known as the Comprehensive Approach. The intent was to get the topic of "civil–military interaction and cooperation with other key actors" on the agenda for the Riga Summit in November 2006. The Danish initiative succeeded, because NATO's leaders declared at Riga that "today's challenges require a comprehensive approach by the international community involving a wide spectrum of civil and military instruments."[2] At Riga, NATO's leaders tasked the permanent representatives "to develop pragmatic proposals . . . to improve coherent application of NATO's own crisis management instruments as well as practical cooperation at all levels with partners, the UN and other relevant international organisations, non-governmental organisations and local actors in the planning and conduct of ongoing and future operations wherever appropriate."[3]

U.S.–Danish Collaboration to Further the Comprehensive Approach

Following the Riga Summit, in early 2007, the Center for Technology and National Security Policy (CTNSP) at the National Defense University in Washington and the Royal Danish Embassy to the United States began a collaboration aimed at further elaborating international perspectives on a comprehensive approach to crisis response. The CTNSP had been engaged in research on postconflict stabilization and reconstruction operations since

2003 and was interested in articulating civilian capacity requirements. The Danish Embassy was eager to continue its national effort and had access to a spectrum of European thinkers willing to participate. From 2007 to 2009 a series of international roundtable discussions were held in Washington to explore the elements and potential methods of implementing a NATO Alliance Comprehensive Approach. Reports were promulgated to attendees, and several publications were published espousing future conceptual development and practical operational ideas for civil–military cooperation.[4] All this work informed NATO staffs and national agencies working on its Comprehensive Approach.

Similar activities took place at the national level for some NATO members, which likewise benefited from the CTNSP–Danish Embassy enterprise. The United States, for example, was successful in establishing in 2008 the initial elements of a Civilian Response Corps under the State Department's Office of the Coordinator for Reconstruction and Stabilization. In 2009 the United States began the Center for Complex Operations (CCO) under the CTNSP. The CCO is designed to link civilian and military educators, trainers, thought leaders, and practitioners to focus on the theoretical and practical problems associated with stability operations, counterinsurgency, and irregular warfare. The CCO's governing structure extends across the Department of State and the Department of Defense as well as the U.S. Agency for International Development. This corporate direction gives the CCO civilian–military oversight and leadership. A part of the CCO initiative will be to reach out to America's international partners and other allies to further civil–military operational response. A related and already-existing program under the CTNSP, called STAR-TIDES, conducts international research on affordable, sustainable support for distressed populations—whether due to postwar, postdisaster, or impoverishment, in foreign or domestic contexts, and for short-term or long-term (multiyear) operations. All these national activities have benefited directly from their association with NATO's Comprehensive Approach.

The Action Plan for the Comprehensive Approach

The NATO Bucharest Summit in April 2008 declared that "many of today's security challenges cannot be successfully met by NATO acting alone."[5] Rather, the Alliance ought to seek "a broad partnership with the wider international community . . . based on a shared sense of openness and cooperation as well as determination on all sides."[6] NATO's leaders went on to declare that "experiences in Afghanistan and the Balkans demonstrate that the international community needs to work more closely together and take a *comprehensive approach* to address successfully the security challenges of today and tomorrow. Effective implementation of a comprehensive approach requires the cooperation and contribution of all major actors, including that of nongovernmental organizations and relevant local bodies. To this end, it is essential for all major international actors to act in a coordinated way, and to apply a wide spectrum of civil and military instruments in a concerted effort that takes into account their respective strengths and mandates."[7]

It is important that NATO seeks to partner across the international community, not only with governmental organizations but also with the vast and capable nongovernmental organization (NGO) community. In seeking to engage as wide a spectrum of civil and military instruments as possible, NATO also committed to the principle of respect for the mandates, autonomy, and decisions of each actor.

With the decision at Bucharest, the Comprehensive Approach and its practical application in critical peace operations in Afghanistan, Kosovo, and elsewhere has now become an integral part of NATO's crisis response strategy. As NATO looks beyond its Sixtieth-Anniversary Summit, the Comprehensive Approach must be a key building block of a new Alliance Strategic Concept. It will do much to set the tone for future cooperation between NATO and the rest of the international community, as well as between the United States and Europe.

In Bucharest, NATO's leaders endorsed an Action Plan to develop its contribution to the Comprehensive Approach. This Action Plan calls for the engagement of NATO's member states and all its staffs and agencies by putting forth pragmatic proposals across four broad areas where it can strengthen its contribution to the Comprehensive Approach: (1) the planning and conduct of operations; (2) lessons learned, training, education, and exercises; (3) enhancing cooperation with external actors; and (4) public messaging.

Developing the Comprehensive Approach in these four areas requires working through NATO's bureaucratic processes, which often appear to proceed at a glacial pace. There are many committees, and each has been enlarged in recent years to include a growing number of Allies. The NATO International Staff has taken the lead in organizing a process that takes account of the decisions made at Bucharest, includes all relevant staffs and agencies, and can accommodate political factors that will affect what can be agreed on. Within these parameters the Action Plan looks to develop proposals at three levels. At the political level NATO will focus on building confidence and mutual understanding between itself and other international actors. At the operational level NATO will begin by seeking to cooperate with other organizations in overall planning for operations where substantial civil and military capabilities will be required. And at the theater level NATO will take steps to provide commanders the authority and means to engage with local leaders and the principals of other international agencies during the conduct of operations. Across all three levels NATO's approach is to make its own crisis management procedures more coherent, to improve its cooperation with every external partner, and to enhance its capacity to bring military support to postconflict stabilization and reconstruction tasks.

The Four Pillars of NATO's Action Plan

NATO's Action Plan is built on four pillars. The first pillar is NATO's internal changes to develop the Comprehensive Approach in the planning and conduct of its operations, thereby revising its operational planning procedures to reflect the Comprehensive Approach's principles and looking for ways to draw more closely together the various bodies that make up the NATO Crisis Response System across the full life cycle of an operation. This would include promoting preoperational planning and exercises, continuous dialogue during operations with relevant players, and the generous exchange of information at all levels. NATO hopes to also develop options for providing support to the planning efforts of other organizations. This would extend to engagement with local actors on steps toward crisis resolution following such proven models as the Joint Coordination and Monitoring Board (JCMB) in Afghanistan.[8] Improvement of planning and operations also means bringing to bear the nonmilitary civilian expertise of NATO's Senior Civil Emergency Planning Committee by integrating that expertise with the activities of the NATO Military Authorities. In addition, the International Staff proposes to compile rosters of national civilian experts available to advise NATO forces on stabilization and reconstruction, and to liaise with external agencies competent in various critical fields, including media, political matters, and providing assistance to alleviate the adverse effects of conflict on populations and their property. The Action Plan also urges more consideration of the roles of NATO senior civilian representatives and political advisers, working alongside military commanders, to bring together NATO's civilian and military resources and expertise.

The Action Plan's second pillar entails deriving lessons learned and taking the Comprehensive Approach to training, education, and exercises. It aims to increase NATO's currently modest inclusion of civilians in joint training and thereby enhance understanding along with mutual respect, trust, and confidence between NATO, its partners, and other international and local actors. NATO already employs Periodic Mission Review (PMR) processes for lessons learned by the Kosovo Force (KFOR) and the International Security Assistance Force (ISAF) in Afghanistan. The PMR process should be expanded to include observations of relevant civilian partner organizations. Another facet of this pillar will be joint civilian and military training of staffs within NATO that are engaged in activities that contribute to the Comprehensive Approach to crises. Along with internal adjustments, training will be extended to the civilian and military personnel of partners, other external actors (including both international organizations and NGOs), and local authorities. Exchanging best practices and lessons learned and the active participation of international actors in NATO crisis management exercises are other steps NATO is considering as part of its Action Plan, including successful implementation of its exercise policy with the EU. Finally, NATO will examine its Joint Analysis Lessons Learned Center to identify shortcomings and potential modifications to optimize its contribution to the Comprehensive Approach.

The third pillar of NATO's Action Plan is to enhance its cooperation with external actors, notably the United Nations, the European Union, other international organizations, relevant NGOs, and local authorities. NATO presumes that these actors accept that operational effectiveness and coherence require continuous close engagement and that they share NATO's interest in building closer ties. NATO plans to focus first on nurturing mutual trust, understanding, confidence, and respect, while fully endorsing local ownership and the UN's appropriate leading role in many areas of coordination. NATO intends to call on its own members to support reciprocal action by other organizations of which they are members. A program of regular conferences, staff talks, and seminars among organizations will be developed. NATO might be able to agree with some organizations to exchange early-warning information or other assessments of evolving crises. Other initiatives leading to enhanced cooperation include new modalities for cooperation across organizations aimed at strengthening heads of state and NATO secretary-general contacts; improving NATO–UN liaison efforts (see below); and proposing to the North Atlantic Council the establishment of arrangements with organizations that are regular cooperation partners, such as key UN agencies—these arrangements could include the exchange of contacts, enhanced information sharing, and the creation of liaison positions at agency headquarters.

In this area, an important initiative would be the establishment of a NATO International Staff civilian liaison at the UN, perhaps with the Office of the UN High Commissioner for Refugees or the United Nations Development Program. Such a civilian liaison would be a valuable complement to the NATO military officer now serving at the Department of Peacekeeping Operations (DPKO). Other initiatives could be strengthening the effectiveness of the NATO Permanent Liaison Team at the EU Military Staff as well as the value of the EU's permanent planning cell at the Supreme Headquarters of the Allied Powers in Europe. Finally, NATO looks to build on the initiative of ISAF's Afghan Country Stability Picture Database as a model for information sharing among the Allies as well as international organizations and NGOs.

Public messaging is the fourth Action Plan pillar, one that is just as critical to operational success. It intends to focus all NATO's agencies and commands on ways to reinforce and expedite the public message of its commitment to working with every participating actor in support of an overall international effort to resolve conflict and restore peace. The Alliance is reviewing its methods of public messaging and institutionalizing processes for systematic updates and rapid promulgation. It looks toward regular sharing of information strategies and campaigns wherever possible with a perspective on complementarity and mutual reinforcement with other actors, both international and local. An early task will be reviewing NATO's media operations to assess the degree of coordination and message synergy among its Media Operations Center, its members contributing to an operation, and its engaged Military Authorities. NATO will also seek to facilitate greater coherence between the messages of the international community and local authorities. Finally, the Action Plan will seek to optimize the use of new technologies and new media in both the gathering and distribution of mission-related message content to local and international audiences.

In addition to these four pillars, the Action Plan calls for enhancing NATO's ability to bring better military support to civilian stabilization operations and reconstruction efforts. A major focus of this task will be to assess the implications of enhanced support of civilian efforts for NATO's military force planning process and operational employment requirements.

Next Steps for NATO

Such an ambitious list of tasks, still under development by staffs at NATO Headquarters and in members' capitals, is a promising start, though the process of implementation will inevitably be a long one. Even with a final Action

Plan approved and implementation under way, the development of NATO's contribution to the Comprehensive Approach will require sustained top-level attention and resources. It will need to take account of developments on the ground and lessons learned by civilian as well as military agencies and instruments. Most of all, as already stated, it will require a shift in organizational culture.

In the spirit of the Comprehensive Approach, NATO is sharing most aspects of its Action Plan with several other states and organizations. A releasable version of the plan has been disseminated to the members of the Euro-Atlantic Partnership Council,[9] the Mediterranean Dialogue countries,[10] the Istanbul Cooperation Initiative countries,[11] and such contact countries as Australia, Japan, and Singapore. NATO has also shared the plan with its international organization partners, including agencies of the UN, the OSCE, and the EU, although as of this writing not with the African Union. NATO also envisions sharing the plan with the key NGOs with which it is working in the Balkans and Afghanistan. The intentions underlying broad promulgation of the plan were to build momentum, to let all potential contributors know what NATO is doing, to seek their views on cooperation, and to set the stage for further involvement as the plan unfolds. It is vital that NATO continues to improve its efforts to share information with partners on its own approach. This is a critical component of any successful civil–military strategy.

In February 2007 the North Atlantic Council tasked the Senior Political Committee (Reinforced) to oversee the development of NATO's Comprehensive Approach. In turn, this committee has tasked other committees and agencies to participate in working groups that have begun to organize NATO's internal capabilities. These working groups have developed a matrix of Action Plan tasks assigned to particular staffs and are cataloging civilian expertise relevant to the Comprehensive Approach within NATO staffs such as the Civil Emergency Planning Directorate. Efforts are also under way to identify areas of NATO planning and operations that must be modified to optimize civilian–military cooperation on a broad basis.

Beyond the optimization of internal processes, getting the most out of the limited civilian capabilities within NATO, and strengthening military support to stabilization and reconstruction, a key component of the Comprehensive Approach lies in the third and fourth parts of the Action Plan—enhanced cooperation with external actors and public diplomacy. In the area of international organizations, in September 2008 the secretaries-general of the UN and NATO signed an agreement to plan together for operations where both organizations will be engaged and to explore joint exercises and training. The details of this inaugural agreement must still be developed; however, the step itself is encouraging. Neither organization has had much preoperational contact, which has hindered early cooperation at the theater level. Experience in Afghanistan shows there is still a long way to go in terms of forging real coordination between the UN and NATO. Thus far NATO has to rely on its one liaison officer at the UN's DPKO, the only international organization at DPKO with access to secure UN documents. Although necessarily small and low profile, this direct link has been useful in NATO's support of antipiracy operations and for its assistance to the UN in Darfur and Somalia. However, the growth of NATO–UN cooperation in operational areas has outgrown the limited capacity of this initial link. An initiative is needed to negotiate more robust NATO–UN liaisons and information exchanges.

NATO–EU planning and cooperation are also too limited. The two organizations cooperate on matters related to Bosnia and Herzegovina, where the EU maintains a force supported by NATO and backed up by NATO's reinforcement plans. However, in Kosovo and Afghanistan, where NATO and the EU are engaged in far more complex operations, achieving more effective cooperation is frustrated by unrelated political factors that thwart the development of regular ties. In lieu of standing agreements, informal sessions produce ad hoc solutions that are suboptimal in terms of resources and even force protection. One of the more pressing issues NATO must address is how to design an acceptable way to cooperate more directly and effectively with the EU.

Currently, there is a limited appetite in the transatlantic community to confront the existing institutional arrangements as defined by the Berlin Plus arrangement, which enabled the use of NATO assets by the EU and vice versa.[12] But this must eventually be addressed by the United States and Europe if meaningful progress toward the Comprehensive Approach is to be achieved. This will require, first, political leadership by key nations that belong to the EU and by Washington in resolving how the EU and NATO can work together and harness the limited resources currently available for stabilization and reconstruction efforts. In the current global economic climate, duplication and inefficiencies needlessly strain the resources of both organizations. Second and similarly, the necessary will and courage must be brought to bear to address the associated political conflicts that limit EU–NATO cooperation, involving Turkey and Cyprus, which are members of NATO but not the EU. A major new initiative will be needed to deal with the impasse created by this dispute.

The Issues and Options Facing NATO

NATO has not stood still in the face of crises; rather, it has changed a great deal in its capacity to respond to conflicts. However, there is much left to do. In many ways the agreements now in place, such as going out of area and including partner forces and capabilities in NATO operations, appear to have been the easier issues. Ahead lie tougher challenges, including NATO–European Union agreements and options for fielding essential civilian expertise. This section explores NATO's achievements and possibilities in building a Comprehensive Approach to crises.

NATO's Post–Cold War Record

Since the end of the Cold War, NATO has been engaged in a transformation, modifying its processes, structures, and missions to meet its members' security interests. Its core mission remains collective defense. However, this mission now requires it to strengthen regional security through engagement, enlargement, and crisis response beyond the borders of its members.

Much has been accomplished during the past fifteen years to turn NATO toward its new missions. Its Partnership for Peace, Euro-Atlantic Partnership Council, and other forums have been added to its institutional base, strengthening European security. It has downsized and reorganized its military command structure. Its Combined Joint Task Forces and the NATO Response Force (NRF) have been operationalized, though tenuously, to meet agreed-on troop requirements. These forces have given it the capabilities to respond to crises on short notice. Its airlift and sealift capabilities are also being organized.

For twelve years, NATO has been continuously engaged in major military crisis response operations, first in the Balkans and Mediterranean, and now in Afghanistan and Africa. These critical land, sea, and air operations have involved tens of thousands of troops deployed well beyond the borders of NATO's member nations, providing it with considerable experience in deployments, strategic sustainability, and complex multinational command-and-control architectures. These operations have also given its military forces considerable interoperability experience, from the tactical to strategic levels of training, planning, and execution. In brief, NATO has remade itself into an unquestionably capable multinational military resource for crisis prevention and conflict resolution while maintaining the commitment to territorial defense based on Article 5 of the Washington Treaty, as it demonstrated in September 2001.

NATO cannot go back; it must continue to adapt both politically and institutionally as a force for transatlantic action when crises or conflicts threaten collective interests. It must become a credible, collaborative player within the context of a far more comprehensive approach to conflict resolution in the Balkans, in Afghanistan, and wherever its members agree to commit themselves under its treaty provisions. The Alliance has gained enough experience since 1995 to replace some of the cobbled-together arrangements that have sufficed for internal planning and coordination as well as limited cooperation with the United Nations, European Union, and other actors. The next steps in NATO's transformation should concentrate on honing its resources to operate more effectively within the framework of the Comprehensive Approach to crisis response and conflict resolution. It is most critical to adopt new accommodations in Afghanistan, where civil–military cooperation must be greatly improved to achieve a successful outcome.

Current Challenges

A key challenge for NATO in moving beyond ad hoc arrangements is the need for its members to embrace a firm agreement on its future roles beyond collective territorial defense—roles such as crisis management. Tensions over these roles have persisted since the Soviet threat disappeared, with some of NATO's members seeking to turn its considerable organizational and other resources to address new risks to its collective interests beyond collective defense, and others desiring to diminish it commensurate with the significantly reduced threat to its members' territories. And with the growing concerns about a more assertive Russia, particularly among those NATO member nations located close to Russia's borders, calls are also being heard for a reemphasis on "NATO's core mission."

For any mission that is undertaken, it is vital to ensure a common political understanding of the strategic objectives. For example, cooperation in Kosovo between NATO, the European Union, the United Nations, and other organizations was eventually effective in part because of an early, high-level political agreement on strategic goals and what each engaged agency needed to accomplish. For operations such as that of ISAF in Afghanistan, mechanisms for determining objectives, roles, and contributions—both in Brussels (the North Atlantic Council and the Council of the European Union) and in the theater of operations (e.g., the Joint Civil Military

Board)—were put in place early but should be better utilized. Thus it is critical that NATO and other organizations clarify the division of labor when working together to manage conflict situations. Many actors are engaged, and if their operations are not coordinated, they risk colliding or at least yielding suboptimal results due to overlaps or gaps. NATO must draw on and cooperate with neighboring countries and regional institutional frameworks.

Notwithstanding these long-running tensions, NATO has engaged in crisis response missions almost since the end of the Cold War, reaching hurried agreements to improvise political arrangements and cooperative mechanisms in lieu of more permanent, more predictable, and more effective procedures. Debates over mechanisms for cooperation stand in stark contrast to the reality of NATO's daunting missions. At this advanced stage, it should be possible to replace some of the most basic expedient arrangements with agreed-on, preestablished procedures that can be counted on for civil–military engagement, both internally and externally. The Alliance should identify some of the most important areas for precrisis planning and coordination, and seek agreements among members as well as with external partners on more permanent processes to address them. These processes should be regularly exercised even as they are put into effect, both to improve on them and to build cross-institutional experience and understanding.

NATO will also need to overcome cultural biases to closer external cooperation, and it will need to recognize that much time and education will be needed for bureaucratic cultures to evolve. Some resist institutionalizing any of the informal cooperative relationships that served NATO and its allies and partners so well in—indeed, were essential for success in—past crises, even as NATO expects to be committed in future crises that will require those same types of relationships. Some believe that a high-level political discussion and a consensus on NATO's future purpose must come first. Once that is reached, they hold, the requisite civil–military and interorganizational mechanisms will readily follow. However, the long and continuing history of NATO's engagement in crises alongside other actors argues for moving beyond ad hoc frameworks without delay. Thus, even if a political consensus remains elusive, NATO should still push forward in important areas. But it must avoid institutionalizing cumbersome arrangements that will frustrate how its civilian resources and military forces are already working together, both internally and externally.

National capacities for the Comprehensive Approach have also developed within the context of NATO's operational experience. Its members and partner countries have responded to the need for civilian capabilities by taking steps to develop some of these capabilities in working with their national military forces. The challenges faced by NATO at the international level in striking the right balance between military and nonmilitary efforts and establishing streamlined and effective cooperative arrangements between different actors are also being faced by each of its member countries at the national level. Based on experiences from Iraq and Afghanistan, most states are in the process of reconfiguring their bureaucratic and institutional framework for crisis management and conflict resolution. These reforms are complex, time consuming, costly, and politically difficult, particularly in changing cultures and traditions, and in reconfiguring budgets to appropriately fund new arrangements. For those NATO members where significant results have been achieved and important lessons have been learned, such information must be shared with all NATO's partners in the context of developing its Comprehensive Approach.

Another pressing task for NATO is coalescing national capabilities at the international level in a way that provides the best possible civilian interagency teammate for multinational military capabilities. Negotiating toward standardized goal setting, planning, operational interfacing, and resourcing will be necessary. Information-sharing modalities will be critical but must overcome national prerogatives. The habit of classifying large volumes of information is strong, especially among national military commands and agencies. This practice should yield to sharing as much information as possible across all civil and military organizations.

NATO's engagement in crises has involved three broad operational areas: combat operations (in Kosovo and Afghanistan), postconflict stability operations (Bosnia, Kosovo, and Afghanistan), and assistance to long-term reconstruction operations (Bosnia, Kosovo, Afghanistan, and Iraq). NATO has thus far organized only for an initial military response, designed primarily for combat operations, that is, the NATO Response Force. The NRF remains NATO's high-water mark in terms of planning, organizing, and training to respond to crises. However, the NRF's operational commitments in Afghanistan, along with the cost, have diluted this capability for the near term, and the NRF concept requires more agreement on mission definition and sustained force commitments.

What NATO still lacks is an organized, deployable civilian and military capacity that is specifically designed to address stabilization and reconstruction operations. Here, the initial solutions may not be a standing civilian capacity or a standing military force tailored to stabilization and reconstruction, but there should be at least preplanned menus of capabilities, exercised together periodically, that constitute a viable and coordinated set of civilian skills and military resources to provide immediate triage to postconflict or crisis areas. In addition, NATO would be well served if its member countries could agree to organize a nucleus of civilians to plan and oversee the full array of civilian resources in an operational environment. A standing civilian cadre, coupled with a menu of available capabilities, would provide the NATO Allies with a readily deployable civilian force for any contingency requiring stabilization and reconstruction. Such a resource would constitute the multinational equivalent of deployable national civilian capabilities. However, realizing these capabilities will require equitable resourcing agreements, basic multinational doctrinal concepts, appropriate command-and-control architectures, sustainable profiles, and deployment flow schemes.

New Tasks Where the Comprehensive Approach Is No Less Essential

Thus far, the Comprehensive Approach being developed by NATO staffs is focused on expeditionary operations where military power is the central component and the application of civilian resources, though no less essential, is complementary—at least in early stages. That remains the cardinal purpose of building up an operational civilian–military teamwork. However, close cooperation across the full spectrum of crisis response (not just military) efforts will, with sustained emphasis, build a broader capacity for cooperation across all NATO operations, including those where military assets are less central.

Many crises of every stripe call for civilian and military responders to act together. It will benefit those at risk if all responders are well linked in their communications and are accustomed to operating together. Whether such a situation arises due to the risk of a pandemic disease, the sudden disruption of essential energy supplies, the loss of critical infrastructure cybernetworks, or an international call for humanitarian relief and/or disaster assistance, each response is likely to involve both civilian and military elements engaged in rapid reaction operations. One example is the 2005 Pakistan earthquake response by NATO military forces, working closely with the UN and international aid organizations and Pakistani civil agencies. Whether assisting a member at home, such as NATO relief operations in the United States after Hurricane Katrina, or responding beyond Alliance territories, it is clear that there will be a substantial benefit in mustering a well-prepared, readily deployable comprehensive response capability. In anticipation of more of these types of operations, NATO should take a broad view of its Comprehensive Approach by including experts on essential civilian capabilities early in all military planning efforts.

NATO's Course of Action in 2009 and Beyond

In this period after its 2009 Strasbourg-Kehl Summit, NATO has a fresh opportunity to move forward in its relationships with those members, organizations, and partners able and willing to deploy civilian resources. In particular, it should focus on undertakings that would contribute significantly to improving its structures for participating with other organizations in its Comprehensive Approach to crises and conflicts. It should formalize those standing political-military and strategic military forums tasked to engage with all appropriate civil actors in crisis response, such as the United Nations, the European Union, the OSCE, and the African Union. These mechanisms should address, as equal partners, top-level policy, planning, and resourcing considerations for integrated civil–military responses in current and future operations.

NATO's structures that seek to provide an optimum interface for civilian counterparts at the operational and tactical levels also need to be adjusted. Its initial efforts should focus on the development of civilian capability goals for its Allies, similar to military force goals. These efforts should include preoperational coordination and planning, as well as doctrine and standards for supporting and being supported by civil entities, such as Provincial Reconstruction Teams and police trainers. NATO's support might include appropriate levels of security, as well as communications, logistical, and transportation resources. Agreements will be needed to establish what is required and how resources will be funded.

The Alliance should continue to hone a common understanding with other actors on its Comprehensive Approach to crisis response and resolution. This can be facilitated through exercising and planning, workshops involving all stakeholders, examining best practices with civil actors, and sharing lessons learned from operations. A comprehensive database of lessons learned should be established and continuously updated by teams in the field, without regard to organizational source. Data collection should go beyond current efforts by NATO's Joint Analysis and Lessons Learned Center. It should also include civil lessons from other agencies, and it should be available to all organizations engaged in planning and operating together. Such a reservoir of collective knowledge would be an ideal topic for an agreement among NATO, the UN, and the EU, as well as other actors.

NATO will also need to keep updated for its potential civilian partners, beginning with its own members, what nonmilitary capabilities it foresees as necessary for its future crisis and/or conflict operations. New civilian capabilities are always being brought to market, just for the military. NATO should encourage its members and, as appropriate, other organizations to indicate what capabilities they might provide and under what conditions. The minimum essential capabilities include the reestablishment of basic services, public safety and security, and institutions of government at the local, regional, and national levels. Finally, NATO should explore ways to reinvigorate its highly successful Partnership for Peace and Euro-Atlantic Partnership Council with the goal of strengthening their influence in conflict prevention. Within these broad undertakings, four initiatives can put the "meat on the bones" of a long-term agenda for implementing NATO's Comprehensive Approach. Some of these initiatives are already under way but require continued emphasis as essential capabilities for civil–military collaboration.

Military Resource Requirements for the Comprehensive Approach

First, NATO must be better at marshaling the military resource requirements of the Comprehensive Approach. The Alliance should develop three or four Comprehensive Approach operational scenarios, involving both military and nonmilitary assets, to provide a framework for preliminary crisis response planning, exercises, and doctrine development. Allied Command Operations/Allied Command Transformation should expand their training and exercises with civilian partners—to include not only the European Union, the OSCE, and the United Nations but also key NGOs. These exercises should take into account the existing training and expertise at the national level and endeavor to make national knowledge available to all NATO members and partners. A key objective should be to enable NATO's deployed military forces to learn to work more closely with civilian experts, such as within Provincial Reconstruction Teams in Afghanistan.

Given that both the police and military capabilities are essential to public security, the North Atlantic Council should discuss how to formalize release authority procedures for the European Gendarme Force at Vicenza, Italy, as well as seek to define commitment modalities for other policing capabilities. As a tenet of military force planning for crisis response, the NATO Military Authorities should plan for crisis response forces sufficient to protect and support essential civilian partners, as called for by conditions of the operational environment.

Training and equipping indigenous security forces is a key component of generating long-term stability in semipermissive environments. NATO should ensure that its schools educate Allied forces on the best practices and lessons learned associated with training and mentoring these forces. Training and concept development, along with the collection of lessons learned, would be best housed in a NATO Center of Excellence for a Comprehensive Approach to Crises.

Civilian Resources for the Comprehensive Approach

Second, NATO must be able to marshal civilian resources for complex operations in a much more systematic and concerted manner. NATO should encourage its members to identify deployable civilian capacity at the national level and compile a database so that all members will realize where their contributions might fit. They can then see where there are gaps and hopefully invest in filling them. Civilian resources would not necessarily be organized or deployed under NATO. However, they would be available to work with NATO operationally, either as national contributions or under other appropriate organizations, such as the United Nations, the OSCE, or the European Union. NATO's interest should be to ensure that the requisite civilian partners are available and ready, and to know what support it will need to provide to civilian partners in potentially hostile and austere environments.

In July 2008 the United States, NATO's principal member outside the European Union framework, dedicated a new interagency Civilian Response Corps under the Department of State, which requested funding in 2009 of almost $250 million for the corps' active, standby, and reserve components. Still, the U.S. Civilian Stabilization Initiative is in its infancy and will require sustained funding and top-level emphasis to flourish. Thus far there is encouraging momentum behind the commitment, which could eventually materialize as the capability elaborated by a team of experts from the National Defense University in its recent publication *Civilian Surge*.[13]

NATO must determine how to bring its International Staff and its Senior Civil Emergency Planning Committee to bear more effectively on the challenges of civil–military coordination, building on initial work done in the middle to late 1990s in response to the Balkan conflicts. Cataloging available commercial resources, capabilities, and standards is one task. Other tasks would include how NATO could mirror at least some of its Cold War processes for civil emergency planning that support its interaction with other agencies in deployed operations. And it should also establish a consolidated database of current and anticipated language requirements and available linguists, both civilian and military, within its staffs and from member nations.

External Resources for the Comprehensive Approach

Third, additional steps should be taken to marshal external resources in support of the Comprehensive Approach. The NATO secretary-general should further both coordination and consultation with other organizations, beginning with the UN and the EU, for civil–military collaboration on crisis response and conflict resolution, with priority given to efforts in Afghanistan. The North Atlantic Council should formally assign the assistant secretary-general for political affairs and security policy to take the lead in external matters related to the development of the Comprehensive Approach.

NATO and each of its members should undertake to strengthen public support for its role in crisis response. This would require vigorous and parallel messaging, diplomacy, and public awareness campaigns to connect NATO's commitments to the collective interests supported by its members' public. In addition, a standing NATO–EU Comprehensive Approach Working Group should be created to propose ways to harmonize both interorganizational initiatives and national interagency initiatives. Currently, discrete processes compete for the same resources to satisfy different and disconnected planning regimes. For example, the EU Civilian Headline Goal Force and NATO's need for police and security sector reform resources in Afghanistan compete for the same police officers from countries that are NATO and EU members or partners.

Information and Communications Resources for the Comprehensive Approach

Fourth, it is essential for NATO to improve its ability to marshal information and communications resources. It should undertake creative and forceful initiatives to share intelligence from its traditional core group when it comes to Comprehensive Approach planning and operations. Its Military Authorities should study how to extend necessary communications and data network connectivity to essential NGOs and international organizations. One way would be to design a portable communications system that can be provided to essential external actors that do not have resources themselves to link to NATO. The NATO Consultation, Command, and Control Agency should inaugurate a Web-based multiservice (blogs, chats, collaboration tools, informational sites, links, etc.) portal for authorized users to share information on civil–military cooperation of immediate interest to others in the field, such as Provincial Reconstruction Teams' best practices. More broadly, NATO should take steps to share its standards in key areas and push for interoperability among all crisis responders, especially for data and communications systems. It should also agree on a process for systematically collecting and sharing lessons learned internally and with its civilian partners on a continuously updated, perhaps interactive web-hosted basis set up and operated in theater by a dedicated service. This would be an expeditious, low-cost tool for strengthening the effectiveness of civil–military cooperation in Afghanistan.

Conclusion

The Comprehensive Approach, first proposed by Denmark in the NATO context, has grown to encompass the full realm of international participants in crisis and conflict management. Today's security challenges require cooperation at the national and international levels to combine civil and military resources and coordinate measures being taken. The effective implementation of this Comprehensive Approach requires the cooperation and contribution of major actors, with a shared sense of openness and determination. This has been the core advocacy pursued by the Danish Embassy in Washington and the National Defense University since 2007.

Actors such as the UN and the EU already play important roles in responding to future crises. NATO should concentrate on developing its relations with these institutions most of all, beginning with the suggestions described in this chapter. The ultimate goal is to work together across all phases of response. This will mean closer and continuous ties at multiple levels, from the strategic to the operational. NATO has established itself as a major contributor to UN operations and a strong partner in EU operations; the trend is that such cooperation will continue in the future and may well grow. The operational advantage inherent in knowing more about each other's capabilities should be justification enough for civilian–military collaboration across all phases of operations.

The early collaborative steps—such as agreeing to an Action Plan and taking the measure of what NATO has at its disposal internally—are encouraging signs. Yet much more needs to be done. More than anything, the NATO Allies and their partners need to take the perspective that realizing the Comprehensive Approach will require a long-term strategic shift, not merely the implementation of a new concept. Institutional cultures and international politics often present the greatest opposition to sharing information, compromising on operational methods, committing to advanced planning, or agreeing that the best solution may be to subordinate one's own agency to an overall representative group or to partner closely with another.

It is likely that the Comprehensive Approach will entail education and training as well as much fresh new thinking among the staffs of all agencies. NATO is off to a respectable start, and it should endeavor to build steady momentum in the months and years ahead. The springboard of NATO's sixtieth anniversary and deliberations to reach agreement on a new Strategic Concept should be seized as opportunities to make substantial progress. The alternative will be operations that are drawn out and more costly. NATO owes its members and its forces a better solution.

NATO's Comprehensive Approach and its practical application in critical peace operations in Afghanistan, Kosovo, and elsewhere have indeed become integral components of the Alliance's crisis response strategy. The Comprehensive Approach can also become the centerpiece for future cooperation between NATO, the UN, the EU, and the rest of the international community. Moreover, it is yet another essential enterprise between Europe and North America that will invigorate transatlantic relations for the future. As NATO moves forward from its Sixtieth-Anniversary Summit, its Comprehensive Approach should be articulated, most visibly in its next Strategic Concept, as a fundamental operating basis for all its future missions.

Notes

The opinions, conclusions, and recommendations expressed or implied within this chapter are those of the contributors and do not necessarily reflect the views of the U.S. Department of Defense or any other department or agency of the U.S. government, or the views of the Danish government.

1. For a full appreciation of the Alliance Reborn initiative, see the Washington NATO Project report: Daniel Hamilton, Charles Barry, Hans Binnendijk, Stephen Flanagan, Julianne Smith, and James Townsend, *Alliance Reborn: An Atlantic Compact for the 21st Century* (Washington, DC: Atlantic Council of the United States, Center for Strategic and International Studies, Center for Technology and National Security Policy at the National Defense University, and Center for Transatlantic Relations at the Paul H. Nitze School of Advanced International Studies of Johns Hopkins University, 2009), www.acus.org/files/publication_pdfs/65/NATO-AllianceReborn.pdf.

2. "Riga Summit Declaration" issued by heads of state and government in the meeting of the North Atlantic Council on November 29, 2006, paragraph 10, www .nato.int/docu/pr/2006/p06-150e.htm.

3. Ibid.

4. See Friis Arne Petersen and Hans Binnendijk, "The Comprehensive Approach Initiative: Future Options for NATO," *Defense Horizons* 58 (September 2007). See also Friis Arne Petersen and Hans Binnendijk, "From Comprehensive Approach to

Comprehensive Capabilities," *NATO Review*, April 2008, www.nato.int/docu/review/2008/03/EN/index.htm; and Friis Arne Petersen and Hans Binnendijk, "NATO Needs New Lease," *Washington Times*, April 2, 2008.

5. Notwithstanding that the process is ongoing at NATO, the actions thus far described articulate a broad menu of what might be undertaken to develop NATO's contribution to the Comprehensive Approach concept of crisis response.

6. NATO, "Bucharest Summit Declaration," April 3, 2008, paragraph 4, www.nato.int/docu/pr/2008/p08–049e.html.

7. Ibid., paragraph 11; emphasis added.

8. The JCMB was established in April 2006 by the Afghan government and the international community for overall strategic coordination of the Afghan Compact, endorsed at the London Conference and pursuant to UNSC Resolution 1659. The JCMB comprises seven key ministries of the Afghan government and twenty-one representatives of the international community in Afghanistan, including donors, troop contributors, and neighboring countries. The major organizations represented are the United Nations (chair), the European Union, NATO, and the World Bank. NGOs are not represented.

9. The Euro-Atlantic Partnership Council is made up of the twenty-six members of NATO and these twenty-four partner countries: Albania, Armenia, Austria, Azerbaijan, Belarus, Bosnia and Herzegovina, Croatia, Finland, Georgia, Ireland, Kazakhstan, the Kyrgyz Republic, Malta, Moldova, Montenegro, Russia, Serbia, Sweden, Switzerland, Macedonia, Tajikistan, Turkmenistan, Ukraine, and Uzbekistan.

10. The countries of the 1994 NATO Mediterranean Dialogue are Algeria, Egypt, Israel, Jordan, Mauritania, Morocco, and Tunisia.

11. NATO's 2004 Istanbul Cooperation Initiative partners are Bahrain, Kuwait, Qatar, and the United Arab Emirates.

12. The Berlin Plus arrangement, which was set out in the EU–NATO Declaration on the European Security and Defense Policy in December 2002, built on earlier NATO decisions, particularly the 1996 European Defense Initiative in Berlin and the 1999 NATO Washington Summit, and made possible the use of NATO assets by the EU and vice versa.

13. See Hans Binnendijk and Patrick Cronin, eds., *Civilian Surge: Key to Complex Operations* (Washington, DC: National Defense University Press, 2008).

CHAPTER 5

NATO–Russia Relations

WILL THE FUTURE RESEMBLE THE PAST?

Martin A. Smith

THE FOCUS OF THIS CHAPTER is on the structures of the NATO–Russia relationship, and the key questions considered here have to do with how this relationship has developed, why it is important, and where it may be going. Russia matters to NATO as its most "significant other" in the broader European context. As such, developing and maintaining at least a tolerably functioning relationship with Russia has come to be seen as an important element underpinning NATO's claims to legitimacy as a core component of the post–Cold War European security architecture. Over time, NATO's members have also come to appreciate the virtues of engaging Russia in the hope that the latter may be willing to act, if not as a full-blown partner, then at least on the basis of perceived shared interests with regard to essential security issues.

The chapter is broadly divided into two sections. The first considers the evolution of the NATO–Russia relationship during the 1990s. Particular attention is paid here to the 1999 Kosovo crisis, which had a profound impact on NATO–Russia relations. The second section considers the first decade of the new millennium. The particular focus here is on the 2008 Georgia crisis and its foreseeable impact on the structures of the relationship.

Today both Russia and the United States are in substantially different situations than during the 1990s. Then, the United States appeared to many as the unchallenged global superpower, while Russia was widely viewed as a weak and chaotic ex-superpower. More recently, perceptions of U.S. decline have grown steadily, as have perceptions that Russia has been "coming back," on the basis of its strengths as a major energy exporter and the often-astute conduct of its foreign policy under then–president Vladimir Putin. The discussions here nevertheless chart the evolution of NATO–Russia relations

99

essentially as a continuum. This approach is adopted to account for the significant elements of longevity, autonomy, and continuity in the basic structures of this relationship and to suggest why it is still relevant today.

NATO–Russia Relations in the 1990s

During the first post–Cold War decade, two key issues dominated efforts to develop a stable and predictable relationship between the NATO institution and Russia. The first was the consistent demand from Russian leaders for some kind of "special" institutional relationship with NATO. By this they meant one that was demonstrably distinct from and closer than that enjoyed by any other non–NATO member state. The second and even more important issue was NATO enlargement.[1]

There were two reasons for these Russian demands for special relations. One was the desire—indeed the need—for Russian leaders to have overt NATO recognition of their state and nation as a great power, if no longer a superpower. The second was more practically focused on attempting to secure a structural way to prevent NATO from agreeing on actions (e.g., in Bosnia) that Russian leaders did not like. If this were not possible, then Russian leaders wanted at least the opportunity to have special consultative rights with NATO and its members, so that Russia's voice would clearly be heard. These concerns were primarily responsible for delaying Russian accession to NATO's Partnership for Peace scheme in 1994, given the partnership's basis on the principle of formal equality among the partners.[2]

The decision to formally proceed with eastward enlargement was made at the NATO Madrid Summit in July 1997. This event served to focus minds among both NATO members and Russian leaders about how best to manage the process, in the sense of preventing it from creating a terminal rupture in NATO–Russia relations. Six months before the summit, bilateral negotiations got under way between the Russian government, represented by then–foreign minister Yevgeny Primakov, and the NATO institution, represented by Javier Solana, then its secretary-general. Insiders reported that these talks were sometimes fraught and difficult, and the eventual agreement in mid-May evidently came as a surprise to some commentators.[3] This agreement could partly be attributed to the good working relationship that Solana had managed to establish with Primakov, an impression confirmed by the pictures of backslapping bonhomie that accompanied press coverage of the announcement that an agreement had been reached.[4] Success was also attributed to the extent to which NATO's member states had deliberately maintained a united front behind Solana and resisted the temptation to cut bilateral deals with the Russian government.[5] This ensured that Russia could not exploit potential divisions among NATO's members and "forum shop" for the best deal from several different possible alternatives.

Most important, however, success had been possible because neither side made a serious attempt to tie the other down to a *specific* interpretation of what their new deal actually meant. Partly this was necessary to reach agreement within the tight deadline before the NATO summit. However, it also reflected a lack of underlying agreement on fundamental principles and issues. Therefore, no real agreed-on conceptual basis for the relationship had been established, and this was to prove an enduring weakness.

A special meeting of NATO leaders with then President Boris Yeltsin was arranged for Paris at the end of May 1997 in order to sign a document ponderously titled the *Founding Act on Mutual Relations, Cooperation and Security between NATO and the Russian Federation.*[6] At the declaratory level, the *Founding Act* gave the Russians a good deal. NATO signed up to multiple pledges for which the Russian side had been arguing. These included revising its core Strategic Concept, continuing to "expand its political functions," and taking on "new missions of peacekeeping and crisis management in support of the United Nations and the Organization for Security and Cooperation in Europe." The underlying purpose, it was grandly declared, was to "build increasing levels of trust, unity of purpose and habits of consultation and cooperation between NATO and Russia."

A new "Mechanism for Consultation and Cooperation" was also established, to be called the NATO–Russia Permanent Joint Council (PJC). It was intended to be "a council of 17,"[7] and hence more inclusive than previous "16 + 1" consultative arrangements between the sixteen NATO member states and Russia. Although not without value, the 16 + 1 formula, by definition, had presupposed that Russia was an institutional outsider.[8] It also suggested that NATO's members would act as a single caucus and "precook" positions before presenting them to their Russian interlocutors. From the Russian perspective, therefore, genuine consultation had been institutionally circumscribed under the 16 + 1 arrangements.

The PJC was to meet regularly at either the ministerial or ambassadorial level, and to that end Russia was to establish a mission to NATO headed by an ambassador. In this respect, its representation would almost be on a par with that of NATO's members themselves. The proviso was that the Russian representatives would not maintain a permanent presence at NATO Headquarters in Brussels, as did member states. Formally, the Russian representatives to NATO would be accredited to Russia's Brussels Embassy to Belgium.

Therefore, the *Founding Act* did give Russia a "special relationship" with NATO, in the sense that its level of representation and rights of consultation were greater than those accorded to any other nonmember state. Its representatives would sit on the PJC on equal terms, at least formally, with their NATO counterparts. There was a crucial caveat, however. It was stated that "provisions of this Act do not provide NATO or Russia, in any way, with a right of veto over the actions of the other nor do they infringe upon or restrict the rights of NATO or Russia to independent decision-making and action."[9] The act detailed "specific areas of mutual interest," which could be placed on the agenda at PJC meetings. Yet the very fact that the scope of the PJC had been limited at all meant that, in the future, NATO's members could keep items *off* the agenda when they did not wish to have Russian representatives discussing especially sensitive or controversial issues. This was to prove especially debilitating for the PJC just before the Kosovo crisis in 1998–99.

From the beginning some in Russia saw Yeltsin's decision to sign up to the *Founding Act* as a defeat for their country. This may appear surprising in view of the institutional successes gained by the Russian negotiators. It is however an indication of the shallowness of support for the new arrangements and the extent to which they were not based on any underlying sense of real rapprochement. An editorial in *Izvestia* argued that "Russia seems to have bidden farewell to a whole era and to any illusions that it could stop the military alliance from drawing closer to its borders. At times this touching scene [the Paris Summit] evoked the picture of a country parting with the role of a great power and consciously shifting to a new capacity."[10] Writing in *Nezavisimaya Gazeta*, meanwhile, Andranik Migranyan, a member of the Presidential Council, argued in a similar vein. His main complaint was that "the NATO countries' fundamental victory is their refusal, on key questions, to make any commitments that might tie the organization's hands."[11]

In countering such accusations from domestic critics, the Yeltsin government argued that everything depended on how the *Founding Act*'s provisions worked out in practice. As the presidential press spokesperson put it, NATO and Russia were at "the beginning of the struggle in interpreting the agreement."[12] The lack of prior agreed-on interpretations might, this argument went, work to Russia's advantage if, in practice, it was able to establish a more assertive role in the relationship than some NATO members may have envisaged.

In this context the lack of agreement on specifics before the Paris Summit could be seen as a potential strength of the new arrangement. Yet conversely, concerns about the possibility of the Russian government taking more from it than intended helped to explain doubts about the *Founding Act* that soon began to appear in the United States. Perhaps most notably, former secretary of state Henry Kissinger claimed in congressional testimony that "it will be argued that if the Permanent [Joint] Council deadlocks, the regular NATO Council remains free to perform its historic functions. That is true in theory, but it will never work in practice. Since, except for the Russian representatives, the membership is identical, each country will assess the grave step of meeting without a Russian presence in terms of its overall relationship with Moscow. Thus, in practice, NATO Council sessions and Permanent [Joint] Council sessions will tend to merge. The free and easy 'family atmosphere' of existing institutions will vanish."[13]

Viewed in the context of NATO's established institutional strengths, Kissinger's concerns seemed wide of the mark even at the time. It is, however, a measure of the anxiety that evidently existed in official Washington about how the new and flexible PJC arrangement might develop that the Bill Clinton administration's attitude began to shift. Whereas, in the period up to and including the Paris Summit, the accent had been on the extent to which Russia–NATO relations might develop, by late 1997 the message was more restrictive.[14] Testifying to the Senate Foreign Relations Committee (shortly after Kissinger), Thomas Pickering, then the undersecretary of state for political affairs and a former U.S. ambassador to Russia, avowed that in the Clinton administration's view, "The PJC is a consultative mechanism, and . . . consultation in diplomatic parlance means just that, talking together. It does not mean a situation in which you are obliged to negotiate. It does not mean you are in a situation where you are obliged to make a decision. . . . In cases where the Russians might suggest subject matter on which there is no NATO position, it is clearly provided that NATO is not required to undertake any such discussion and certainly can, if it wishes and chooses to make such a discussion, first agree among itself, its members, as to what its position is."[15]

The clarity that Pickering claimed here was in fact not as evident in the text of the *Founding Act* as he suggested. This, in itself, was a demonstration of the studied ambiguity of key provisions in that document and the consequent scope for differing interpretations. Specifically, the *Founding Act* did *not* provide for NATO's members to precook positions among themselves before taking them to the Russians. Indeed, talk of a "council of 17" seemed to have ruled this out. Conversely, and crucially, the adoption of prearranged common positions was not *explicitly* prohibited either. At the least, therefore, the Russian leaders could be forgiven for thinking that the apparent shift in position on the part of NATO's most powerful member state indicated bad faith and suggested that the *Founding Act* and PJC were never intended to be much more than tactical ruses designed to sublimate official Russian opposition to NATO enlargement.

However, there are grounds for doubting whether the Russians were prepared to engage constructively and substantively themselves. The very first meeting of the PJC in July 1997 was postponed for a day. This occurred because the Russian representatives raised eleventh-hour objections to the chairing arrangements, despite the fact that these had been set out in the *Founding Act* itself.[16] During the first six months of PJC meetings, the Russian representatives threatened to walk out several times. The Russian government also displayed a persistent reluctance to conclude an agreement on the opening of a NATO Military Liaison Mission in Moscow, as provided for in the *Founding Act*.[17]

There were indications, nonetheless, that by mid-1998 the PJC was beginning to show some promise as a venue for useful and substantive discussions, at least on occasion. Colonel General Leonid Ivashov, director of the Russian Defense Ministry's Chief Administration for International Military Cooperation (and a noted NATO skeptic), warmly praised a PJC defense ministers' meeting in June of that year. He described it as having been "highly appraised by both sides in terms of substance and transparency."[18] Six months later, then–foreign minister Igor Ivanov stated that Russia–NATO relations had "come a long way, from distrust to mutual understanding and joint efforts to resolve the issues confronting them." He paid tribute to the PJC in helping to bring this about.[19] Public assessments on the NATO side were also upbeat during 1997 and 1998.[20] The emerging optimism was about to be rudely curtailed, however.

The Kosovo Crisis

It is easy to view the decision by NATO's members to go ahead with air operations against the Federal Republic of Yugoslavia (FRY) over Kosovo in March 1999 as dealing a blow to the PJC from which it never fully recovered. In his first official response to the bombing, President Yeltsin accused NATO's leaders of violating the terms of the *Founding Act* and announced the suspension of Russian participation in the PJC.[21] The Russian government had some grounds for making this accusation. According to the *Founding Act*'s provisions, both NATO's members and Russia pledged to respect "the primary responsibility of the UN Security Council for maintaining international peace and security," yet NATO had launched its bombing campaign without an explicit UN mandate. Further, the *Founding Act* pledged both parties to refrain "from the threat or use of force against each other as well as against any other state, its sovereignty, territorial integrity or political independence in any manner inconsistent with the United Nations Charter."[22]

The main indictment against the PJC from more detached observers is that it failed completely to function as an early-warning consultative mechanism in the critical weeks leading up to the commencement of the NATO bombing action. There can be little doubt as to where most of the blame for this lay. NATO's members had, allegedly, not wanted to "complicate" their decision making over Kosovo by granting the Russians any kind of formal input.[23]

Taking the longer view, it can be argued that the Kosovo crisis did not cause the breakdown of the PJC all by itself. By then it was apparent to many informed observers that it was *already* floundering. Thus, for example, Peter Trenin-Straussov argued frankly that the PJC had turned into a "failure." He noted that NATO's members had been caucusing in advance of meetings and presenting their Russian interlocutors with pre-agreed-on positions. As a result, "the Russians for their part, soon discovered that dealing with individual NATO member states outside the PJC was more effective and satisfying." In consequence, "the PJC . . . [had] turned itself into a talking shop for rather stale dialogue."[24] NATO's members were also accused of being unwilling to routinely discuss "main political issues" in depth within the PJC, as favored by the Russians. The former allegedly preferred to stick to narrower technical matters.[25]

Such criticisms illustrate the extent of the failure of the *Founding Act* and the consultative mechanisms based upon it. Broadly speaking, they had been bedeviled by two problems. The first—noted above—arose from the fact that both sides preferred to avoid pinning themselves down to agreed-on understandings during the negotiations in the first half of 1997. In retrospect this simply left too much to chance. Put a little more charitably, it presumed a significant degree of mutual goodwill and a willingness to utilize the new arrangements for the shared good.

Second, by the late 1990s and in spite of the fact there had been institutional links of one kind or another between NATO and Russia since 1991, no real sense of "partnership" or "community" had emerged. The text of the *Founding Act* simply presumed that these did in fact exist. Thus its preamble eloquently hailed "the beginning of a fundamentally new relationship between NATO and Russia," which "on the basis of common interest, reciprocity and transparency" would produce "a strong, stable and enduring partnership."[26] The overall record of the PJC between May 1997 and March 1999 suggested that neither common interest nor reciprocity nor transparency had loomed large in its short history. As a result, when faced with its first serious test, it became irrelevant almost immediately.

Having said all this, it should be remembered that the suspension of the PJC did not result in the termination of all contacts between Russia and the NATO member states themselves. Indeed, as is well known, Russia played an instrumental—some would say vital—role in the diplomacy that eventually resulted in the FRY government's accepting terms to end the NATO bombing. The increasing Russian involvement occurred, furthermore, with the active encouragement of leading NATO member states.[27]

NATO–Russia Relations in the New Millennium

Notwithstanding what has been argued above, the rupturing of the specific structural relationship between NATO and Russia in March 1999 illustrates the ongoing failure to underpin it with a shared normative basis. Its subsequent revival, however, points to a second essential truism of the relationship—that at no point since 1991 have the leaders on either side wished to see it end irrevocably and permanently. In the aftermath of the Kosovo air campaign, it seemed apparent to both sides that serious challenges to Europe's security would likely require significant de facto cooperation, if not full de jure partnership, in order to be tackled effectively. Structures designed to provide for joint consultations and potential common action when agreement was reached could be, it was felt, one important element in facilitating such cooperation.

Evidence for this thinking can be seen in the extent to which the Kosovo rupture proved to be both more limited than it might have at first appeared and also short term. In July 1999, less than a month after the end of the NATO bombing of the FRY, the newspaper *Vremya MN* summed up the prevailing sentiment in Russia when it argued that "during the Balkan war, Russia made the most important choice in our country's recent history. We didn't ally ourselves with NATO, but, thank God, we didn't become its enemy either. Now, Russia and the West can become partners who may not have any reason to love each other, but have to work together if only because there's no getting away from each other."[28]

Russia's political leaders at the time publicly accepted that their state would need to learn—again—to live with NATO. Igor Ivanov conceded that "like it or not, NATO is a reality in today's international arena, primarily in Europe but also in the world in general." Yevgeny Primakov stated that "we have to talk, as NATO is a real force and this should be taken into account."[29] Whatever else it may have done, the NATO bombing of the FRY evidently served to persuade the Russian leaders that NATO was likely to remain a leading actor on the European security stage for the long term.

The PJC was reconvened before the end of July 1999. The Russian side emphasized that it saw the reactivation as being for the sole purpose of discussing issues "in a clearly defined sphere: interaction within the framework of KFOR [the NATO-led Kosovo peacekeeping force]."[30] Nevertheless, the reactivation of the PJC did indicate that both sides accepted that it was not in their interest to see a continuation of the complete freeze on institutional links that Yeltsin had imposed at the start of NATO's bombing campaign.

On the NATO side, then–secretary-general Lord Robertson evidently saw an opportunity to further invigorate relations in the aftermath of Yeltsin's resignation at the end of 1999 and the consequent advent of the presidency of Vladimir Putin. In February 2000, when Putin was still acting president, Robertson made the first official high-level NATO trip to Russia since the Kosovo crisis. He met with Putin and Ivanov, and the two sides agreed on a statement pledging to "intensify their dialogue in the Permanent Joint Council . . . on a wide range of security issues."[31] Thus, it was agreed that consultations within the PJC would henceforth take place on other issues in addition to those specifically related to Kosovo.

Robertson was careful to avoid giving the impression of triumphalism. He restricted his public assessment to the understated comment that "we've moved from permafrost into slightly softer ground."[32] Indeed, it should be borne in mind that the moves made between July 1999 and February 2000 resulted in nothing more than the restoration of the status quo ante bellum, rather than moving the NATO–Russia relationship in any qualitatively new direction.

Anybody familiar with the trajectory of the relationship in the first decade of the new millennium will know that a significant qualitative enhancement did not occur until after the September 11, 2001, terrorist attacks on the United States. It is of course impossible to know whether and how the relationship would have evolved in the absence of September 11. Nevertheless, it can be argued that a desire to see qualitative progress was in evidence from early in the Putin era. In March 2000, Putin had made international headlines following a television interview with David Frost. Most of the attention focused on his response to a question about possible Russian membership in NATO. "Why not?" was his brief but pointed reply.[33]

The significance of this apparently innocuous response was that it recalled the approach taken in a letter that President Yeltsin had addressed to NATO's members in December 1991, at the start of Russia's existence as a post-Soviet state.[34] Putin was, no doubt, *intentionally* emulating his predecessor in seeking to send a strong political signal to NATO's members at the start of his own period in power. As with Yeltsin in 1991, it is doubtful that he was seriously interested in actual NATO membership for Russia. Rather, the new leader was likely seeking to capture Western attention and focus it on the question of how the existing bilateral NATO–Russia relationship could be qualitatively enhanced.

The signaling purpose of Putin's remarks was widely recognized and acknowledged, both inside Russia and among the governments of the NATO member states.[35] The latter may thus have shown a certain degree of "institutional learning." In 1991, there had been no official acknowledgement of the Yeltsin letter. This had possibly caused a degree of resentment among Russian leaders and policymakers, and contributed to the depth of their opposition to the subsequent NATO enlargement process.

The NATO–Russia Council

In March 2000, Lord Robertson, speaking on behalf of NATO, said that although "at present Russian membership of NATO is not on the agenda," nevertheless NATO's members recognized "the need for partnership between the Alliance and Russia, and will work hard to build on our existing links."[36] Thus, "partnership" was officially back on the agenda. Yet it is arguable that NATO and its members missed the underlying signal that Putin was really seeking to convey. This was that the "existing links" between Russia and NATO were not sufficient and should be superseded by something more substantial. In his Frost interview, Putin had stated that "we believe we can talk about more profound integration with NATO, but only if Russia is regarded as an equal partner."[37] This suggested a desire for something better, from Russia's point of view, than the PJC. NATO, however, was not yet prepared to offer anything more. A better offer did not come until after September 11.

In view of what has been argued here, it is surely significant that, in the immediate aftermath of the events of September 11, Putin once more raised the question of possible Russian membership in NATO.[38] Following a meeting with Lord Robertson in early October 2001, Putin was quoted as saying that "we have got the impression that our signals in favour of closer cooperation have been heard."[39] Among the NATO member governments, there was now talk that Russian representatives might be given some co-decision-making rights in a new "council of twenty" at NATO. Then–British prime minister Tony Blair was often credited with this idea, perhaps because he was reckoned to have a particularly good working relationship with the Russian president.[40] In fact, on a visit to Moscow immediately after the proposal became public knowledge, Secretary-General Robertson attributed similar ideas to the United States, Germany, Italy, and Canada.

In effect, Robertson used this November 2001 visit to formally propose the council of twenty to the Russian government. This new body, he said:

> Would involve Russia having an equality with the NATO countries in terms of the subject matter and [it] would be part of the same compromising trade-offs, give and take, that is involved in day-to-day NATO business. That is how we do business at 19 [NATO members] . . . we get compromises. We build consensus. So the idea would be that Russia would enter that. That would give Russia a right of equality but also a responsibility and an obligation that would come from being part of the consensus-building organization. That is why I say a new attitude is going to be required on both sides if this is going to work. But if it works, it obviously is a huge change, a sea change in the way in which we do business.[41]

From these remarks, it was clear that Robertson envisaged the new body serving, in part, to "discipline" the Russians into acting "responsibly." Hopefully, this might prevent them from repeating what some Westerners had regarded as a dilettantish approach to the terms of the *Founding Act* (e.g., by repeatedly holding up the opening of the NATO Military Liaison Mission in Moscow).

Negotiations in early 2002 on establishing the new council were comparable to those that had taken place in 1997 on the *Founding Act* and PJC in the sense that they were taking place within a fairly tight time frame. In December 2001, the NATO foreign ministers had pledged that the creation of the council would be formally announced at, or even before, their next gathering, which was scheduled for May 2002 in Reykjavik. There was thus a risk of repeating the same significant mistake made in 1997—which had been, as noted, a failure to ensure that there was a genuinely shared conceptual and normative basis for the enterprise. Too much had been left to chance and possibly conflicting interpretations after the new forum was established.

The details formally announced in Reykjavik (and shortly thereafter confirmed at a NATO–Russia Summit in Rome) were indeed rather sketchy.[42] The new forum was to be called the NATO–Russia Council (NRC). It would give the Russian government formal co-decision-making responsibilities with NATO member states in nine issue areas, including significant ones such as military crisis management, counterterrorism, the nonproliferation of weapons of mass destruction, and missile defense.

Important provisos were reportedly included in the new consultative arrangements. One was a "safeguard" mechanism. This would reportedly allow "any single NATO member to veto any continuation of the discussion with Russia" in meetings of the NRC.[43] It was, in addition, unclear as to whether NATO's members would maintain the option of formulating common positions in advance of meetings with Russian representatives.[44] This had been a major bone of contention in previous consultative formats, as noted. Overall, it did indeed seem as if both NATO's members and the Russian government had again avoided trying to tie the other side down to agreed-on understandings and interpretations of key issues before their new joint forum was up and running.

The NRC's Track Record

As the NRC was being established, the Russian analyst Alexander Goltz set out what would prove to be a prescient yardstick for measuring its underlying success, or otherwise: "The problem is that we can come to mutual understanding and mutual decisions even without this body. . . . What Russia needs is the opportunity to participate in a decision-making process when [there is] some problem, some controversial issues, something like war in Yugoslavia. [It is] not a problem to reach an agreement when you have the same points of view. The problem is to reach an agreement and to come to a consensus when you have different views on the same problems. That is the task."[45]

The early years of the NRC were generally appraised positively on both the NATO and the Russian sides, certainly when compared with what had gone before. In November 2002, despite reports of continuing opposition to NATO's enlargement from prominent Russian military figures,[46] the Putin government sent Foreign Minister Ivanov to Prague to participate in an NRC ministerial meeting. This was part of NATO's Prague Summit program, for which further enlargement was a key item on the agenda. Notwithstanding this backdrop, the NATO secretary-general publicly declared that Ivanov had "offered a glowing assessment" of progress made in the NRC in its first six months.[47]

Just as significantly, the NRC was not noticeably affected by the Iraq crisis of 2002–3, notwithstanding official Russian opposition to the use of military force against Saddam Hussein's regime. This stood in marked contrast to the collapse of the PJC at the outset of NATO's bombing of the FRY in 1999. Lord Robertson drew the comparison explicitly: "I think that the existence of the NRC has prevented differences over Iraq from becoming a crisis, like the NATO–Russia relationship suffered during the Kosovo crisis in 1999. It has brought about a new maturity. It has created a new equality and a new respect for each other, so that we are now capable of disagreeing without falling out, of having different opinions without walking out of the room . . . . The NATO nations and Russia . . . have established a working relationship of such durability that it can survive and move on from even passionately held differences of opinion."[48]

On the face of it, therefore, Goltz's "test" for the new council seemed to have been passed in the case of Iraq. It should be noted, however, that the NRC had not actually served as a forum within which NATO's members and the Russian government had actively tried to resolve their differences on this issue. It would have been difficult for this to have happened because NATO's members themselves were fundamentally divided, with France and Germany in the vanguard of opposition to military action. In this sense the Goltz test had been only partly met. A fresh breakdown in relations had been avoided, but there still had not been an instance of NATO and Russia effectively consulting and agreeing on a common position or course of action with regard to a significant international crisis. In the case of Iraq they had effectively agreed to differ and not let it impair their relationship.

In two respects, the evolution of the NRC since 2002 has been relatively impressive. One problem with the PJC was that it had never become significantly institutionalized. It had, for example, no Preparatory Committee to prepare the ground for its formal meetings, and it spawned only two subordinate working groups. In contrast, the NRC machinery has featured a "Prep-Com" from the start. The institutional significance of this is that the PrepCom includes Russian as well as NATO representatives. Russians are therefore involved in the crucial agenda-setting and preparation stages of the consultative process. In practice this constitutes a structural safeguard against precooked NATO positions simply being presented to NRC meetings as faits accomplis. By 2008 the NRC's institutional "family" had also grown to embrace twenty-seven subordinate committees and working groups.[49] This is one indication of the breadth and depth of its consultative agenda.

The second area in which the NRC has evolved impressively is in the number and range of cooperative activities that have developed under its auspices.[50] Particularly noteworthy have been instances of actual operational cooperation. The two most important of these have been, firstly, the participation of the Russian Navy in NATO's Operation Active Endeavor. This is the name given to antiterrorism patrols in the Mediterranean by multinational maritime task forces from NATO states. They have been ongoing since 2001. It is a particularly significant operation for NATO because its origins lie in the first-ever invocation of Article 5 of its treaty on September 12, 2001. Active Endeavor is the only ongoing NATO military operation deriving directly from that pivotal event. Even more important in security terms has been the NATO-led operation in Afghanistan since 2003. Consultation with Russia in the NRC has yielded two practical benefits with regard to this. One is agreement on transit rights to allow matériel for the International Security Assistance Force to be transported through Russia. The second has been cooperation in providing counternarcotics training for personnel from Afghanistan and Central Asia.

Overall, therefore, to brusquely write off the NRC, as Dmitri Trenin has done, as "merely a low-key technical-cooperation workshop operating at NATO's side" fails to do full justice to its achievements.[51] Having said this, it should be noted that some of the cooperation that has materialized has been less impressive than its billing has sometimes suggested. It has also proved to be enduringly fragile and vulnerable to political and strategic differences or disputes between NATO's members and Russia. Thus, for example, the actual Russian contributions to Operation Active Endeavor have been limited. It has been reported that the Russian Navy's initial participation in 2006 was limited to one frigate operating with the NATO flotilla "for about a week." In 2007 a single frigate took part for just three weeks,[52] and the following year the planned Russian participation was canceled by NATO in the wake of the war in Georgia.[53]

Indeed, the ongoing NATO maritime operations had increasingly become a bone of contention before the August 2008 crisis erupted. This can be traced back to the NATO members' decision, announced at their Istanbul Summit in June 2004, to "put special focus on engaging with our Partners in the strategically important regions of the Caucasus and Central Asia."[54] This decision does not appear to have been the subject of consultations in the NRC. Reflecting upon it at the time, one Russian commentator bemoaned that "nothing is being done to coordinate Moscow's and Brussels' efforts in the Transcaucasus and Central Asian area."[55] The practical implications of this were manifested the following year, when it was reported that NATO's members were interested in extending the scope of Operation Active Endeavor to the Black Sea. This revelation generated statements of official Russian opposition.[56]

With regard to the cooperative efforts in counternarcotics training, these remained ongoing but also fragile. The sense of fragility derived mainly from the extent to which the specific cooperative programs became caught up in an ongoing dispute caused by the NATO members' failure to agree to direct contact and cooperation between NATO and the Collective Security Treaty Organization, the putative military arm of the post-Soviet Commonwealth of Independent States. The mutual misperception, if not plain incomprehension, that has existed on this issue can be seen in the extent to which, on the one hand, it has become an important bone of contention in Russian debates about cooperation with NATO, whereas, on the other hand, Western sources have virtually ignored it.[57]

Thus, the NRC's track record has been crucially circumscribed. In academic terms, there has been little evidence of a "spillover effect" between "low" and "high" politics. The many practical activities initiated and developed within the NRC have not demonstrably helped to stimulate a broader strategic or political rapprochement between the NATO member states and the Russian government.[58] In consequence, and despite the NRC's achievements, the overall NATO–Russia relationship has remained constantly prone to disruption as a result of disputes or disagreements over long-term unresolved "big picture" issues.

Over the course of the NRC's life to date, and indeed in some cases since the 1990s, four major contentious issues have hung over the NATO–Russia relationship: the status of Kosovo, the future of the Treaty on Conventional Armed Forces in Europe (CFE), missile defense, and NATO enlargement. As the communiqué issued at the NRC's last major meeting before the conflict in Georgia candidly acknowledged, not one of these issues had yet been resolved.[59]

The Georgia Crisis and Its NATO Dimension(s)

In view of what has been argued in this chapter thus far, it was disappointing but hardly surprising that, when confronted with the outbreak of conflict in Georgia, the NRC in August 2008 proved to be as deficient as the PJC had been at the time of the Kosovo crisis in 1999. Most significantly, it evidently failed to function as an effective early-warning mechanism and also to act as a forum for NATO–Russia crisis management consultations.

Although the immediate triggers of the August 2008 conflict were bilateral disputes between the Russian and Georgian governments, there was nonetheless a clear and important NATO dimension.[60] In fact there were several NATO dimensions. Indeed, of the four major sources of ongoing contention between NATO and Russia noted above, each one had either a distinct Caucasian element or at least a resonance there.

The unilateral declaration of independence by the Albanian authorities in Kosovo in February 2008, supported by most NATO member states and actively promoted by the United States, was widely cited in Russia as a precedent for possibly also recognizing the territories of Abkhazia and South Ossetia as states.[61] A second argument, which appeared once the August conflict was under way, held that Russia was justified in intervening militarily in response to Georgian "ethnic cleansing" in South Ossetia. This, it was asserted, followed the same logic and justification that NATO's members had used with regard to Kosovo in 1999.[62] In another indication of misperception, there is little evidence that the NATO member governments had taken the Russian "precedent" arguments seriously, still less made any real effort to engage with and assuage them in the NRC or elsewhere. Generally, they simply asserted that the Kosovo case was sui generis.

The long-running NATO–Russia impasse over the CFE Treaty is directly linked to disputes over "frozen conflicts" in the Caucasus. This dates back to 1999, when the NATO member governments insisted on establishing linkage between adapting the original CFE Treaty regime of 1990 (to reflect the breakups of the USSR and Warsaw Pact together with subsequent NATO enlargement), and the withdrawal of Russian military forces from Abkhazia, South Ossetia, and the Transdniestrian region of Moldova. The danger with a linkage of this kind is that it can complicate and magnify the original source of disagreement so that it becomes both more difficult to resolve and also more likely to bedevil overall relations. This seems to have happened with the CFE issue in the context of the NATO–Russia relationship. In July 2007, immediately after President Putin announced his intention to "suspend" Russian compliance with CFE, one Russian commentator argued grandiloquently that "Moscow is dissatisfied with more than just the West's refusal to ratify the adapted CFE Treaty. For all practical purposes, it is unhappy with all of the politico-military arrangements that have come about in Europe and the world over the past 15 years."[63] More pertinently, Putin himself had linked the ongoing CFE dispute to a strong condemnation of NATO enlargement in a fiery speech to the Munich Security Conference five months before his decision to suspend Russian participation.[64]

The failure to resolve the CFE Treaty dispute can also be seen in part as a failure by the NRC to function as an effective consultative forum on an issue of major contention. Putin had flagged up the possibility of suspending Russian participation in the CFE three months before he actually did so. At that time he made a point of proposing that the issue be referred to the NRC for consultation.[65] Subsequent reports suggested that it had indeed been discussed there, but evidently to no significant ameliorative effect.[66] The July 2007 suspension decision was confirmed at the end of the year.

With regard to missile defense, on the face of it the Caucasian element appears least significant, although not wholly irrelevant. In the summer of 2007 President Putin made a series of proposals for the creation of joint United States–Russia missile defense facilities in Azerbaijan and in southern Russia. His proposal envisaged these serving as an alternative to U.S. plans to base missile defense facilities in the Czech Republic and Poland. It might also be seen as an attempt to institutionalize a joint U.S.–Russian strategic interest and presence in the Caucasus and thus forestall possible moves to turn the region into a mainly U.S.–NATO sphere of influence. For some observers, the 2004 NATO Summit decision to "put special focus on engaging with our Partners in the strategically important regions of the Caucasus and Central Asia" had presaged moves in this direction.[67]

What is of most interest here is evidence of another NRC failure on a key issue. Missile defense was an area where a disinterested observer might have expected the NRC to play an important and positive role. It was, as noted above, one of the specific issue areas identified for NRC discussion and possible co-decision in 2002. Indeed, missile defense had been suggested as an area of potential cooperation with NATO by Putin as early as February 2001.[68] Granted, the main focus of the NRC subject strand was theater missile defense, as opposed to the more strategic version with which the United States was preoccupied. Additionally, as Sean Kay notes in chapter 6 of this volume, there have been enduring differences between the United States and many of its European Allies that are also NATO members over the appropriate scope for, and capabilities of, a missile defense system in Europe. Kay shows that there has been no strong and settled "NATO view" on the issue. Nevertheless, and given genuine political will, it is still reasonable to expect the NRC to have been able to play some role in reconciling differences— both within NATO and between NATO and Russia—on missile defense.

Clearly, however, this has not been the case. During 2007, as decision time approached on deploying elements of the U.S. system in Central Europe, Russian leaders repeatedly professed themselves eager to see missile defense issues discussed as a matter of some urgency in the NRC.[69] What consultations did take place there obviously failed to produce an agreement, and the issue became one of open antagonism in November 2008, as Kay notes. At that time, President Dmitry Medvedev greeted the election of Barack Obama in the United States with a speech threatening to deploy nuclear capable missiles in Russia's Kaliningrad region in response to U.S.–Czech–Polish agreements to proceed with the deployment of missile defense components in Central Europe.[70]

In a conciliatory move in September 2009, Obama announced that the first stages of the proposed U.S. system in Europe would be based at sea rather than on land, although the eventual deployment of some land-based components was not ruled out. At the time of writing it remained to be seen whether this initiative would succeed in defusing missile defense as a contentious issue in relations with Russia, or whether the difficult questions surrounding possible land-based systems had merely been postponed. In any event there was not evidence that consultations within the NRC had played a significant role in formulating this presidential initiative.

The failure of consultations in the NRC to yield agreement on the missile defense issue can arguably be attributed to the existence of a "values gap" on the issue between the two sides. This term has tended to be used by Western analysts and commentators rather patronizingly, to denote problems in developing cooperation caused by Russian leaders showing themselves to be insufficiently respectful of Western normative constructs of supposedly common values such as security and democracy.[71] In the example under consideration here, however, the gap seemed if anything to be working the other way round. The Russian diplomatic effort in favor of Putin's proposals for a joint missile defense system heavily stressed the extent to which acceptance of this "new international security model"[72] would move Russia's relations with the United States and NATO to a new level of "strategic partnership."[73] The negative Western response failed markedly to pick up on the declared normative element of the Russian pitch. It focused instead on faulting Putin's proposals on the grounds of technical feasibility. This was accompanied by sotto voce suggestions that his initiative was actually designed to try to open divisions among NATO's members.[74]

It was of course perfectly possible that the grandiose Russian rhetoric did lack real substance, or perhaps it did disguise an intention to try to divide and weaken NATO, in view of the U.S./European differences noted above. In addition, there were genuine technical questions about the viability of Putin's proposal. What was striking, however, was the absence of any serious attempt—or even serious interest—on the NATO side in exploring the Russian ideas systematically and thus exposing and quantifying actual problems and difficulties that may have existed. There is no evidence of thoroughgoing consultations of this kind taking place on missile defense issues in the NRC.

Since the early 1990s, NATO enlargement has been the hardy perennial among all the problematic issues that have bedeviled relations between NATO and Russia. Given that an extensive literature exists on the enlargement debates—and also that the issue is covered in detail by Roger Kanet in chapter 7 of this volume—it is not necessary to discuss it in depth here. Nevertheless it is important to note that official Russian opposition to NATO enlargement to eventually include Georgia (and Ukraine) was well established. The Russian military intervention in Georgia in August 2008 can thus be seen at least partly as a dramatic warning to NATO's members against opening the way to Georgian accession.

In this context it is worth recalling the timing of the intervention. It occurred almost exactly midway between the NATO Summit in Bucharest in April 2008 and the meeting of foreign ministers scheduled for December of that year. One of the major topics at the summit had been the issue of eventual NATO membership for Georgia and Ukraine. "Instant" analysis in Western states had tended to interpret the summit's outcome as a blow to the membership aspirations of these two governments.[75] However, such an assessment was not really borne out by a close examination of the agreed summit communiqué. The key paragraph read as follows:

> NATO welcomes Ukraine's and Georgia's Euro-Atlantic aspirations for membership in NATO. *We agreed today that these countries will become members of NATO.* Both nations have made valuable contributions to Alliance operations. We welcome the democratic reforms in Ukraine and Georgia and look forward to free and fair parliamentary elections in Georgia in May. A MAP [Membership Action Plan] is the next step for Ukraine and Georgia on their direct way to membership. *Today we make clear that we support these countries' applications for MAP.* Therefore we will now begin a period of intensive engagement with both at a high political level to address the questions still outstanding pertaining to their MAP applications. *We have asked Foreign Ministers to make a first assessment of progress at their December 2008 meeting. Foreign Ministers have the authority to decide on the MAP applications of Ukraine and Georgia.* (emphasis added)[76]

It is actually difficult to imagine a clearer statement of intent on the part of member states of an international institution than "we agreed today that these countries will become members of NATO." Nor was the time frame left entirely open ended. It could be argued that the specific reference to the December foreign ministers' meeting and the official delegation of authority to them to grant Georgia and Ukraine formal candidate status (via their participation in the Membership Action Plan) was a clear indication that such status would in fact be awarded then.[77] Given the well-publicized presummit skepticism of leading NATO members' governments—principally the German and the French—about offering anything concrete to Georgia and Ukraine, the Bucharest declaration was remarkably robust. All things considered, it was understandable if rather undiplomatic of Georgian president Mikheil Saakashvili to boast publicly at the summit that "we got a 100-percent guarantee, at least formally, for membership. That's very unusual."[78]

Even if the argument that the August 2008 Russian intervention was partly designed to derail Georgia's route to NATO membership proves ultimately unconvincing, it is not easy to deny that NATO enlargement generally has been a source of ongoing debilitation to the NRC. Despite—indeed, because of—its status as the most significant ongoing issue of contention between NATO and Russia, enlargement had not been included as one of the specific issues subject to joint consultation and decision making in the NRC. Instead, it has always been a potential "deal breaker" as far as the NRC's effectiveness and overall value are concerned.

The Future of NATO–Russia Relations

The 2008 Georgia crisis revealed in a dramatic way the key limitations on the institutional relationship between NATO and Russia that had developed since the NRC's inception in 2002. Georgia mattered because it was the first significant crisis since then in which both sides perceived that they had essential stakes. With regard to this crisis, the NRC failed the Goltz test. As noted above, Goltz argued that the core challenge for a consultative forum like the NRC "is to reach an agreement and to come to a consensus when you have different views on the same problems." This manifestly did not happen in the case of Georgia, with reference either to the ongoing disputes over Abkhazia and South Ossetia or to the question of possible Georgian membership in NATO. Further, when the crisis came to a head, the NRC was sidelined as thoroughly as the PJC had been in 1999.

James Sherr has suggested that the NRC might actually have made crisis consultation and management *more* difficult just before the 2008 war. Sherr has argued that NATO was partly culpable for the events of August 2008 because "the elaborate architecture of NATO–Russia 'cooperation' and the focus on 'programmes' and process substituted for negotiation, blunted

warnings and marginalised analysis of Russian policies and plans."[79] His contention draws attention to the ever-present risk of institutional structures
and processes becoming overly bureaucratized. It can be argued with some
justification that there is no certain way to prevent this altogether. Its impact
can, however, be mitigated if participants in an institutional process display
the degree of political will required to maintain a significant and consistent
results-oriented focus over the longer term. This challenge had been alluded
to at the time of the NRC's creation by then–NATO secretary-general Robertson. He argued that the key to making the new body work effectively
would be "chemistry rather than arithmetic, as even the best format and seat-
ing arrangement can be no substitute for genuine political will and open mind
on both sides."[80]

Notwithstanding Robertson's prescience, since 2002 substantial agreement and cooperation have *not* been achieved within the NRC on significant
issues, as discussed above. Cheerleaders for the NRC have tended to emphasize the degree to which it has become institutionalized. Thus, for example,
reference has been made to the substantial number of subsidiary committees
and working groups that have been created under the NRC's auspices. Less
impressive, however, has been practical NATO–Russia cooperation on the
ground. As noted above, much has been made of the Russian contribution
to NATO's maritime Operation Active Endeavor. In reality this has so far
amounted to the deployment of a single Russian ship for a period of a few
weeks at most. The fragility of even this minimal level of cooperation was
demonstrated in the aftermath of the Georgia crisis when the United States
blocked plans for a third round of Russian participation in the autumn of
2008.

On land, there is no current instance of a combined military operation
involving Russian troops working within a NATO-led framework. In this
respect the situation has deteriorated since the late 1990s and early 2000s,
when there was a significant Russian contribution to the NATO-led operations in both Bosnia and Kosovo. These were both withdrawn in 2003.

Such has been the limited nature of the NATO–Russia rapprochement
that it begs the question as to whether this is solely or even mainly due to
bureaucratic ossification. It was argued above that such ossification is less
likely to take hold if a sufficient dynamic is generated by mutual political will.
Such will in turn can both develop from and reflect an underlying sense of
shared beliefs, values, and objectives. More than anything else, these are what
have thus far been absent from the NATO–Russia relationship.

There has been a tendency to simply assume that viable and significant
normative commonality does in fact exist between the United States and its

European Allies that are also NATO members on one side and Russia on the other. Stephen Sestanovich—citing Henry Kissinger—has referred to this as the "moral consensus" view. Sestanovich argues that such a consensus was temporarily apparent in the immediate aftermath of September 11. It might also be argued that it was detectable, at least on the Russian side, during the early years of Boris Yeltsin's time in the Russian presidency. What is clear, according to Sestanovich, is that the moral consensus, insofar as it ever existed, "is now a distant memory."[81] One important reason for its fading is that little practical effort appears to have been devoted in the "good times" to systematically conceptualizing which shared beliefs and values might actually exist and how these could effectively be operationalized to ensure that their impact was sustained. In the context of NATO–Russia relations, the most obvious and debilitating consequence of the enduring lack of genuine normative rapprochement has been failure to rise to the Goltz test when required. This has been evident most notably over Kosovo in 1999 and Georgia in 2008.

At their meeting in December 2008, the NATO foreign ministers justified their post-Georgia decision to suspend formal consultations with Russian representatives in the NRC by asserting that "in a partnership based on common values, the lack of a shared commitment to those values must naturally cause the relationship and the scope for cooperative action to suffer."[82] This assertion completely glossed over the fact that the NATO–Russia relationship has never been "a partnership based on common values" in any real sense.

Both parties have been culpable in this failure. On the NATO side there has long been a tendency to assume that "common values" are really Western ones. This approach was typified in the influential and controversial 2006 report *Russia's Wrong Direction*, sponsored by the Council on Foreign Relations. With regard to the NRC, the report recommended its possible abolition if Russia showed itself to be "lacking in commitment to democratic principles or to the goal of collective responses to meet common challenges."[83] From the general tenor of the report, it was clear that its authors and contributors defined "democratic principles" and "common challenges" on the basis of prevailing American understandings, as opposed to envisaging efforts being made to achieve *shared* understandings. With no little conceit, the report also recommended that "the existence of the NATO–Russia Council needs to be justified on terms that parallel NATO membership."[84] This was in spite of the fact that no Russian government had shown serious interest in actually applying for NATO membership and thus taking on the commitments that this would entail.

On the Russian side, the official response to the breakdown in relations following the military action in Georgia contrasted significantly with the aftermath of NATO's bombing of Serbia nine years earlier. In 1999, it may be recalled, the dominant strand in political and informed opinion in Russia accepted that it was in the Russian interest to repair relations as a matter of urgency. In the aftermath of Georgia, in contrast, political leaders from President Dmitry Medvedev on down appeared to make a deliberate effort to convey the impression that they frankly did not care if relations were ruptured for the long term—or perhaps even permanently.[85]

This contrast can be explained by reference to the impact of Russian domestic politics and, in particular, the approach adopted by Vladimir Putin during his tenure as Russia's president from 2000 to 2008 and, it would seem, maintained so far by the Medvedev-Putin duumvirate. Putin's overarching objectives have been, first, to prevent an internal weakening of the Russian Federation. Second, and related to this, Putin has striven consistently to reestablish Russia as a great power on the international stage. Apropos of these twin goals, the key feature of Putin's style of rule has been the so-called power vertical, based on the centralization of control in the hands of the Russian president and a small coterie of advisers and senior officials.

States and governments that strive to maintain a high degree of central control over a significant period of time often rely in part on creating and maintaining the perception that their wider society is menaced by external enemies. NATO—particularly an expanding NATO—presented an obvious candidate for this kind of enemy imaging, in view not only of its condemnation of Russian military action in Georgia but also the long-running disputes with Russia that were discussed in detail above.

However, this attitude has not become *wholly* dominant, even in the Putin era. On the more positive side, there have been occasional official hints of new and alternative constructs being put forward as the basis for discussion with Russia's Western interlocutors. Yet, thus far, these have not proved to be of enduring substance. One prominent instance occurred in 1994, when the Yeltsin government advanced for a time suggestions for creating a pan-European security community on the basis of the Conference on Security and Cooperation in Europe. Little came of these Russian proposals, however, other than the entity's name change to the Organization for Security and Cooperation in Europe. In retrospect, it seems that they were designed mainly as a tactical means for trying to head off the momentum toward the eastward enlargement of NATO, which was then just getting under way.[86]

More recently, in 2008 President Medvedev hinted at a fresh proposal for some kind of pan-European security arrangement. At the time of writing, however, little in the way of either practical suggestions or systematic engagement with NATO's members and others had been forthcoming from the Russian government. Indeed, in July 2008 "sources at the Russian Foreign Ministry" were quoted in *Kommersant* as apparently disavowing any intention of putting forward particular proposals. Rather, their "chief objective was to toss out the idea and see how they [Western governments] reacted to it."[87] Under these circumstances, potential Western interlocutors could be forgiven for viewing the Russian initiative as lacking in substance.

Overall, it is clear that prevailing attitudes on *both* sides have not been conducive to laying a shared normative basis for a more substantial and enduring partnership between NATO and Russia. The dominant tendency on the NATO side has been to measure the value of the relationship in terms of Russian acquiescence to Western understandings of core values and concepts such as democracy and security. Though increasingly bridling against this, the Russian government has made no obvious systematic effort to either come up with alternatives or seriously engage with Western perspectives with a view to promoting possible normative rapprochement.

Nevertheless, the news is not all bad. As noted above, a continuing theme in the story of NATO–Russia relations since 1991 has been that neither side has proved willing to allow the relationship to deteriorate to the extent that a permanent rupture becomes a real possibility. This became apparent in the aftermath of the NATO bombing of the FRY over Kosovo in 1999. It was also becoming apparent a few months after the events of August 2008. By the end of that year, both NATO's and Russian leaders had made moves designed to ensure that the suspension of elements of cooperation in the NRC that had followed the Georgia conflict did not become permanent. Despite Russia's blast of rhetoric in the aftermath of the war suggesting that a complete breakdown in relations was something it could live with, its response was calibrated so that substantive institutional engagement within the NRC framework was left intact.[88] This approach constituted de facto reciprocation of that taken by NATO, which had declared at a special meeting of foreign ministers that "we cannot continue with business as usual" in the NRC.[89] This was a deliberate choice of words and not the same as saying that NATO's members were intending to discontinue business altogether. Even this relatively limited sanction was soon being eroded. At their meeting in December 2008, the NATO foreign ministers "mandated the Secretary General to reengage with Russia at the political level; agreed to informal discussions in the NRC; and requested the Secretary General to report back to us prior to any decision to engage Russia formally in the NRC."[90] By early 2009, NATO officials were openly talking about steps being taken to promote the full "normalization" of NATO–Russia relations.[91] The NATO Summit in Strasbourg-Kehl in April 2009 blessed the formal revival of NRC activities at all levels.

Conclusion

Since 1991 the NATO–Russia relationship has existed in a kind of limbo. On the one hand, it has never been fully consummated, in the sense of becoming any kind of norm-based partnership. An important litmus test for the existence of such a partnership would be the extent to which its structures and processes could provide a framework for helping to defuse crises of the kind that erupted in August 2008. As has been discussed, the Georgia crisis, as with the crisis over Kosovo nine years previously, in fact substantially paralyzed these structures, even if only temporarily. On the other hand, there is no real evidence to suggest that the relationship will decline to complete irrelevance. It has now survived two major crises—Kosovo and Georgia— along with a number of protracted disputes, as discussed above.

It would be foolish to discount simple bureaucratic inertia as being part of the explanation for the relationship's endurance. In this context it may be recalled that James Sherr has criticized "the elaborate architecture of NATO–Russia 'cooperation' and the focus on 'programmes' and process."[92] Nevertheless, it is unlikely that either the NATO or Russian side would have continued to invest their joint structures with significant *political* attention if this were the only or major factor keeping them alive.

The bottom line is existential—NATO and Russia are likely to continue to exist as the other's most significant interlocutor on key security issues. Such an assertion may appear intuitively more obvious in the case of Russia. Barring an unforeseeable catastrophic collapse, the Russian Federation is not going anywhere. Predictions of disintegration had some plausibility during the chaotic Yeltsin regime in the 1990s. Since the Russian revival under Putin, however, virtually no serious observer still believes that it is likely to happen.

As regards NATO, normal-seeming debates about—and predictions of— its demise have continued. Increasingly, however, they lack credibility—at least in the eyes of Russian leaders. In this context it is worth recalling the statements made quite publicly by figures such as Igor Ivanov and Yevgeny Primakov in the aftermath of the Kosovo crisis. They and others were explicit in their view that, however much some might wish it were not so, NATO was and would remain a central feature of the European and wider security landscapes. Such public statements were less in evidence in the aftermath of the Georgia conflict in 2008. Nevertheless, the actions of the Russian government in calibrating its response to NATO's declaration of "no business as usual" for the foreseeable future indicated a desire not to totally undermine the NRC and its associated structures and processes.

All things considered, it is clear that a structural and institutional relationship between NATO and Russia has become a permanent feature of the European security scene. Given the history of this relationship, however, it is much less clear that it will ever become firmly or definitively premised on a common vision of security goals and objectives, or shared underlying values. It is more likely to remain periodically bedeviled by the two sides' essentially unilateral—and sometimes conflicting—formulations of their own strategic and national interests.

Notes

The views expressed here are personal and should not be taken to represent the policy or views of the British government, Ministry of Defence, or the Royal Military Academy Sandhurst.

1. For a more detailed analysis of the course of relations during this period, see M. A. Smith, *Russia and NATO since 1991: From Cold War through Cold Peace to Partnership?* (Abingdon, U.K.: Routledge, 2006), chap. 3; and M. A. Smith, "A Bumpy Road to an Unknown Destination? NATO–Russia Relations, 1991–2002," *European Security* 11, no. 4 (2002): 59–77.

2. For more on the issues and debates raised in this paragraph, see Smith, *Russia and NATO since 1991*, chap. 3.

3. N. Afanasievskii, "On the NATO–Russia Founding Act," *International Affairs* (Moscow) 43, no. 4 (1997): 159ff.

4. "Javier Solana, NATO's Master-Builder," *The Economist*, October 17, 1998, 60.

5. On this, see S. Talbott, *The Russia Hand: A Memoir of Presidential Diplomacy* (New York: Random House, 2002), chap. 9; J. Goldgeier and M. McFaul, *Power and Purpose: US Policy toward Russia after the Cold War* (Washington, DC: Brookings Institution Press, 2003), 203; and "A New European Order," *The Economist*, May 17, 1997, 43.

6. NATO, *Founding Act on Mutual Relations, Cooperation and Security between NATO and the Russian Federation* (Brussels: NATO, 1997), www.nato.int/docu/basic txt/fndact-a.htm.

7. This phrase was attributed to the then German foreign minister, Klaus Kinkel. See "Wooing a Bear," *The Economist*, December 14, 1996, 47.

8. See Smith, *Russia and NATO since 1991*, 66.

9. NATO, *Founding Act*, part II.

10. *Izvestia*, May 28, 1997, trans. in *Current Digest of the Post Soviet Press* (hereafter *CDPSP*) 49, no. 21 (1997): 5.

11. *Nezavisimaya Gazeta*, May 27, 1997, trans. in *CDPSP* 49, no. 22 (1997): 10–11.

12. Quoted by Assembly of the Western European Union, *Russia and European Security (Document A/1722)* (Paris: Assembly of the Western European Union, 2000), www.assembly-weu.org/en/documents/sessions_ordinaires/rpt/2000/1722.html. See also *Segodnya*, May 16, 1997, trans. in *CDPSP* 49, no. 20 (1997): 2–4.

13. "Testimony of Hon. Henry Kissinger," in *The Debate on NATO Enlargement* (Washington, DC: Committee on Foreign Relations, U.S. Senate, 1997), available at http://frwebgate.access.gpo.gov/. See also K.-H. Kamp, "The NATO–Russia Founding Act: Trojan Horse or Milestone of Reconciliation?" *Aussenpolitik*, no. 4 (1997): 320–21.

14. Following the successful conclusion of the Solana–Primakov negotiations, an unnamed "NATO source" was quoted as saying that "we have . . . told the Russians that this agreement is just the beginning and that, as the relationship improves, their role could become even more significant." See M. Evans, "Deal Grants Russians Unique NATO Access While Denying Veto," *The Times* (London), May 17, 1997.

15. "Ambassador Pickering Response to Question from Senator Hagel," in *Debate on NATO Enlargement*.

16. Kamp, "NATO–Russia Founding Act," 324.

17. NATO Parliamentary Assembly, *NATO–Russia Relations and Next Steps for NATO Enlargement (Document AS277PCED-E)* (Brussels: NATO Parliamentary Assembly, 1999), www.nato-pa.int/publications/comrep/1999/as277pced-e.html.

18. Colonel General L. Ivashov, "Russia-NATO: Matters of Cooperation," *International Affairs* (Moscow) 44, no. 6 (1998): 113.

19. *Segodnya*, December 10, 1998, trans. in *CDPSP* 50, no. 49 (1998): 19.

20. See, inter alia, K.-P. Klaiber, "The NATO–Russia Relationship a Year after Paris," *NATO Review* 46, no. 3 (1998): 16–19.

21. *Rossiiskaya Gazeta*, March 26, 1999, trans. in *CDPSP* 51, no. 12 (1998 [*sic*]): 2–3.

22. NATO, *Founding Act*, part I.

23. Goldgeier and McFaul, *Power and Purpose*, 253.

24. P. Trenin-Straussov, *The NATO–Russia Permanent Joint Council in 1997–1999: Anatomy of a Failure* (Berlin: Berlin Information Center for Transatlantic Security, 1999), www.bits.de/public/researchnote/rn99–1.htm.

25. Assembly of the Western European Union, *Russia and European Security*.

26. NATO, *Founding Act*, "Preamble."

27. Russia's role during the Kosovo crisis is discussed more fully by P. Latawski and M. A. Smith, *The Kosovo Crisis and the Evolution of Post–Cold War European Security* (Manchester: Manchester University Press, 2003), chap. 4.

28. *Vremya MN*, July 5, 1999, trans. in *CDPSP* 51, no. 27 (1999): 8.

29. The quotation from Ivanov appeared in *Nezavisimaya Gazeta*, October 12, 1999, trans. in *CDPSP* 51, no. 41 (1999): 3. Primakov was quoted by E. MacAskill, "NATO and Russia Re-establish Ties as Tensions Ease," *The Guardian* (London), February 17, 2000.

30. Assembly of the Western European Union, *Russia and European Security*. See also *Kommersant*, July 24, 1999, trans. in *CDPSP* 51, no. 30 (1999): 19.

31. NATO, *Joint Statement on the Occasion of the Visit of the Secretary General of NATO, Lord Robertson, in Moscow on 16 February 2000* (Brussels: NATO, 2000), www.nato.int/docu/pr/2000/p000216e.htm.

32. Quoted by MacAskill, "NATO and Russia."

33. Quoted by G. Whittell, "Putin Uses Frost to Begin Thaw with West," *The Times* (London), March 6, 2000.

34. This Yeltsin initiative is discussed by Smith, *Russia and NATO since 1991*, 51–52.

35. See, inter alia, *Izvestia*, March 7, 2000, trans. in *CDPSP* 52, no. 10 (2000): 5; *Kommersant*, March 7, 2000, trans. in *CDPSP* 52, no. 10 (2000): 5; and "The Fist Unclenched," *The Times* (London), March 7, 2000.

36. NATO, *Statement by Lord Robertson, NATO Secretary General, on Acting President Putin's Interview with the BBC (Document [2000] 02)* (Brussels: NATO, 2000), www.nato.int/docu/pr/2000/p00–023e.htm.

37. Quoted by Whittell, "Putin Uses Frost."

38. R. Boyes, "Putin Is Impatient for NATO Welcome," *The Times* (London), September 27, 2001; "Russia: Putin Backs Antiterrorism Effort, Seeks to Join NATO," *Radio Free Europe/Radio Liberty* (hereafter *RFE/RL*), www.rferl.org/nca/features/2001/09/260926122945.asp.

39. Quoted by C. Bremner, "Russia and West to Work More Closely on Security," *The Times* (London), October 4, 2001.

40. See, inter alia, *Noviye Izvestia*, November 20, 2001, trans. in *CDPSP* 53, no. 47 (2001): 20–21; and M. Evans, "Blair Plans Wider Role for Russia with NATO," *The Times* (London), November 17, 2001.

41. NATO, *Press Conference with NATO Secretary General, Lord Robertson, 22 November 2001* (Brussels: NATO, 2001), www.nato.int/docu/speech/2001/s011122b.htm.

42. The Reykjavik communiqué simply stated that the new council would be created and in it "NATO member states and Russia will work as equal partners in areas of common interest, while preserving NATO's prerogative to act independently." See NATO, *M-NAC-1(2002)59* (Brussels: NATO, 2002), www.nato.int/docu/pr/2002/p02–059e.htm.

43. I. Straus, "The New NATO–Russia Council in Context: One Step in a Series, Many More to Come," *Johnson's Russia List* (hereafter *JRL*), no. 6276, www.cdi.org/russia/johnson/6276-9.cfm. See also *Noviye Izvestia*, May 16, 2002, trans. in *CDPSP* 54, no. 20 (2002): 5; and *Trud*, May 30, 2002, trans. in *CDPSP* 54, no. 22 (2002): 4.

44. For differing views on what NATO members had agreed to on this score, see M. Evans, "Russia to Move into NATO HQ," *The Times* (London), May 15, 2002; and J. Dempsey and R. Wolffe, "In from the Cold," *Financial Times*, May 15, 2002.

45. Quoted by K. Knox, "NATO: Alliance Mulls Details of Larger Role for Russia," *RFE/RL*, www.rferl.org/nca/features/2002/02/27022002095238.asp.

46. *Nezavisimaya Gazeta*, September 26, 2002, trans. in *CDPSP* 54, no. 39 (2002): 16; *Vremya Novostei*, November 21, 2002, trans. in *CDPSP* 54, no. 47 (2002): 4–5.

47. NATO, *A New Russian Revolution: Partnership with NATO* (Brussels: NATO, 2002), www.nato.int/docu/speech/2002/s021213a.htm.

48. NATO, *Press Conference by NATO Secretary General, Lord Robertson, following the Meeting of the NATO–Russia Council* (Brussels: NATO, 2003), www.nato.int/docu/speech/2003/s030513a.htm.

49. H. Adomeit and F. Kupferschmidt, *Russia–NATO Relations: Stagnation or Revitalization?* (Berlin: Stiftung Wissenschaft und Politik, 2008), 9.

50. For the details, see, inter alia, ibid., 10–14; P. Fitch, "Building Hope on Experience," *NATO Review*, no. 3 (2003), www.nato.int/docu/review/2003/issue3/english/art3_pr.html; S. Blank, *The NATO–Russia Partnership: A Marriage of Convenience or a Troubled Relationship?* (Carlisle, PA: U.S. Army War College Strategic Studies Institute, 2006), 46–53; P. Williams, "NATO–Russia Military Co-operation: From Dialogue to Interoperability?" *RUSI Journal* 150, no. 5 (2005): 44–47; *Nezavisimaya Gazeta*, September 15, 2005, trans. in *CDPSP* 57, no. 37 (2005): 13; and NATO Parliamentary Assembly, *NATO's Developing Partnerships (Document 165PCNP08E)* (Brussels: NATO Parliamentary Assembly, 2008), 2.

51. D. Trenin, "Russia Leaves the West," *Foreign Affairs* 85, no. 4 (2006): 90.

52. Adomeit and Kupferschmidt, *Russia–NATO Relations*, 14.

53. "Russian Ship Barred from NATO Antiterror Patrol," *RFE/RL*, www.rferl.org/articleprintview/1190977.html.

54. NATO, *Istanbul Summit Communiqué*, paragraph 31 (Brussels: NATO, 2004), www.nato.int/docu/pr/2004/p04–096e.htm.

55. *Izvestia*, June 30, 2004, trans. in *CDPSP* 56, no. 26 (2004): 8.

56. *Rossiiskaya Gazeta*, June 10, 2005, trans. in *CDPSP* 57, nos. 23–24 (2005): 3. See also Blank, *NATO–Russia Partnership*, ix.

57. For the flavor of Russian views on the issue see, inter alia, *Vremya Novostei*, December 9, 2005, trans. in *CDPSP* 57, no. 49 (2005): 16; *Izvestia*, May 3, 2006, trans. in *CDPSP* 58, nos. 18–19 (2006): 27; *Vremya Novostei*, March 13, 2008, trans. in *CDPSP* 60, nos. 10–11 (2008): 15–16; and M. Kokeyev, "Russia–NATO Relations: Between the Past and the Future," *Russia in Global Affairs* 5, no. 2 (2007): 95–96. During research for this chapter, the author found no reference to the NATO–Collective Security Treaty Organization issue in any Western source material.

58. This is the major theme of Adomeit and Kupferschmidt, *Russia–NATO Relations*. See also J. Edwards, J. Kemp, and S. Sestanovich, *Russia's Wrong Direction: What the United States Can and Should Do* (New York: Council on Foreign Relations, 2006), 29.

59. NATO, *Meeting of the NATO–Russia Council at the Level of Heads of State and Government Held in Bucharest* (Brussels: NATO, 2008), www.nato.int/docu/pr/2008/p08-050e.html.

60. It is not necessary here to enter the debates about who was to blame for triggering the conflict. Illuminating discussions are given by, inter alia, O. Antonenko, "A War with No Winners," *Survival* 50, no. 5 (2008): 23–35; J. Sherr, *Culpabilities and Consequences* (London: Chatham House, 2008); and C. W. Blandy, *Georgia and Russia: A Further Deterioration in Relations* (Shrivenham, U.K.: Defence Academy of the United Kingdom, 2008).

61. See, inter alia, "Kosovo May Influence Russian Ties with Georgia Breakaway Regions," *JRL*, no. 2008–33, www.cdi.org/russia/johnson/2008–33–42.cfm; and "Georgia: South Ossetia Cites Kosovo 'Precedent' in Call for International Recognition," *JRL*, no. 2008–50, www.cdi.org/russia/johnson/2008–50–40.cfm.

62. *Kommersant*, August 9, 2008, trans. in *CDPSP* 60, no. 31 (2008): 5; *Vremya Novostei*, August 11, 2008, trans. in *CDPSP* 60, no. 32 (2008): 4.

63. *Kommersant*, July 16, 2007, trans. in *CDPSP* 59, no. 29 (2007): 8.

64. "Speech at the 43rd Munich Conference on Security Policy," www.securityconference.de/konferenzen/rede.php?sprache = en&id = 179&print = &.

65. "The End of Arms Control? Russia's Attempts to Renegotiate the CFE Treaty Have Yet to Produce Results," *JRL*, no. 2007–137, www.cdi.org/russia/johnson/2007-137-28.cfm.

66. "Russia Suspends Participation in Key Arms Treaty," *RFE/RL*, www.rferl.org/articleprintview/1077619.html.

67. See J. Simon, "NATO Enlargement and Russia," in *NATO–Russia Relations in the Twenty-First Century*, ed. A. Braun (Abingdon, U.K.: Routledge, 2008), 96–97.

68. Adomeit and Kupferschmidt, *Russia–NATO Relations*, 11.

69. See, inter alia, *Vremya Novostei*, June 4, 2007, trans. in *CDPSP* 59, no. 23 (2007): 1; "No Claws Bared as 'Lobster Summit' Ends with Putin Proposal," *RFE/RL*, www.rferl.org/articleprintview/1077446.html; and "Moscow Seeks Missile Defense Talks in Russia–NATO Council," *JRL*, no. 2007–215, www.cdi.org/russia/johnson/2007-215-28.cfm.

70. "The Return of Missile Diplomacy," *JRL*, no. 2008–207, www.cdi.org/russia/johnson/2008-207-22.cfm.

71. See, inter alia, S. Sestanovich, "What Has Moscow Done?" *Foreign Affairs* 87, no. 6 (2008): 12–13; and Blank, *NATO–Russia Partnership*, ix–x.

72. *Izvestia*, July 4, 2007, trans. in *CDPSP* 59, no. 27 (2007): 2.

73. *Kommersant*, July 4, 2007, trans. in *CDPSP* 59, no. 27 (2007): 4; *Izvestia*, July 5, 2007, trans. in *CDPSP* 59, no. 27 (2007): 5; "Russia Offers NATO Strategic Missile Defense Partnership—Official," *JRL*, 2007–162, www.cdi.org/russia/johnson/2007-162-36.cfm.

74. See, inter alia, *Kommersant*, June 9, 2007, trans. in *CDPSP* 59, no. 23 (2007): 5–6; and "US/Russia: NATO Wary of Entering Missile-Defense Dispute," *RFE/RL*, www.rferl.org/articleprintview/1077454.html.

75. See, inter alia, "Commentary: Did Ukraine and Georgia Lose a NATO Battle, or the War?" *RFE/RL*, www.rferl.org/articleprintview/1109559.html.

76. NATO, *Bucharest Summit Declaration (Document [2008] 049)* (Brussels: NATO, 2008), paragraph 23, www.nato.int/docu/pr/2008/p08–049e.html.

77. On this, see, inter alia, "NATO: What Is a Membership Action Plan?" *RFE/RL*, www.rferl.org/articleprintview/1079718.html; and "NATO Diary: Bucharest, You Are No Munich!" *REF/RL*, www.rferl.org/articleprintview/1079724.html.

78. Quoted in "NATO: No MAP for Georgia or Ukraine, but Alliance Vows Membership," *RFE/RL*, www.rferl.org/articleprintview/1079726.html.

79. Sherr, *Culpabilities and Consequences*, 2.

80. NATO, *NATO in the 21st Century: Speech by NATO Secretary General, Lord Robertson at the Charles University in Prague* (Brussels: NATO, 2002), www.nato.int/docu/speech/2002/s020321a.htm.

81. Sestanovich, "What Has Moscow Done?" 16–17.

82. NATO, "Final Communiqué, Meeting of the North Atlantic Council at the Level of Foreign Ministers Held at NATO Headquarters, Brussels," NATO Press Release (2008) 0153, paragraph 25, www.nato.int/docu/pr/2008/p08–153e.html.

83. Edwards et al., *Russia's Wrong Direction*, 49.

84. Ibid., 40.

85. See, inter alia, *Kommersant*, August 20, 2008, trans. in *CDPSP* 60, no. 33 (2008): 2; *Nezavisimaya Gazeta*, August 26, 2008, trans. in *CDPSP* 60, no. 34 (2008): 1; and "Medvedev Says Russia Ready to Cut Ties with NATO," *JRL*, 2008–157, www.cdi.org/russia/johnson/2008-157-7.cfm.

86. See Smith, *Russia and NATO since 1991*, 10–13.

87. *Kommersant*, July 29, 2008, trans. in *CDPSP* 60, no. 30 (2008): 14.

88. "Russia-NATO Logistics Cooperation Being Put on Hold—Rogozin," *JRL*, no. 2008–158, www.cdi.org/russia/johnson/2008–158–15.cfm.

89. NATO, *Statement (Document [2008] 104)* (Brussels: NATO, 2008), www.nato.int/docu/pr/2008/p08–104e.html.

90. NATO, "Final Communiqué, Meeting of the North Atlantic Council at the Level of Foreign Ministers Held at NATO Headquarters," paragraph 25.

91. See "Weekly Press Briefing by NATO Spokesman, James Appathurai—28 Jan. 2009," www.nato.int/docu/speech/2009/s090128a.html.

92. Sherr, *Culpabilities and Consequences*, 2.

CHAPTER 6

Missile Defenses and the European Security Dilemma

Sean Kay

As NATO MOVES TO IMPLEMENT a new Strategic Concept for twenty-first-century security challenges, it will need to continue to manage effectively its relationship with Russia. New threats, particularly the proliferation of weapons of mass destruction and associated missile delivery technology, can only be managed effectively with the full and constructive engagement of Russia. As the first decade of the twenty-first century drew to a close, the problem of Iran and its nuclear ambitions had become particularly acute. By 2008, NATO's members were in fragile agreement that ballistic missile defense might be an important component of collective defense and thus central to the credibility of Article 5 of the North Atlantic Treaty. Nonetheless, as this chapter demonstrates, the effort to address one set of security challenges related to weapons proliferation had a negative impact on the Alliance's relations with Russia—at a time when Russia's role in European security had been increasingly questioned following its invasion of Georgia in the summer of 2008. The dilemma confronting NATO's strategic planning for its collective defense was thus clear—a threat was emerging, but the existing policy options for threat management were having a negative effect on general European security interests. By early 2009, a major policy shift in the development of NATO's new Strategic Concept regarding nuclear weapon and missile technology proliferation—especially regarding Iran—was needed. More broadly, NATO was in need of a more comprehensive approach toward renewed arms control and enhanced efforts to substantially reduce the threat of nuclear weapons as a regional and global concern.

131

The Missile Defense Puzzle

The United States and its European Allies that belong to NATO confront a dilemma. There is an emerging security threat posed by the proliferation of ballistic missile technology and the efforts by states such as Iran to develop nuclear weapons programs. In an era of asymmetrical threats, many states wonder whether classic deterrence still applies, and they do not want to wait to test that proposition. Thus NATO achieved a consensus by 2008 to endorse the development of European ballistic missile defense programs, as planned by the United States, for deployment in Poland and the Czech Republic. These systems are not tested or proven, and many European NATO Allies are skeptical of the benefits. Even if these systems did eventually work, they would not address the spectrum of related threats. Furthermore, they have damaged the NATO–Russia relationship in ways that risk undermining the existing balance of power in the European area. This chapter explains the evolution toward NATO's consensus on supporting the deployment of ballistic missile defense capacities. It then examines primary rationales for these systems to illustrate the dilemmas that NATO's member states must manage. A final section examines an alternative approach to Iran, Russia, and threat management. The central conclusion of the chapter is that, by 2009, a major revision of NATO's approach to missile defenses was needed.

Why Missile Defense?

The idea of missile defense has its origins in American political opposition to the 1972 Anti–Ballistic Missile Treaty, which resulted in the United States and the Soviet Union agreeing not to deploy ballistic missile defense capacities. Missile defenses were problematic because if one side in a potential conflict attained them and could eliminate an enemy's first-strike or retaliatory capacity, it could make war more likely. However, advocates see missile defenses as necessary to removing constraints on the exercise of American power and as an alternative to needing to negotiate with distasteful governments.

By the 1980s this calculus changed under the administration of Ronald Reagan, who advanced the Strategic Defense Initiative, whereby he envisioned creating a shield against nuclear missiles that would eventually make nuclear weapons obsolete. This idea remained active through the 1990s, with bipartisan political support for research and development—but disagreement over deployment. In 2001 the administration of George W. Bush began a concerted effort to move forward with national missile defense programs. President Bush thus withdrew from the Anti–Ballistic Missile Treaty and commenced to deploy lead elements of radar and site locations for missile defenses, initially based in California and Alaska with support elements in Greenland and the United Kingdom. In 2007 a decision was made to seek agreement to deploy interceptors in Poland and a radar station in the Czech Republic.

It is difficult to argue with the idea that a state should be able to knock down incoming nuclear missiles targeted at its population. Consequently, missile defense concepts have momentum across the Atlantic—as NATO and the United States have agreed to an implementation phase. NATO began with an agreement to coordinate command-and-control elements for existing theater-based national programs. For the United States, however, deployments in North America and planned deployments in Europe proceed on an acquisition model of "spiral development," which includes the deployment of existing capabilities before their effectiveness is proven. This plan assumes that an initial threshold capacity will gradually be improved over time.[1] The result is that systems are being deployed without a clear end cost, without a proven capacity for success, and with major questions for how American Allies might be engaged. As testing has progressed, limited theater missile defense capacity has improved. Ballistic missile defense testing has also yielded technological advances, including against incoming missiles with decoys attached. The U.S. Missile Defense Agency of the U.S. Department of Defense asserts that between 2001 and mid-2008, , it conducted successful tests with thirty-four out of forty-two attempted intercepts. Six of nine tests were successes in eliminating long-range targets. Of those six, four used warhead decoys as countermeasures.[2] However, there has also been a reduction in the complexity of tests involving decoys. Furthermore, the actual number of intercepts is more realistically eight out of fourteen, because the Missile Defense Agency does not include tests where interceptors did not launch.[3] In the fall of 2008, for example, an intercept successfully occurred. However, the decoys on the inbound missile failed to deploy. Thus what is a "successful" test is open to interpretation—but the system is not battle tested for serious war-fighting conditions.

There is no doubt that the proliferation of weapons of mass destruction and missile delivery systems is a serious international security threat in the early twenty-first century. Of particular concern is the acquisition of these systems by states that have not abided by expected norms of behavior within the international system. By 2007 there were more than 120 ballistic missile launches worldwide—though most of these states are American and European Allies.[4] Iran, however, has a long record of hostility toward the interests of NATO's member states and has the largest force of ballistic missiles in the Middle East and the second-largest in the developing world after North Korea.[5] About thirty countries worldwide have missiles with ranges of up to 1,000 kilometers, and eleven have ballistic missiles with longer ranges. There are roughly an additional 75,000 cruise missiles around the world, for which ballistic missile defense systems have no relevance.[6]

Despite this proliferation threat, there is disagreement over whether missile defenses are the best policy response—particularly given technological limitations. As Philip Coyle and Victoria Samson state: "Shooting down an enemy missile is like trying to hit a hole-in-one in golf when the hole is moving at 17,000 mph. . . . And if an enemy uses decoys and countermeasures, missile defense is like trying to hit a hole-in-one when the hole is moving at 17,000 mph and the green is covered with black circles the same size as the hole."[7] At a strategic level, some states worry that rather than provide for purely defensive postures, missile defenses would make offensive military action more likely by states that possess defensive systems because they will not be concerned about retaliation. Even limited systems could cause states to perceive this threat and thus build more offensive missiles to overcome defenses. This could lead to costly arms races that might eventually include the deployment of weapons in space and other costly technologies. Finally, even if ballistic missile defense were effectively deployed, these systems would not stop cruise missiles, which fly low and fast and can carry a nuclear payload, or terrorists with a weapon parked on a boat in a harbor.[8]

Despite the range of difficulties and technological barriers, the high degree of danger inherent in the proliferation threat makes it impossible to discount the need for some kind of policy response—of which missile defense is one important consideration. As Victor Utgoff writes, "Widespread proliferation is likely to lead to an occasional shoot-out with nuclear weapons, and that such shoot-outs will have a substantial probability of escalating to the maximum destruction possible with the weapons at hand. . . . This kind of world is in no nation's interest."[9] Missile defenses also might serve as a component of deterrence—dissuading states from developing ballistic missile and weapons of mass destruction programs in the first place, if they are persuaded that their utility will be minimized. Finally, by providing extended missile shields, the United States believes that it will assure its Allies of its commitment to their defense.

Why Europe?

There is agreement in Europe that there is a common threat of missile proliferation, combined with weapons of mass destruction programs—especially those involving Iran. However, there is disagreement on the pace with which this threat is emerging and about the methods that are most effective in managing it. NATO has mainly emphasized the development of theater-based defensive systems for troop deployments and the coordination of existing national theater defense systems. The United States, however, has also pursued bilateral agreements with Poland and the Czech Republic to install ballistic missile and radar capabilities. These systems would support North American defense capabilities and aim to protect the European members of NATO. However, there is also a concern in Europe that ballistic missile defenses are not worth alienating Russia. Moscow has made clear that it strongly opposes the American missile defense plans—to the extent that it threatens withdrawal from the landmark Intermediate-Range Nuclear Forces Treaty and has suspended its participation in the Conventional Armed Forces in Europe Treaty. These treaties established the parameters for the nuclear and conventional balance of forces in Europe at the end of the Cold War. Russia has also threatened to redeploy medium- and short-range nuclear-capable missiles that would target missile defense installations in Poland.

The American concept of missile defense deployments in the European theater of operations was detailed in October 2007 by the Missile Defense Agency. The plans include a ground-based midcourse defense element of the national Ballistic Missile Defense System. The system would incorporate ten two-staged ground-based interceptors in Poland and an X-band radar in the Czech Republic (plus a likely forward-deployed X-band radar installation at a site to be determined, though one has been deployed by the U.S. European Command in Israel). Iranian missile capabilities are identified as the primary rationale for these deployments. The official assessment by the director of operational tests and evaluation (who works at the Defense Department) makes clear that there were serious technological problems relative to this planned deployment: "The proposed expansion of Ground-based Midcourse Defense to the European theater has not accomplished system engineering adequate to support the development of a test program sufficiently detailed to certify a high probability of working in an operational effective manner once deployed."[10]

European operations are intended to address Iranian missile threats to the United States and to Europe. However, as the Defense Department initially noted, war-fighting deficiencies unique to the European theater of operations include the proximity and reduced time for deployment in the geometry between Iran and Europe versus that between Iran and the continental United States. It was also unclear how a European ballistic missile defense program would interact with existing shorter-range missile defense capabilities in Europe, including the Aegis Ballistic Missile Defense, Terminal High Altitude Area Defense, and Patriot Advanced Capability-3. The integration of these systems was an important objective, because the United States' planned ballistic missile defense would leave southeastern Europe geometrically and geographically vulnerable.

There are technical issues relative to the actual interceptor missiles, which would (of geometric necessity) be two-stage rockets. These missiles are very different from the three-stage rockets that would be deployed for North American defense. Two-stage rockets are untested and unproven, and they are unreliable at the three-stage level. Also, within NATO, battle management and command-and-control issues remain unresolved.[11] Additional operational problems include a question of priorities for the United States relative to its European Allies. For example, would the United States employ its own national ballistic missile defenses to ensure that European countries are protected? Would it keep them in reserve to protect North America, hoping that European theater defenses would work? Even more problematic, would a European missile defense, if it worked, shoot down a missile headed for London but have its debris rain down on France? A missile launched from Iran would provide only 20 minutes to detect, track, and intercept. Thus launch decisions would have to be made quickly and with precision command-and-control procedures.[12] Finally, there is no element in this array of radars and interceptor plans to defend against cruise missiles, which, if combined with ballistic missile capacity, would prove a very serious threat to the European theater of operations. In fact, the greater the emphasis placed by the United States and Europe on missile defense, the higher the incentive for adversaries to invest instead in cruise missile technology. But with a shorter range, cruise missiles would be a particular problem for southern and southeastern Europe.[13]

Missile defense plans for Poland and the Czech Republic have provoked a strong negative response from Russia. A limited missile defense capacity in Poland and the Czech Republic poses no serious threat to Russia's strategic nuclear arsenal. In part, this reality is due to the fact that the planned missile defense systems show little evidence to date of actually working, and even if they did, ten interceptors in Poland would not be relevant to Russian strategic rocket forces in terms of both numbers and geometry. Nonetheless, Russia views the encroachment of American military capacity into Central and

Eastern Europe as a violation of the premises on which it accepted German unification and the enlargement of NATO in the 1990s. Russia also sees missile defense capacities as platforms that could be expanded and eventually neutralize its strategic deterrent. Indeed, some Russian officials assert that the missiles intended for deployment in Poland would have a capacity to intercept Russian intercontinental ballistic missiles launched over the North Pole on paths from missile locations based west of the Ural Mountains.[14] In geostrategic terms, forward missile defenses are seen by Russia as a further means of expanding American primacy in the international system.[15]

Moscow has long presented a tough line on missile defense as part of a strategy of achieving concessions from the West on other strategic priorities—recently to inhibit progress by Georgia and Ukraine toward NATO membership.[16] By 2008 there were substantial indicators that Russia was preparing to back its diplomatic rhetoric with military capacity in response to American and European missile defense plans. In particular, the Russian Ministry of Defense announced in November 2008 that by 2015 it would have five Iskander missile brigades in the Kaliningrad area. These missiles have a solid-propellant single-stage capacity with an extended flight-path control at ranges up to 400 kilometers. This range means Russia could target most of Poland and parts of Germany and the Czech Republic. Moreover, the flight trajectory for these missiles does not exceed 30 miles, thus making them hard to detect and difficult to intercept.[17] Russia has also commenced production of a new intercontinental ballistic missile, the Bulava. This is a submarine-launched ballistic missile that can range up to 5,000 miles. The Russian prime minister, Vladimir Putin, has claimed that this missile can penetrate missile defenses planned for deployment in Poland and the Czech Republic.

Meanwhile, Russia has announced that a new generation of RS-24 intercontinental ballistic missiles would be in service by December 2009 and that it is developing a range of new weapons systems intended to circumvent American missile defense systems.[18] The U.S. secretary of state, Condoleezza Rice, characterized Russian threats of military redeployments, especially those that would target Poland with nuclear weapons, as "pathetic rhetoric" that reflected views that "border on the bizarre."[19]

NATO's Role in Missile Defense

NATO's member states have long agreed that the proliferation of weapons of mass destruction represents a fundamental threat to international stability and to the security interests of the Alliance members with the end of the Cold War.[20] NATO has, however, not achieved a strong consensus on the best means to engage the problem. Certainly, any country threatening a NATO member with ballistic missiles would represent a fundamental concern for the core function of the Alliance—collective defense. This was highlighted for NATO's member states when the United States presented its Allies with a computer simulation of a long-range ballistic missile attack from Iran against each member's capital city.[21] NATO continues to place deterrence at the core of its strategic doctrine, indicating that "the Allied defense posture must make it clear to any potential aggressor that NATO cannot be coerced by threats or use of weapons of mass destruction, and that the Alliance has the capability to respond effectively."[22] NATO officials have argued that "dissuasion" is an important element of missile defense in "dissuading countries from developing missile capabilities in the first place, secondly in deterring an adversary who might think well, we've got missiles we potentially could use them but we can't be sure that we're going to have the intended effect and, you know, does it still make sense from . . . the adversary's perspective, to launch an attack."[23]

NATO has conducted feasibility studies and awarded contracts for the development of a test bed for theater missile defense, although deployment is a distant reality. NATO has also agreed to develop enhanced coordination for existing national short-range missile defense systems and conducted missile defense feasibility studies, and it has completed collective missile threat assessments. In April 2008 NATO agreed that the planned American deployments in Poland and the Czech Republic should be an integral part of any future NATO-wide missile defense architecture. Final decisions on how that architecture might work were deferred, likely with an eye toward a new American administration and also toward whether the U.S. Congress was likely to fund these programs. This deferral suggested agreement on the theory of the threat, but ongoing disagreement among NATO's member states about the urgency and the response. In grappling with missile defense, its members have struggled with a range of challenges, beginning with high levels of concern among the European members regarding technological feasibility. Many of these European members were especially uncomfortable with Washington's decision to pursue bilateral negotiations with Poland and the Czech Republic, rather than engage in a consultative and consensus-building process within NATO. Meanwhile, Poland and the Czech Republic had their own concerns that they would now become primary targets for Russian missiles. Poland eventually leveraged Washington to agree to more substantive bilateral security guarantees, although neither country had finalized approval of these systems in their national legislatures by the end of 2008.

A central concern for NATO is that the planned ballistic missile defense system would not physically cover all its member states—especially those in southeastern Europe that are closer to Iran and more likely targets for Iran's medium- and short-range missiles. As its secretary-general, Jaap de Hoop Scheffer, indicated in 2007, "When it comes to missile defense, there shouldn't be an A League or a B League within NATO."[24] Yet some members argue that it is essential to have missile defense capacities in the European theater. As Czech deputy prime minister Alexander Vondra noted in October 2008, "If the Europeans say no, then you will inevitably build just the national shield, and it will contribute to the transatlantic divide and that's something that we do not want."[25] There are, nevertheless, divisions between old and new members of NATO over how to respond to proliferation threats. Many of the new members believe that the primary threat is Russia. They are thus driving NATO toward a more assertive defensive posture, which could in turn further alienate Russia.[26] This view became especially pronounced after Russia's invasion of Georgia in the summer of 2008. As the Polish prime minister said in August 2008, "Poland and the Poles do not want to be in alliances in which assistance comes at some point later—it is no good when assistance comes to dead people."[27] Poland successfully negotiated a commitment by the United States to deploy Patriot missile batteries and approximately 100 American support troops in Poland. Warsaw also received a bilateral statement reinforcing America's commitment to defend Poland. Meanwhile, France believes that its independent nuclear force is a reliable deterrent for any Iranian missile threat to Europe, although, at the same time, it is considering developing its own missile defense derived from the Exoguard exoatmospheric interceptor system.[28]

NATO's internal discussion about missile defense has raised an existential crisis for NATO over its role in the post–Cold War world and the credibility of collective defense.[29] Similar tensions are likely to rise if this discussion also moves into the debates about the future of the European Union and its security dimension. Equally difficult for NATO's European members is that many have a high dependence on Russia for energy supplies and can ill afford to overly provoke Russia so long as this persists. In July 2008 Russia dramatically cut the flow of oil to the Czech Republic—three days after Prague signed accords codifying the U.S. missile defense radar deployment.[30] Nonetheless, recognizing that the United States, Poland, and the Czech Republic were moving forward without NATO, its remaining members concluded that it is better to have influence in that decision. Consequently, NATO agreed to endorse ballistic missile defense concepts in the spring of 2008. As Secretary-General de Hoop Scheffer had earlier stated in 2007, "NATO is the right place to have this discussion on missile defense."[31]

American officials saw the NATO endorsement as a political victory for their long-standing effort to gain legitimacy for missile defense. Nevertheless, subsequent problems emerged—especially involving estimated funding costs, which have opened new burden-sharing debates in the U.S. Congress. In 2008, Congress cut the $85 million allocated to the Polish and Czech deployments, pending final approval by each country and independent evaluations of the technology. Congress also required that the Defense Department certify that two-stage interceptors have "demonstrated, through successful, operationally realistic flight testing, a high probability of working in an operationally effective manner" before acquisition and deployment could begin.[32] Existing technology transfer constraints simultaneously make it more difficult for other NATO members to participate in the program.[33]

In the fall of 2008, the United States elected Barack Obama as its new president. During the campaign and after the election, Obama stressed that he supported European missile defense systems, but only to the extent that they are proven effective and enhance regional security.[34] Given technical limitations, financial constraints, and new diplomatic priorities, it is possible that the NATO missile defense debate will be indefinitely shelved as other approaches to Iranian nuclear programs are engaged. Ironically, a primary motivator for continuing missile defense plans for Europe is the question of the credibility of what NATO has already said about the benefits of the proposed system and the credibility of America's bilateral agreements with Poland and the Czech Republic. Nevertheless, these commitments alone are not likely to be sufficient to prevent a major reassessment within NATO by the Obama administration. In November 2008, French president Nicolas Sarkozy said that missile defenses in Poland and the Czech Republic will "bring nothing to security" but rather will "complicate things and move them backward."[35] Two weeks later, France's minister of defense, Hervé Morin, raised cost questions, asking what money Europe would have left if it committed to the "huge cost" of missile defense, and he also asked "Who would hold the key" to their use. He added: "There are risks, yes, but to say that there is a threat today would need to be checked."[36]

The Obama administration began quickly to calibrate America's European missile defense position. Speaking in Munich in February 2009, Vice President Joseph Biden noted that missile defense deployments in Europe would go forward so long as they were proven and cost-effective. Undersecretary of State William J. Burns indicated also in February 2009 that regarding Iran:

"If through strong diplomacy with Russia and our other partners we can reduce or eliminate that threat, it obviously shapes the way at which we look at missile defense."[37] Subsequently, multiple press reports indicated that President Obama had sent a letter to the Russian leadership specifying that if Russia engaged in serious efforts at diplomacy that produced effective results in turning back Iran's nuclear program, there would be no need for the European ballistic missile deployments. Meanwhile, Russia began making overtures suggesting that it might need to make new missile deployments in the European area—accepting the Obama administration's desire to "reset" the relationship. The Obama administration also engaged in its own independent review of the missile defense systems. In its 2009 defense budget, a new emphasis was placed on prioritizing spending on theater-range missile systems rather than ballistic missile defense priorities.

Significantly, at the Sixtieth-Anniversary NATO Summit in April 2009, the year-long review of NATO ballistic missile defense concepts produced a statement highly reflective of the new look that the United States had brought to the systems. Summarizing a year of study of the ballistic missile defense issue, the best NATO could offer was a conditional statement that "a future United States contribution of important architectural elements could enhance NATO elaboration of this alliance effort." NATO further added that "based on the technical and political military analysis of these options, we judge that missile threats should be addressed in a prioritised manner that includes consideration of the level of imminence of the threat and the level of acceptable risk. We received a comprehensive analysis of the technical architecture options and agree to its overall assessment that, even though some of these options do not meet the Bucharest tasking, each of them has its strengths and shortcomings."[38] NATO went on to specify an emphasis on working to expand existing theater defense programs to include both troops deployed in the field and territorial defense.

Aligning Threats and Responses

It had generally become clear that plans for a European-based missile defense system that is folded into NATO were problematic. By 2009 the United States had persuaded two Allies—Poland and the Czech Republic—to support the deployment of missile defense capabilities via bilateral negotiations. Subsequently, NATO provided a general endorsement of the concept. This situation came about despite several basic facts: First, there remains uncertainty about Iran's nuclear ambitions and capabilities. Moreover, ballistic missile defense as planned would not protect those NATOs member nations most in range of Iranian capabilities nor would it stop cruise missiles or nuclear terrorism. Additionally, the technology of European ballistic missile defense does not fully exist, is untested, and the U.S. Congress has placed limitations on both funding and capacity. Meanwhile, public opinion in Poland and the Czech Republic has opposed hosting this capacity on their territory, and some NATO members worry that the plans create a multitiered level of collective defense. Other members believe that diplomacy and deterrence will represent better first and second stages of threat management.

Moreover, policy has proceeded while producing high levels of concern in Russia. This development has significantly complicated relationships between NATO and Russia. Yet Russian cooperation is needed on a range of international issues—especially Iran's nuclear program. Although there is relatively little for Russia to actually fear from the current deployment plans, Russian fears are high enough to threaten unraveling key post–Cold War arms treaties and to assert planned redeployments of short-range and ballistic missile capabilities. The entire process has also lacked consultation and transparency, both within NATO and between NATO's member countries and Russia— further heightening fear-driven assessments and response. Finally, national constraints on sharing missile technology, uncertain architectures for command-and-control arrangements, and growing concern in the U.S. Congress about program costs and burden sharing all create further consensus difficulties for deploying ballistic missile defense via NATO.

By 2008, it was tempting to discount the idea of ballistic missile defenses as "much ado about nothing," for the program remained at the planning stage. However, there were measurably negative security effects unfolding in Europe. These trends portend major consequences for NATO and its collective defense requirements, force projection capacity, and relationship with Russia. Two specific dilemmas requiring a hard, realistic assessment of how missile defenses were already affecting the European security environment were (1) how to approach Iran and (2) the Russia problem.

Iran

Iran has made substantial regional gains since the 2003 U.S. invasion of Iraq bogged down in a counterinsurgency battle. Iran is a growing regional power, but with serious limitations on its capabilities. Its conventional military force is containable by the collective military power of NATO's member nations.

Nevertheless, Iran possesses a wide range of asymmetrical capabilities. Ambiguity about Iran's nuclear program serves as a force multiplier given uncertainty about what Iran might, or might not, possess in conventional and unconventional war fighting.[39] Iran's main missile capacity focuses on older-generation Soviet-era SCUD missiles. Iran has, however, also been seeking to acquire Russian nuclear-capable, intermediate-range, strategic air-launched cruise missiles (KH-55 Granat).[40]

Iran has not hidden its effort to mine uranium deposits in Saghand, and it has been constructing a uranium enrichment facility at Natanz. By 2003 it had as many as 10 centrifuge machines assembled, parts for another 1,000, and plans for up to 5,000. Nonetheless, Iran remained substantially removed from having a weaponized nuclear program combined with an effective ballistic missile delivery system. In Arak, Iran was constructing a heavy water plant that could make up for the lack of this capacity at other facilities, especially in Bushehr.[41] The International Atomic Energy Agency indicates Iran has not been fully cooperative or transparent in its weapons programs. However, in 2008, the United States declared that in its national intelligence estimates, Iran had suspended its nuclear program designs in 2003—though perhaps with the intent of moving to a new stage focused on developing fissile material.

Of particular concern to Europe are Iranian efforts to upgrade and expand its missile capacity. Iran has an older generation of ballistic missile technology purchased largely from North Korea during the 1980s. This program includes components from North Korea's No Dong program, which could provide foundations for an eventual intercontinental ballistic missile system. Iran has also developed an internal ballistic missile program, which includes the Shahab-3 missile, claimed by Iran to have a range of up to 1,300 kilometers. Unconfirmed reports imply that Iran is also researching a Shahab-5 with a 2,500-kilometer range.[42] Iran has also launched suborbital rockets, which suggests a nascent capacity for intercontinental ballistic missiles, though its attempts at space launches have been technically problematic. Strategically, Iran could employ missile systems mainly for deterrence. However, given the radical nature of its regime and links to international terrorist movements, it could transfer missile technology and weapons for asymmetrical use against NATO's members. Iran could also pursue more assertive conventional power in the Persian Gulf region with less fear of retaliation.

Meanwhile, an Iranian nuclear missile program could prompt Israel to preemptively attack Iran—or set off a chain reaction of nuclear weapons programs spreading to Egypt, Saudi Arabia, Syria, and Turkey. One Saudi diplomat was asked how to respond to a nuclear Iran and answered: "With another nuclear weapon."[43] There is no question that an Iran with nuclear weapons is a dangerous outcome, in particular because of the risk of further nuclear proliferation. It is also clear that some members of the international community are not prepared to accept the idea of Iran with nuclear weapons—thus increasing the likelihood and associated danger of preemptive attacks on Iranian nuclear facilities. Consequently, NATO is left with a serious security challenge—for which the existing approach, missile defenses, actually cedes the initiative to Iran, rather than engaging forward in a way to create incentives for Iran to pursue alternative approaches to its own perceived security requirements regarding nuclear weapons and associated missile systems.

Russia

The United States' and NATO's plans for European missile defense systems are neither deployed nor proven to work. Thus they really are not a threat to anyone. Once in place, ten interceptor missiles would not be a match for the strategic rocket forces of Russia. As the NATO secretary-general asserts, "Ten interceptors will not, cannot and will not affect the strategic balance and 10 interceptors can also not pose a threat to Russia."[44] American and NATO officials have consulted often with Russia over the planned deployments. These officials note that in their private discussions on missile defense, Russian officials are much less belligerent.[45] In particular, U.S. secretary of defense Robert Gates offered specific proposals to build confidence in the systems. Secretary Gates offered in 2007 that the United States and Russia could colocate radars, conduct joint threat assessments, and have a Russian expert presence at missile shield sites. He also suggested that the entire system could be kept nonoperational until an actual identifiable threat appeared from Iran or elsewhere.[46] Russia did not take advantage of these proposals.

However, Moscow did offer a counterinitiative, suggesting that the United States and Russia work jointly to develop a warning radar system that Russia currently maintains in Azerbaijan and that has a range of 6,000 kilometers.[47] The United States did not follow up on initial indicators of interest in this proposal because it was presented as an alternative to the U.S. missile plans, not as a complement to them. This failure to respond heightened skepticism in Moscow about the intent behind the American missile defense plans.

There are some technical rationales for Russian concern that facilities in Poland and the Czech Republic could eventually create serious problems for Russia's strategic defenses. This would be particularly true for the radar in the Czech Republic, which would provide advance launch notice and tracking of Russian missiles. Russian experts fear that these radar systems could target three hundred times more missiles than current American capacity. Russian experts may also be concerned that once the capacity for missile interceptors in Poland existed, the numbers deployed there could be expanded. Furthermore, the ground-based interceptors themselves could be refitted as intercontinental ballistic missiles because their two-stage capacity will be based on the Minuteman series of missile capabilities. It is also possible that the interceptors in Poland could be targeted at Russian nuclear launch sites west of the Ural Mountains. Finally, Russian experts assert that Poland and the Czech Republic are not the most logical locations in Europe for defenses against Iranian capability. This leads them to conclude that the deployments are a means of neutralizing Russia's nuclear deterrent.[48]

A Return to Realism: Threats, Responses, and Alliance Interests

The United States and its fellow NATO members have approved a ballistic missile defense deployment for which there is only a developmental technological capacity and an emerging, but unrealized, threat not likely to come to fruition until 2015.[49] At the same time this policy has had a measurably negative effect on relationships with Russia and risks creating layered degrees of collective defense. By 2009 three interrelated challenges required effective policy responses and creative calibration of resources. First, the United States and its allies needed to employ a full-spectrum approach to engaging Iran based on diplomacy and deterrence. Second, the United States and NATO needed to refocus missile defense priorities onto theater missile defense systems. Simultaneously, the United States would benefit from a freeze of planned missile defenses for Poland and the Czech Republic until technology justified the deployments and they could be done in a way that would enhance regional security. Third, the United States and NATO needed to reemphasize building a strong working relationship with Russia that renewed efforts toward reducing reliance on nuclear weapons and made NATO and Russia reliable partners in the pursuit of common security interests.

Diplomacy and Containment

By 2008, the United States and NATO were not addressing the Iran security dilemma with a coherent strategy designed to persuade Iran to change its current policies. The existing prioritization of ballistic missile defense assumed that diplomacy with Iran would fail without having made the effort.

However, Barack Obama was elected U.S. president in 2008 on a mandate that included engaging directly with Iran using carrots-and-sticks diplomacy. There is historical evidence that suggests that this approach can work. A range of states have voluntarily given up weapons programs (e.g., Libya and South Africa), through either a change in priorities or a change in government.[50] A key player in securing a diplomatic success in changing Iranian intentions would need to be Russia. Yet the Russian "card" would be much harder to play so long as Moscow feared NATO's ballistic missile defense. Moscow was thus in the regrettable, but powerful, position of now being able to condition its Iran policy on concessions on missile defense deployments. Without question, diplomatic engagement guarantees no results. A basic "economic incentives versus sanctions" approach has been in place for some time but has not yielded breakthroughs. Iranian intransigence that any negotiations include Israeli disarmament is likely to stall any serious progress. Some middle-ground concepts would include persuading Iran to adhere to an intrusive inspection regime under the Comprehensive Test Ban Treaty while the West acknowledges a right of Iran to develop peaceful nuclear energy with oversight by the International Atomic Energy Agency. A next layer of diplomacy might emphasize a situation in which Iran is understood to have a capability to test but does not actually move forward with testing nuclear weapons.[51]

If diplomacy does not succeed, there exists a substantial deterrent force that should make Iran think hard about the utility of its nuclear weapons program. The nuclear capabilities of Israel, the American forces in the region and beyond, and the nuclear forces of Britain and France provide Iran with ample deterrent and dissuasion incentives.[52] Deterrence and containment would require a clear and credible statement to Iran that the use of nuclear weapons or the proliferation of weapons or missiles to third parties will be met with a forceful and devastating response.[53]

Theater Missile Defenses

A layered perspective is needed to address the problem of missile technology and nuclear proliferation in Iran and elsewhere. Ballistic missile defenses might eventually be a relevant part of a layered system of defenses. However, until the technology is proven to work, the theater-based missile defense systems that NATO members have deployed and are being integrated in southern and southeastern Europe are likely to be the most effective initial layer of collective defense. Rather than deploying the planned interceptors and radar in Poland and the Czech Republic, the United States and NATO would be better advised to deploy a mix of mobile midcourse (Aegis SM-3) systems and terminal theater defenses (PAC-3, Terminal High Altitude Area Defense). The Aegis system is especially optimal as it is mobile, highly accurate, and could also intercept Iranian missiles in their ascent phase before they reach maximum velocities—with potentially as few as four ships with redundant capacity in nearby areas of operation.[54] There are range/accuracy ratio problems regarding these shorter-range systems. However, if accompanied by enhanced European radar capabilities (and perhaps Russian radar locations), these limitations could be minimized. There is also a problem of low-altitude intercepts raining missile parts and payloads down on untargeted territory and populations, which could create significant political difficulties in developing effective command-and-control systems for NATO.

NATO and Ballistic Missile Defenses

The study of, and research into, ballistic missile defense is a legitimate concern for NATO's collective defense given evolving technology-driven threats. However, relative costs must be considered. Effective diplomacy costs virtually nothing and can create major gains. Containment would be expensive, but the costs of going nuclear would also be very high for Iran. Crossing the nuclear threshold would lead to even more political and economic isolation of Iran from the international community. Even if Iran did develop capabilities, it would still have to weigh the obvious massive retaliation that it would confront if it did attack a NATO member. The United States and its fellow NATO members also must be mindful of the financial costs of missile defense in uncertain economic times. Already, the United States spent $115 billion on ballistic missile defense research and testing up through 2008. Given global economic concerns, and given relative threat timelines and tactical weaknesses in existing concepts, the deployment to Poland and the Czech Republic could be on sustained hold while research and development continues.

Engaging Russia in Common Threat Management

The primary reason the United States and NATO would benefit from a freezing of deployment plans for Poland and the Czech Republic is that it is in the United States' and NATO's interests to do so. Russia cannot have a veto over how NATO prepares for its defensive requirements. Nonetheless, if NATO is pursuing security policy that is fundamentally counterproductive to the interests of its member states, then the states have an obligation to make adjustments. An added benefit to a freeze on deployments by the United States would be that it would ease tensions with Russia and likely facilitate Russian support for diplomatic and economic pressure placed on Iran. Given the existing trends, Russia is threatening military responses to missile defenses via new missile deployments targeted at NATO's member countries. The new members of NATO are thus going to be even more worried about Russia's behavior.

Ironically, Russia's political hand has gotten stronger because it is in an increasingly powerful position to divide the NATO member states over missile defense. Russia would be wise, however, to tread carefully, because the more it is exposed in such efforts, the more likely they are to backfire. Both NATO and Russia would benefit from a "time out" over their increasingly confrontational posture as each goes through a period of significant economic challenges. The United States, Europe, and Russia share a wide range of common interests, and a return to first-order principles in the relationship is needed. As former U.S. senator Sam Nunn has stated: "The United States and Russia need to pause—take a deep breath and realize that we are at a crossroads in our strategic nuclear relationship. . . . We could stumble to the precipice of strategic danger if we and our Russian friends play a foolish zero-sum game with missile defense."[55]

Conclusion

The nexus between weapons of mass destruction and missile proliferation had by 2009 reached a dangerous crossroads between the United States, Europe, Iran, and Russia. For reasons associated with strategy, technology, diplomacy, and general international stability, an alternative framework was needed. This chapter has demonstrated a set of individual security relationships that have logic in isolation. However, when placed in the complex international security environment, they create a substantial security dilemma. A new architecture would include a focus on regional diplomacy that builds a stronger missile control and nonproliferation regime across the Middle East and Central Asia, as well as direct diplomatic efforts to engage Iran over its missile and nuclear programs combined with effective containment strategies. It might also include the development of medium-range theater missiles for NATO, beginning with the Aegis system, perhaps enhanced by new radar installations in Europe and potentially in Russia, while placing planned ballistic missile defense deployments for Poland and the Czech Republic on hold. Finally, there should be a return to more cooperative and transparent relations with Russia based on a prioritization of common interests.

Common sense dictates that these approaches would require clear measures of success and should be adapted or discarded as necessary depending on the external threat environment. However, NATO's member states, including the United States, and Russia would also be well served to deepen efforts in two additional strategic objectives. First, NATO needs a new concept for achieving energy security. By cooperating on this objective via coordination through NATO and other relevant international institutions, NATO's members will remove the primary strategic vulnerability that rests underneath some of their concerns regarding the need for missile defense systems. Second, the United States and Russia need to enter into a new phase of nuclear arms reduction negotiations. New initiatives are needed to develop a tighter missile and technology control regime and develop new and enhanced standards for nuclear weapons and missile safety and security. As Henry Kissinger, George Shultz, Sam Nunn, and William Perry state: "In some respects, the goal of a world free of nuclear weapons is like the top of a very tall mountain. From the vantage point of our troubled world today, we can't even see the top of the mountain, and it is tempting and easy to say we can't get there from here. But the risks from continuing to go down the mountain or standing pat are too real to ignore. We must chart a course to higher ground, where the mountaintop becomes more visible."[56] What this path requires is a clear strategic vision that it is possible to work toward a world without nuclear weapons—and that this vision needs to begin with the United States, NATO, and Russia as cooperative partners working toward a safer twenty-first century.

Notes

1. Victoria Samson and Nick Schwellenbach, "Spiraling Out of Control: How Missile Defense's Acquisition Strategy Is Setting a Dangerous Precedent," *Defense and Security Analysis* 24, no. 2 (June 2008): 203–11.

2. Lieutenant General Henry A. Obering III, "Online Exclusive, Response to 'Missile Defense Malfunction': Setting the Record Straight," Carnegie Council for Ethics in International Affairs, www.cceia.org/resources/journal/22_1/special_report/002.html. Also see "Missile Defense Agency Fact Sheet," December 12, 2008, www.mda.mil/mdalink/pdf/testrecord.pdf.

3. See Victoria Samson, "Flight Tests for Ground-Based Midcourse Defense (GMD) System," www.cdi.org/pdfs/GMD%20IFT3.pdf.

4. See Joseph Cirincione, "The Declining Ballistic Missile Threat," U.S. House of Representatives Committee on Oversight and Government Reform," March 5, 2008, http://nationalsecurity.oversight.house.gov/documents/20080305141 211.pdf.

5. Lieutenant General Henry A. Obering III, "Testimony before the House Oversight and Government Reform Committee, National Security and Foreign Affairs Subcommittee," April 30, 2008, http://nationalsecurity.oversight.house.gov/documents/20080430170 809.pdf.

6. Anthony Seaboyer and Oliver Thranert, "What Missile Proliferation Means for Europe," *Survival* 8, no. 2 (Summer 2006): 86–87. Also see John Liang, "DOD Finds Cruise Missile Defense 'Gaps'," *Military.com*, August 17, 2006, www.military.com/features/0,15240,110199,00.html.

7. Philip Coyle and Victoria Samson, "Missile Defense Malfunction: Why the Proposed U.S. Missile Defenses in Europe Will Not Work," *Ethics and International Affairs* 22, no. 1 (Spring 2008), at www.cceia.org/resources/journal/22_1/special_report/001.html.

8. See Scott D. Sagan and Kenneth N. Waltz, *The Spread of Nuclear Weapons: A Debate Renewed* (New York: W. W. Norton, 2002).

9. Victor A. Utgoff, "Missile Defence and American Ambitions," *Survival* 44, no. 2 (Summer 2002): 85–102.

10. U.S. Department of Defense, "European GMD Mission Test Concept," October 1, 2007, www.cdi.org/pdfs/EuropeanGMD.pdf.

11. Command and control issues are still a major challenge for American ballistic missile systems designated for North America. See U.S. Government Accountability Office, *Ballistic Missile Defense: Actions Needed to Improve Process for Identifying and Addressing Combatant Command Priorities*, Report GAO-08–740 (Washington, DC: U.S. Government Printing Office, 2008).

12. Lieutenant General Robert G. Gard Jr. (U.S., ret.), "National Missile Defense in Europe: Premature and Unwise," Center for Arms Control and Non-Proliferation, July 2007, www.armscontrolcenter.org/policy/missiledefense/articles/european_missile_defense_premature.

13. See Dennis M. Gormley, "Missile Contagion," *Survival* 50, no. 4 (August–September 2008): 137–54.

14. Jack Mendelson, "European Missile Defense: Strategic Imperative or Politics as Usual?" Arms Control Association, available at www.armscontrol.org.

15. For detailed discussion of the Russian approach toward European missile defense systems, see John P. Caves Jr. and M. Elaine Bunn, "Russia's Cold War Perspective on Missile Defense in Europe," *Foundation por la Recherche Strategique*, May 3, 2007, www.frstrategie.org/barreFRS/publications/pv/defenseAntimissile/pv_20070503_eng.pdf.

16. See Richard Weitz, "US: Russia's Missile Defense Fears Driven by More than Security," *Eurasia Insight*, March 6, 2007, www.eurasianet.org/departments/insight/articles/eav030607a.shtml.

17. "Russia to Equip 5 Brigades with Iskander Missile Systems by 2015," *RAI Novosti*, November 7, 2008.

18. Guy Faulconbridge, "Russia Starts Production of New Ballistic Missiles," Reuters, December 1, 2008.

19. Liam Stack, "Russia Threatens to Suspend NATO Cooperation," *Christian Science Monitor*, August 22, 2008.

20. For further details, see "Countering Weapons of Mass Destruction," www.nato.int/ebookshop/briefing/weapons_mass_destruction/weapons_mass_destruction2008-e.pdf.

21. Joris Janssen Lok, "NATO Struggles with Missile Defense," *Aviation Week*, July 10, 2007, www.aviationweek.com/aw/generic/story_channel.jsp?channel = def ense&id = news/aw061107p2.xml.

22. NATO, *Briefing: Weapons of Mass Destruction*, www.nato.int/ebookshop/ briefing/weapons_mass_destruction/weap ons_mass_destruction2008-e.pdf.

23. "Press Briefing by the NATO Spokesman James Appathurai, and Technical Briefing on Defense against Terrorism and Missile Defense by NATO Assistant Sec-retary-General for Defense Investment, Peter Flory," March 12, 2008, www.nato.int/ docu/speech/2008/s080312b.html.

24. Barcin Yinanc, "Turkey's Position on US Missile Defense Program," *Turkish Daily News*, March 14, 2007, www.turkishdailynews.com.tr/article.php?enewsid = 68232&contact = 1.

25. Emily Harris, "Europeans Cool to U.S. Missile Defense Plan," National Public Radio, October 20, 2008.

26. Kingston Reif, "Russia Looms over U.S.-Poland Missile Defense Agreement," Center for Arms Control and Non-Proliferation, August 20, 2008, www.armscontrol center.org/policy/missiledefense/articles/082008_russia_looms_us-poland_missile_ defense/.

27. Thom Shanker and Nicholas Kulish, "Russia Lashes Out on Missile Deal," *New York Times*, August 15, 2008.

28. Lok, "NATO Struggles with Missile Defense."

29. See Benjamin Schreer, "NATO and Strategic Defense," *International Politik*, Summer 2008, www.ip-global.org/archiv/2008/summer2008/download/1dd234392 c8ebb4234311dd9dfa4f3ed50aed8ded8d/original_2_schreer.pdf.

30. Harry de Quetteville, "Russian Oil Supplies to Czech Republic Cut after Mis-sile Defense Deal with U.S.," *Daily Telegraph* (London), July 19, 2008, www.tele graph.co.uk/news/worldnews/europe/russia/2403798/.

31. "Opening Statement of Senator Carl Levin at Armed Services Committee Hearing on Posture of U.S. European Command," May 17, 2007, http://levin.senate .gov/newsroom/release.cfm?id = 274537.

32. Reif, "Russia Looms."

33. Robert G. Bell, "Addressing NATO's Missile Defense Challenges," Remarks to NPA Science and Technology Committee, May 29, 2004, http://transatlantic.sais-jhu.edu/PDF/speeches/bellspeech.pdf.

34. See "Obama Denies Poland Missile Vow," BBC News, November 8, 2008, http://news.bbc.co.uk/2/hi/europe/7717669.stm.

35. Quoted by Steve Erlanger, "NATO Chief Defends Opening to Russia," *New York Times*, December 4, 2008, www.nytimes.com/2008/12/04/world/europe/ 04nato.html?ref = world&p agewanted = print.

36. Quoted by Julian Hale, "French DM Casts Doubt on Need for Missile Defense," *Defense News*, December 2, 2008, www.defensenews.com/story.php?i = 3846066.

37. Quoted by Peter Paker, "Obama Offered Deal to Russia in Secret Letter," *New York Times*, March 3, 2009.

38. Strasbourg/Kehl Summit Declaration, NATO, April 4, 2009.

39. See Anthony Cordesman, "Iranian Weapons of Mass Destruction: The Broader Context," Center for Strategic and International Studies, December 5, 2008, www.csis.org/media/csis/pubs/081208_irannucstratcon.pdf.

40. Nuclear Threat Reduction Initiative, "Iran Profile," www.nti.org/e_research/profiles/Iran/Missile/index.html.

41. International Institute for Strategic Studies, *Military Balance: 2003–2004* (Oxford: Oxford University Press, 2004), 102–3.

42. Ze'ev Schiff, "New Iranian Missiles Put Europe in Firing Range," Haaretz, April 27, 2007, www.haaretz.com/hasen/pages/ShArt.jhtml?itemNo = 709937.

43. Daliea Dassa Kaye and Frederic M. Wehrey, "A Nuclear Iran: The Reactions of Neighbours," *Survival* 49, no. 2 (Summer 2007): 114.

44. "NATO Chief Dismisses Russia Fears," BBC News, April 19, 2007 http://news.bbc.co.uk/2/hi/europe/6570533.stm.

45. Off-the-record briefing with a senior official from the U.S. Department of State, April 2008, Washington.

46. Stephen Hildreth and Carl Ek, "CRS Report to Congress: Long Range Ballistic Missile Defense in Europe," February 19, 2008, http://assets.opencrs.com/rpts/RL34051_20080219.pdf, 18.

47. Matthew Collin, "Azeri Radar Eyed for US Shield," BBC News, June 18, 2007, http://newsvote.bbc.co.uk/mpapps/pagetools/print/news.bbc.co.uk/2/hi/europe/6764079.stm.

48. These Russian perspectives are detailed by George N. Lewis and Theodore A. Postol, "European Missile Defense: The Technological Basis of Russian Concerns," Arms Control Association, 2007, available at www.armscontrol.org.

49. "Vice Admiral Lowell E. Jacoby, U.S. Navy Director, Defense Intelligence Agency Statement for the Record," U.S. Senate Armed Services Committee, March 17, 2005, www.dia.mil/publicaffairs/Testimonies/statement17.html.

50. See Scott Sagan, "Why Do States Build Nuclear Weapons? Three Models in Search of a Bomb," *International Security* 21, no. 3 (Winter 1996–97): 54–87.

51. For a detailed survey of diplomatic initiatives and options toward Iran, see Mark Fitzpatrick, *The Iranian Nuclear Crisis: Avoiding Worst-Case Outcomes*, Adelphi Paper 398 (London: International Institute for Strategic Studies, 2008).

52. The Israeli role in deterrence would be likely enhanced if it were to develop a visible second-strike capacity. Even with existing assumed capacity, Israel has a spectrum of forces that are sufficient to make Iran think very hard before launching any attacks on Israel or supporting attacks by nonstate actors that could be traced back to Tehran. See Kaye and Wehrey, "Nuclear Iran," 112.

53. For further discussion, see Barry Posen, "We Can Live with a Nuclear Iran," *New York Times*, February 27, 2006.

54. This proposal was initially advanced by U.S. representative Ellen Tauscher in June 2007.

55. "Former Senator Sam Nunn, Co-Chairman of the Nuclear Threat Initiative," Spaso House Discussion Forum, Moscow, August 27, 2007, www.nti.org/c_press/speech_samnunn_spaso082707.pdf.

56. Henry Kissinger, George Shultz, Sam Nunn, and William Perry, "Toward a Nuclear Free World," *Wall Street Journal*, January 15, 2008, http://online.wsj.com/public/article_print/SB120036422673589947.html. Also see Ivo Daalder and Jan Lodal, "The Logic of Zero," *Foreign Affairs* 87, no. 6 (November–December 2008): 80–95.

CHAPTER 7

The "New" Members and Future Enlargement

THE IMPACT OF NATO–RUSSIA RELATIONS

Roger E. Kanet

ALTHOUGH NATO HAS TRIED to retain its momentum of transformation and relevance in an ever-changing world, the new strategic environment in Europe poses an essential dilemma for the normative basis of NATO's continuity given its 1990s template. Recent events in the Caucasus and the crisis over Russia's August 2008 intervention in Georgia and its subsequent recognition of the breakaway Georgian republics of South Ossetia and Abkhazia, followed by NATO's condemnation of Russia's behavior, have created a dilemma for the West in dealing with the growing discrepancy between the realpolitik of regional geopolitics and the expansionary nature of a global system of values and norms based on Western-led principles of democracy, human rights, and free markets. Because human rights and democratic governance have been largely abandoned by most of the former Soviet states and as free markets are being seriously challenged by the ongoing global financial crisis, the return of regional geopolitics challenges NATO's 1990s project of expanding a Western system of normative values with like-minded governments bonded to each other through the power of international institutions.

For almost two decades now, ever since the end of the Cold War and the implosion of the Soviet Union, the question of the rationale for NATO's continued existence has persisted. Despite the reinvention of NATO in the 1990s by redefining its major objectives away from the collective defense of its member states against the now-defunct Soviet Union to a form of general collective security, the questions of its raison d'être and the likelihood of its continued existence have continued to emerge.[1] Yet notwithstanding the arguments that the rationale for its continued existence has disappeared, that the divisions within it are irreparable,[2] and that its continued expansion eastward could only lead to a direct confrontation with Russia,[3] it has continued its seemingly inexorable drive eastward, with Georgia and Ukraine, along with various countries in the Western Balkans, on Washington's list of candidates for membership in the near future—although by no means on the lists of all its other major members.[4]

The central questions addressed in this chapter are the role of NATO's new and possible future members in its policy, in particular concerning the relations between NATO and its member states and Russia, as well as the likely impact of Russian policy on future plans for NATO's continued expansion. Before proceeding with an examination of these core questions, however, it is important to trace briefly the dramatic changes in the policy commitments and the capabilities of Russia—changes that culminated in August 2008 in Russia's military intervention in Georgia and in the clear and hostile rhetoric emanating from Moscow throughout the fall of 2008 that targeted the United States, NATO, and Europe more generally.[5] Russia's January 2009 natural gas "war" with Ukraine, with its strong negative impact on a number of other European states, was but a continuation of Russia's attempt to demonstrate that it is willing to employ whatever instruments it has available to accomplish its objectives.[6]

As many analysts have argued, since the collapse of the Soviet Union in 1991, some in Moscow have asserted that Russia remains and must be recognized as a major world power. During the 1990s, as Russia's economy and state structures were in the process of disintegration, these claims seemed farfetched at best. Yet most important for a clearer understanding of Russia's recent more assertive foreign policy is the fact that the countries of the West, led most visibly by the United States, seemingly wrote off Russia as a major power during the first decade of its independence—both then and for the foreseeable future. Although Russia was invited to join some of the West's major clubs—for example, the Group of Eight and a special arrangement with NATO—it was as a second-class partner, whose voice was heard but whose influence on policy decisions was virtually nonexistent.[7] On those issues where Russia had major concerns, such as the wars in the former Yugoslavia and NATO's expansion eastward toward Russian territory, they were de facto ignored. By the time, therefore, that President Boris Yeltsin turned over power to his successor, Vladimir Putin, on January 1, 2000, Russia's relations with the United States, and its relations with NATO and the West

more broadly, had deteriorated significantly from the euphoria of the immediate post-Soviet period. A broad range of issues, from human rights abuses
in Russia to a possible U.S. antimissile shield, clouded those relations.

One of the very first things that Putin noted after assuming the presidency
was his commitment to reestablishing Russia as a respected great power, one
whose interests would not be ignored by others and whose voice would be
heard on issues of major global importance. As Russia's economic situation
improved during Putin's presidency, in particular his second term, Moscow
became more assertive in voicing its positions, more critical of the West, and
more assertive in dealing with some of its nearby neighbors.

Russia as a Revisionist State

Early in his presidency Putin made clear his commitment to reestablishing
Russia's position as the preeminent regional power and as an important international actor. The essential preconditions for the fulfillment of these objectives, as outlined in the *Foreign Policy Concept* that he approved, were the
internal political stability and economic viability of Russia.[8] Russia had to
overcome all evidence of and inclinations toward separatism, national and
religious extremism, and terrorism. Putin moved forcefully, and in most cases
effectively, to reassert central governmental control in Russia. The economy,
though still not flourishing, had shown strong signs of turning around, with
growth rates of 4.5, 10.0, and 5.0 percent in the years 1999–2001.[9] These
high growth rates continued, and even expanded, in the subsequent years—
and not merely in the oil and gas sector but also across broad sectors of the
economy.[10]

In the foreign policy realm Russia continued to seek allies that shared its
commitment to preventing the global dominance of the United States, which
represents, in the words of the *Foreign Policy Concept*, "a threat to international security and to Russia's goal of serving as a major center of influence
in a multipolar world."[11] Most of the issues on which Russia and the United
States disagreed already in the mid-1990s continued to plague their relationship, and after a very brief hiatus immediately after the September 11, 2001,
terrorist attacks on the United States, these issues reemerged and continue
to undermine Russian–U.S. relations today.

However, Putin's success in dealing with the major domestic problems
challenging the Russian state meant that Russia increasingly faced Europe
and the United States from a position of vastly increased stability and

strength. His reassertion of central control over Russian territory—by eliminating the election of provincial governors, by suppressing domestic opponents and critics (especially the independent media), and by playing on the
fears of Russian citizens of domestic terrorism, crime, and general chaos—
were important in strengthening the Russian state, which under his predecessor at times seemed on the verge of becoming a failed state. Besides
rebuilding the foundations of the Russian state at great cost to political liberty and democracy as a precondition for Russia's ability to reassert itself as
a major power, he and his associates benefited greatly from the exponential
rise in global demand for natural gas and oil—at least until the fall of 2008—
and the ensuing revitalization of the Russian economy. This, in turn, has
contributed to Russia's ability to pursue a much more active and assertive
foreign policy, as many analysts have noted.[12]

Thus Putin was quite successful, and fortunate, during the eight years of
his presidency in establishing the economic and political foundations for a
strong centralized state as the prerequisite for Russia's reasserting itself as a
major player in international political and security affairs. Though the voices
calling for Russia to resume its role as a great global power in the 1990s were
strident but not realistic, similar voices have today taken over the dominant
position in Russian politics, and now they have realistic expectations of
achieving many of their goals. Supporters of this policy position begin with
former president Putin himself, as was made clear in his statement to the
Russian parliament and people that "the collapse of the Soviet Union was the
greatest geopolitical catastrophe of the century."[13] This comment had been
preceded in 2007 by his broad attack on virtually all aspects of U.S. policy,
delivered at the annual international Munich Security Conference, which
made clear Russia's new assertive and nationalistic approach to foreign policy, beginning with its relations with the United States.[14] As Mark Beissinger
notes, Putin's comments imply that the "persistence of the Soviet empire
would have been preferable to the East European democracies or to the current fifteen states that now cover former Soviet space."[15] The rhetoric emanating from Moscow since the military incursion into Georgia, in particular
that of President Dmitry Medvedev, confirmed the image of a revisionist
state intent on reestablishing its dominant role, at least along its periphery,
and one that simply will no longer deal with the rest of the world on any
other terms except those that it sets.[16]

By 2008, when Putin handed over the presidency to his handpicked successor Medvedev, Russia had become a revisionist state—at least in the sense
of being committed to reversing the dramatic geopolitical changes that had
occurred after the collapse of the Soviet Union. As the West—through its

major institutions, such as NATO and the European Union—has incorporated the countries of the former Soviet empire in Central Europe and the Baltics and contemplates admitting other countries along the Russian periphery, Russian leaders have become more concerned about the implications of this shift in power relationships. Directly related to this concern with status and relative power is the fact that under presidents Putin and Medvedev, Moscow has abandoned all pretense of democratization and has reestablished many of the institutional arrangements of a traditional authoritarian political system.

This development has led to two important shifts in Russian foreign policy. First, the turn toward democracy in the so-called color revolutions in Ukraine and Georgia, even though this has been a flawed process of democratization, is seen as a threat to Russia's stability because of its potential for "contaminating" Russia.[17] Second, in the absence of any overriding ideological justification for the reimposition of authoritarian political structures in Russia, the leadership has turned to a focus on external threats to Russia supposedly emanating from the West, in part at least to generate public support for, or at least acceptance of, the existing political system.[18] The West, in particular the United States, has supposedly orchestrated a program that has been aimed at undermining Russian interests, at weaning away from Russian influence areas that are legitimately a part of a Russian sphere, and at attempting to ensure the permanent weakening of Russia. For President Putin, as he noted in his now-famous speech of 2005 to the Russian Duma already quoted above, "the collapse of the Soviet Union was the greatest geopolitical catastrophe of the century."[19] Russia's further slide into economic and political decline during the Yeltsin years is viewed by some in Russia as the direct result of Western advice intended, in effect, to weaken Russia permanently.

President/now–Prime Minister Putin and President Medvedev, along with other key Russian figures, have lost little opportunity in recent years to emphasize to the Russian population the ill intentions of the West—NATO's expansion, the United States' encirclement and containment, and the subversive activities of Western nongovernmental organizations operating in Russia.[20] During the natural gas "war" between Russia and Ukraine, for example, the deputy director of Gazprom even implied that the United States was behind Ukraine's policy, presumably as a means of undermining Russia's reputation as an economic partner with Western Europe and strengthening its argument that Europe should diversify its energy suppliers.[21]

The key point here, however, is the fact that under the Putin-Medvedev administrations Russia has moved far toward rebuilding what Bertil Nygren refers to as "Greater Russia," a reassertion of Russia's influence across the former Soviet space as an integral part of reestablishing its role as a major power and also revising the power structures and power relationships that have emerged in the post-Soviet period.[22] However, at this point it is not clear whether the likely negative implications for Europe of Russia's recent policy in its western borderlands and the impact of the global financial and economic meltdown on the Russian economy will enable Moscow to continue its assertive approach to its relations with the West.

The Reinvention of NATO after the Cold War

Because an alliance is created to maximize the capabilities of its member states to accomplish objectives important for their national interests, major changes in the international system or changes in objectives of key members of such an alliance will undermine its raison d'être and contribute to its eventual dissolution. Precisely for this reason, analysts predicted the demise of NATO after the end of the Cold War and the dissolution of the Soviet Union in 1991.

Yet NATO did not disappear. In fact, as Gülnur Aybet has ably documented, NATO was reinvented in the first half of the 1990s and given an entirely new set of objectives that had little to do with the factors that had initially led to its creation in 1949—namely, the threat represented by a presumably aggressive and expansionist Soviet Union.[23] NATO was no longer responsible for warding off a Soviet invasion force from the east, but rather now assumed responsibility for maintaining peace among disruptive, predominantly ethnically divided, peoples on the eastern and southeastern peripheries of Europe and for helping to socialize populations that had long suffered under authoritarian oppression into an appreciation of liberal democratic and free market political and economic institutions.

So, even though NATO had lost its original purpose, it obtained a new one. In addition to the public rationale presented for the retention of NATO and its political and security structures, another factor of significance to the United States was also at work. Over the more than forty-year history of NATO, important institutional arrangements tied its member countries and their military forces closely together. As the largest and most important of these members and the one that provided all others with an effective security guarantee, the United States gained through the Alliance important levers with which to influence political and security developments in Europe. In other words, the United States' leaders were committed to retaining NATO because it provided the United States with the means to influence its long-term European Allies and to continue to play an important role in the security politics of Europe.[24] Thus, before the end of the 1990s, NATO had already gained a new set of purposes, but ones that were not necessarily of parallel importance for the United States, on the one hand, and some of its European Allies, on the other.

For the purposes of this chapter, the key developments during the past two decades that have most strongly affected the U.S.–Russian and the Russia–NATO relationships have concerned the extension of NATO membership to the countries that comprise the western borderlands of Russia, the use of NATO's forces against Russia's "ally" Serbia, and most recently the United States' decision to deploy portions of its planned antimissile defense system in Poland and the Czech Republic. All these developments have been viewed by Moscow as challenges to its long-term security, while Washington and its NATO allies have viewed them generally from a very different perspective.

Differences between Russia and NATO in the 1990s

After a brief period of associating Russian foreign policy almost completely with U.S. and Western initiatives, the Yeltsin government was forced by its domestic opponents to begin revising its policy orientation. President Yeltsin's appointment in early 1996 of Yevgenii Primakov as foreign minister to replace Andrei Kozyrev did not really usher in a new era in Russian foreign policy, although Primakov emphasized more than had his predecessor the fact that Russia had been and remained a great power, despite its current economic and political problems, and that its foreign policy should be based on this reality. He argued that Russia would not accept dependence on outside powers and was committed to the creation of a stable multipolar world in which its relations with the United States would be based on an "equal partnership."[25]

The Russians increasingly opposed United States–initiated United Nations economic sanctions against a number of countries—all viewed as Russia's important potential international partners. At the time of U.S. and British military strikes in Iraq in retaliation for repeated Iraqi refusals to cooperate with UN weapons inspectors in late 1998, President Yeltsin spoke of "gross violations of the UN Charter." When the West began to pressure Yugoslavia in 1998 over the issue of Kosovo, the Russians placed Yugoslav territorial integrity far above the issue of human rights and threatened various forms of retaliation if the West bombed Yugoslavia.

The issue that raised the most serious Russian concerns at this time—an issue that is even more important a decade later[26]—was NATO's decision to proceed with eastward expansion into former Soviet-controlled Europe. With the dissolution of the Warsaw Pact in 1991 and the dissolution of the Soviet Union later that year, the Russian Federation was no longer a member of an organized security bloc. By the summer of 1994, 600,000 Soviet/Russian troops from Central Europe and 140,000 troops from the Baltic states, together with 400,000 civilian personnel and 500,000 family members, had been withdrawn to Russia. As part of an effort to build confidence in the western regions, this withdrawal of Russian military power in Europe 1,500 kilometers eastward was coupled with a more defensive reconfiguration of Russia's remaining military capability.[27] At this time Moscow was proposing the creation of a new Europe-wide security system that would include Russia as a full and equal partner.[28] However, this was not the intention in Washington. No such system emerged. As Berryman notes: "Washington had no intention of winding up NATO or inviting Russia into NATO and no interest in a geopolitical deal which would recognize Russia's primacy in its neighborhood. Contrary to what, in the Russian view, were categorical assurances given to [Mikhail] Gorbachev and [Eduard] Shevardnadze at the time of German unification that there would be no extension of NATO eastward, in January 1994 NATO launched the Partnership for Peace program and committed itself to eastward enlargement."[29]

Moscow's multifaceted campaign against the extension of NATO membership to Central European states before NATO's 1997 Madrid Summit included pressure on the applicant countries and threats that the expansion would in effect initiate a new cold war in relations between Russia and the West. However, when NATO invited the Czech Republic, Hungary, and Poland to join the Alliance, Russia reluctantly accepted the decision without any of the retaliatory responses that had been threatened. Once it became obvious that their efforts to forestall the expansion of NATO eastward were doomed to failure, the Russians seem to have accepted the reality and attempted to gain whatever benefits they could out of that acceptance. They shifted their opposition to NATO's expansion from Eastern and Central Europe to the Baltic states, despite the fact that the entry of Poland extended NATO's security commitments to the very border of Russia's Kaliningrad region and changed the strategic status quo in Europe. This opposition also failed to stop the extension of NATO membership to the Baltic states seven years later. The push in Washington in 2008 to extend NATO membership to Georgia and Ukraine no doubt was important in triggering the much more aggressive Russian response, when it invaded Georgian territory.

Although NATO and Russia signed the Russia–NATO Founding Act in May 1997, which was to provide a clear framework for Russian–NATO relations, and Russia was granted membership in an expanded Group of Eight, in fact neither of these relationships fulfilled Russian objectives.[30] The Russia–NATO Founding Act failed to serve as an effective means for Russia to pursue its foreign policy interests. Although the act did not provide Russia with anything approximating veto power over NATO's decisions, it did call for consultation on important security issues. In fact, NATO largely ignored Russia's increasingly vehement complaints about its refusal to consult on issues including NATO's attempts to arrest Serbs as war criminals and to implement various aspects of the Dayton Peace Accords. At the same time, Moscow was excluded from full participation in those Group of Eight meetings at which meaningful decisions concerning international financial matters were likely to be made. But given the disastrous state of its economy, Moscow had little hope of exercising any real influence within the group.

When President Yeltsin plucked Vladimir Putin from political obscurity in August 1999 and began to groom him as his successor, the state of Russia's relations with the United States and with NATO had reached a post–Cold War low. However, although many of Russia's stated policies were in direct conflict with U.S. foreign objectives, the central component of bilateral Russian relations with the United States remained stable. Moreover, given its generally weak position because of its economic dependence on the West, Moscow often was forced to back down when faced with Washington's opposition. As should be clear, most of the issues that divide Russian–American relations in 2009 have their roots in political and security developments a decade earlier. What has changed is the unwillingness of Moscow to accept a position of weakness or dependence in its relations with the West. It is important to recall that throughout the prior decade the United States, and the West more generally, had benefited geopolitically from the weakness of Russia and, from Moscow's perspective at least, were encroaching on Russia's legitimate sphere of influence and, in effect, pursuing policies that, de facto at least, were designed to contain future Russian influence.

The Bush Doctrine and Russian–NATO Relations

The November 2000 election of George W. Bush as president initiated major shifts in American foreign policy, which exacerbated the tensions in

Russia's relations with both the United States and NATO. The commitment of President Bush and his key advisers to assuring the "permanent" hegemony of the United States in global affairs soon brought Washington into direct conflict with Moscow, as well as with key long-term Allies such as France and Germany. The approach to foreign affairs pursued by the Bush administration, the so-called Bush Doctrine, including its global objectives and its willingness to engage in preemptive attacks and to pursue a unilateralist approach to accomplish them, was laid out in 2002 in *The National Security Strategy of the United States.*[31] It is that of a "coercive hegemon" using raw power politics to cow both rivals and friends in an effort "to impose its will and preference on all who oppose it, on those that would prefer to remain neutral or hide, and on those who are enlisted in coalitions of the moment to bandwagon on American power."[32] This new approach to foreign policy and to relations with long-term friends and Allies met with serious resistance in Europe among those states derided by U.S. secretary of defense Donald Rumsfeld as "old Europe." France and Germany, as well as other NATO members and Russia, resisted the United States' attempts to impose its worldview and its interpretation of how best to accomplish its own objectives. The result was disagreement on policy in Iraq, but probably more serious, a growing divide between the United States and its key long-term partners in European security, as well as a major contribution to the souring of relations between the United States and Russia.

After a short-lived improvement in Russian–U.S. relations immediately after the terrorist attacks in New York and Washington in September 2001, amid the decisions of the Bush administration to decline assistance from NATO states in taking on al-Qaeda and the Taliban in Afghanistan and, even more important, to destroy the regime of Saddam Hussein in Iraq, relations deteriorated again. In part this resulted from Washington's initiatives; in part, however, it resulted from the decisions made in Moscow as Russia emerged from the economic and political chaos of the 1990s, and was able to achieve its major foreign and security policy objectives on its own without continuing to defer to the United States and Europe.

Already before Bush's inauguration as president in January 2001, planning for the next stage in the expansion of NATO—including the three former Soviet republics of Latvia, Lithuania, and Estonia—was well under way.[33] Despite strongly voiced opposition to further expansion and conciliatory security policies aimed at convincing the United States and its NATO Allies not to offer membership to the three Baltic states, at its November 2002 Summit, NATO offered full membership, effective in 2004, to ten new members, including the Baltic states.[34]

By the time that the Baltic states were admitted to membership in NATO, the United States had decided to move ahead with the further development and deployment of portions of an anti–ballistic missile system—a decision that had strongly negative implications for the United States' and NATO's relations with Russia. In his final years in office President Bill Clinton, in the face of growing pressures from the Republican-dominated Senate to expand a commitment to developing an effective anti–ballistic missile system, had finally decided to defer the decision to the incoming administration. Bush made clear, even before his election, that he was committed to pursuing the development of such a system. Once in office he moved immediately to eliminate the restrictions on testing by withdrawing from the 1972 Anti–Ballistic Missile Treaty and eventually proceeded with plans to deploy the first stages of an antimissile defense system in the Czech Republic and Poland to defend against missiles possibly launched from Iran in the future. The speed with which the Poles and Czechs finally ratified the agreements with the United States in August 2008—after long domestic debates—made clear that the Russian military intervention in Georgia and their revived concerns about the long-term nature of their relations with Russia had played a major role in their decisions.[35] No doubt President Medvedev's announcement in his address to the Russian Parliament on November 5, 2008, reinforced concerns throughout Central Europe, as he stated the likely deployment of Russian missiles in the Kaliningrad region along the Polish border and that capabilities for electronic warfare against NATO would be expanded in the area.[36] But the central issue from the perspective of the United States' and NATO's relations with Russia is the fact that a series of post–Cold War U.S. decisions ignored Russia's stated concerns, and this contributed to a continuing deterioration of relations.

New NATO Members and Russia–NATO Relations

In the discussions of the implications of NATO's expansion—as well as that of the European Union—little attention was given to the issue of the possible impact of the new members on decision making within the organizations or on the influence that they would likely have on relations between NATO and the EU and Russia. Given the decision-making procedures of the two organizations, new members are likely to have greater influence in decision making within the European Union, where unanimity is required. Joan DeBardeleben has pointed to the role of Poland and several of the Baltic states in complicating relations between the EU and Russia, as they refused to back negotiations for a new framework agreement until Russia responded to their own concerns.[37] These countries brought to the European Union experiences in the post–World War II era that simply did not overlap with those of the original fifteen EU members. Most bring a fear of a resurgent Russia and a concern for the ways in which Russia has used its economic leverage, especially its control over energy, to bully neighboring states.[38] They have, therefore, attempted to influence their EU partners to be aware of Russian intentions and to protect their interests.

In different ways the policy concerns of the new members of NATO can also be seen in their governments' support of U.S. initiatives, even at times of substantial domestic opposition to U.S. policy within their populations. All the new members of NATO supported the U.S. decision to invade Iraq, and all except Slovenia sent troops to Iraq, most notably Poland. In fact most of the countries were not yet NATO members, but they were part of NATO's Partnership for Peace when they sent forces. No doubt a central reason many of these countries sent troops was to shore up their relations with NATO and the United States to ensure membership, as well as strengthen their longer-term security ties with the United States. In the policy disagreements that have divided NATO since the fall of 2002 and that have threatened to make it irrelevant, its new members have almost always sided with the United States—and the United Kingdom—against many of its other European members, and also against Russia.[39]

Georgia, Ukraine, and NATO–Russian Relations

During 2008 and early 2009 several developments had direct relevance to the issues of continued NATO expansion, as well as the likely course of Russian–NATO relations. First, there was the escalating tension in the relationship between Moscow and Tbilisi that had been growing, more or less, ever since the Rose Revolution of 2003 that eventually brought to power the Western-oriented government of Mikheil Saakashvili. Over the ensuing four years or so, the two countries were at increasing odds with one another, as Saakashvili pursued attempts to assert Georgia's full independence, clamored for entry into NATO and the EU, and jockeyed to reassert central government authority over the breakaway republics of Abkhazia and South Ossetia.[40]

In the midst of this escalating conflict President George W. Bush, during a visit to Ukraine in April 2008, announced his support for immediate NATO membership for both Georgia and Ukraine, regardless of Russian opposition to further expansion of NATO into the former Soviet space.[41] At the NATO

meetings in Bucharest several days later, Bush's proposal that the two countries should be offered a Membership Action Plan leading to full membership
was opposed by Germany, France, and several other member states, which
argued that the two countries had not yet met the expected criteria for membership.[42] No doubt the issue of Russia's likely response played a role in the
views of many of the members. Throughout the final year of his presidency,
Bush continued his effort to convince his NATO partners to begin the process of admitting Ukraine and Georgia to NATO.[43]

Related to the possibility of Georgia and Ukraine being offered NATO
membership were the conflicts between Russia and the two countries, which
exploded, respectively, in August 2008 and January 2009. By 2008 the processes discussed here were well under way. On the one hand, President Putin
and Russia's leadership had made clear its commitment to reestablishing its
position as the major actor in the post-Soviet region and its willingness to
use the instruments at its disposal to bring neighboring states into line and
to stop the expansion of Western influence on its periphery.[44] Until the
August 2008 Russian invasion, Russia's control of the natural gas, natural gas
pipelines, and electricity needed by Georgia had been the most important
instrument at its disposal to bring pressure against Georgia, in order to
coerce Tbilisi into policies more in line with Moscow's interests. However,
these pressures did not cow the Georgian government into accepting Russian
dominance in the region, or into accepting the de facto autonomy of the
Russian-backed secessionists in South Ossetia and Abkhazia. This resulted in
military hostilities in August 2008 that in effect wiped out Georgian military
capabilities developed in recent years with U.S. military assistance and training and made clear that Russia would use whatever means it had at its disposal
to ensure that its interests on its western periphery were protected.[45]

Although the issues involved in the January 2009 confrontation over natural gas prices between Russia and Ukraine were quite different from those
leading to the military incursion into Georgia five months earlier, at root was
the issue of Kyiv's defiance of Moscow's preferences across a broad range of
issues and not simply the disagreement over the price of natural gas exported
to Ukraine. For example, Ukraine had insisted on Russia's removal of its
Black Sea Fleet from its bases in Sevastopol, currently scheduled for 2017.[46]

Parallel to this process of Moscow's attempt to bring neighboring states
into line with its foreign and security policy preferences was the commitment
of the Bush administration, backed by many of NATO's new Central European and Baltic members, to respond to the calls of Western-oriented governments in the two countries to extend membership to Ukraine and
Georgia. Although the stated goal was to respond to the desire of the peoples

of Ukraine and Georgia to integrate into existing Euro-Atlantic institutions and helping to stabilize the countries over the longer term, the desire to contain expanding Russian influence was no doubt a factor in Washington, as it had been ever since the collapse of the USSR. The fact that a substantial portion of the Ukrainian population opposed NATO membership and that the Georgian government did not exercise effective control over large portions of its territory were factors largely ignored by Washington.[47]

An Unclear Future

Before turning to a discussion of the likely future of NATO–Russian relations and the place of NATO's new members in this relationship, I would like to note briefly that relations between Russia and the United States and NATO might have developed differently—that the confrontation between the two was not preordained. At various points in its first ten years, the post-Soviet Russian government made concessions and introduced proposals intended to create a new European security environment that would include Russia as a full partner. After these actions, coupled with growing Russian concerns—paranoid though they might at times appear to decision makers in Washington—were systematically ignored, Putin and his colleagues opted for a new approach to Russian security, which in effect wrote off the importance of collaborative relations with the West and focused on a return to the great-power politics of the past. Rising global demand and prices for oil and natural gas generated the economic revival in Russia that provided the foundation for this new assertive approach to dealing with the West. A less triumphalist and more cooperative U.S. approach to dealing with Russia during the 1990s that extended beyond mere rhetoric and a less aggressive approach early in the current decade could have created an environment in which Russian leaders might not have decided to pursue the type of assertive, revisionist policy that has characterized the past several years. But even if such a policy had been pursued, there is no guarantee that Russia under Putin would not have developed much the same domestic and foreign policy orientations.

This brings us to the question of the likely future evolution of NATO's policy on the issue of its continued expansion and on the nature of Russia's relations with the United States, NATO, and Western Europe. First, it is very important to recognize the fact that two basic objectives should underlie NATO and U.S. decision making. On the one hand, it is essential that states in the area be able to pursue their own political and security interests, as long as they do not threaten others, and that Russia not be permitted, in effect, to hold veto power over their ability to join either NATO or the European Union. On the other hand, the future of European, and even global, security requires the effective integration of Russia into a broader, European-wide, security system where it is not marginalized and is able to operate as an equal partner. At this time these two objectives appear to be at odds with one another. In fact, developments over the course of the past five or six years have illustrated not only growing friction between Russia and the West but also growing divisions within the Western community on ways to deal with Russia. NATO's and the EU's lack of a response to Russian military operations in Georgia and to its later diplomatic recognition of the breakaway republics and its decision to establish permanent military bases in both South Ossetia and Abkhazia[48]—beyond temporarily breaking off direct contacts—demonstrated their impotence in the face of clear evidence of Moscow's "resolve to maintain its position in the region and send a strong message to the leaderships in the Caucasus, Central Europe, the Baltics and Central Asia."[49]

The new Barack Obama administration in Washington has provided some initial hints that it plans to alter the policy of the United States toward Russia by considering a delay in the deployment of an anti–ballistic missile system in Central Europe and by calling for a resumption of bilateral negotiations on the elimination of nuclear weapons.[50] NATO's 2009 Strasbourg-Kehl Summit made no decisions about future membership for countries such as Ukraine or Georgia. At the summit the Obama administration took future expansion, as well as the earlier planned missile defense, off the agenda. More attention was given to improving relations with Russia and, therefore, the need for transparency.[51] Yet the issue of NATO's continuing eastward expansion remains open. Given the instability of the domestic political situation in both Ukraine and Georgia, the dissatisfaction of a growing number of Western officials with the behavior of the leaders of the two countries, and the concerns about the likely impact of the extension of such an offer of membership on relations with Russia, it is highly unlikely that NATO will in fact offer to either country a Membership Action Plan in the foreseeable future. Whether or not the Obama administration will push such a plan as did its predecessor—something that appears unlikely at the present time—those of NATO's European members that voiced their opposition to this further enlargement at its meetings in 2004 are not likely to abandon their position. This means that the objective of not further alienating Russia by continuing to challenge its self-proclaimed interests in its western borderlands will for the foreseeable future trump the self-determination of states in the region to the right to join Euro-Atlantic institutions.

This brings us to another question of importance for the future of NATO. The heightened level of security concerns in NATO's new Central European and Baltic members resulting from Russian pressures on Estonia and Poland, followed by the intervention in Georgia and the natural gas "war" with Ukraine, are likely to push these countries closer to the United States and further from the position of other European members of NATO—and the European Union. The cohesion of the transatlantic Alliance has been challenged ever since the end of the Cold War. Although the moderation in the tone of relations with Europe in the George W. Bush administration's second term and since the change of presidential administrations in Washington has smoothed over some important differences, strong divergences of perspective and interest still divide the Alliance. Relations with Russia have become a key aspect of these divisions, added to growing concerns about the pursuit of the war in Afghanistan. Finally, even though NATO may continue to exist largely for reasons of inertia, these and other factors are likely to make it increasingly irrelevant to the central security interests of many of its members, especially the United States. As I have argued elsewhere, even though NATO's organizational structure may continue to exist, in the future it is likely to serve more as a pool of states from which temporary coalitions can be created to deal with specific security issues. Differences among its members on policy toward Russia and on its further expansion simply contribute to the likelihood of such a development.[52]

Notes

1. For an excellent analysis of the reinvention of NATO in the 1990s, see Gülnur Aybet, *A European Security Architecture after the Cold War: Questions of Legitimacy* (New York: St. Martin's Press, 2000). See also David S. Yost, *NATO Transformed: The Alliance's New Roles in International Security* (Washington, DC: U.S. Institute of Peace Press, 1998). Rajan Menon has been among those who have pronounced the imminent death of NATO. See, e.g., Rajan Menon, "NATO: R.I.P.," *The American Interest* 4, no. 2 (2008): 52–59; and Rajan Menon, *The End of Alliance* (New York: Oxford University Press, 2007). It is important to note that the Russians simply do not accept the depiction of NATO's expansion as an extension of collective security. They view it, rather, as a continuation of Western efforts to contain Russia's legitimate role in its Western borderlands and to challenge Russia's security interests. See, e.g., John Berryman, "Russia, NATO Enlargement and the Western Borderlands," in *A Resurgent Russia and the European Union*, ed. Roger E. Kanet (Dordrecht: Republic of Letters Publishing, 2009), 163–88. The present author has benefited greatly from reading this excellent analysis.

2. Among the numerous discussions of the future of the transatlantic relationship, see the symposium "Still Mars, Still Venus? The United States, Europe and the

Future of the Transatlantic Relationship," *International Politics* 45, no. 3 (2008): 231–397.

3. See J. L. Black, *Russia Faces NATO Expansion: Bearing Gifts or Bearing Arms?* (Lanham, MD: Rowman & Littlefield, 2000).

4. See Paul Taylor, "Europeans Souring on Ukraine, Georgia," Reuters, January 14, 2009, www.reuters.com/article/vcCandidateFeed2/idUSTRE50D2VO20090114. Albania and Croatia were formally welcomed to NATO membership at the Strasbourg-Kehl Summit meeting of NATO in April 2009. See NATO, "NATO Secretary General Welcomes Albania and Croatia as NATO Members," www.nato.int/cps/en/natolive/news_52342.htm.

5. Vladimir Shlapentokh has provided in some detail an overview of the hostile rhetoric that has characterized Russian discussions of the United States and the West in recent years in "Behind the Five-Day War: The Ideological Backing of Putin's Regime," *Johnson's Russia List*, JRL 2008–195, October 23, 2008, www.cdi.org/russia/johnson/2008–194–30.cfm.

6. On the January 2009 gas war, see Marc-Antoine Eyl-Mazzega, "The Gas Crisis between the Ukraine and Russia: One Crisis Too Far That Obliges a Humiliated Europe to React," *European Issues*, no. 125, *Les Policy Papers de la Fondation Robert Schuman*, January 26, 2009, www.robert-schuman.org/question_europe.php?num =qe-125.

7. Andrei Tsygankov makes this argument quite strongly; see, e.g., Andrei Tsygankov, "The West Needs to Make Up for Past Mistakes on Russia," *Radio Free Europe/Radio Liberty*, August 27, 2008, www.rferl.org/content/West_Make_Up_Past _Mistakes_Russia /1194339.html.

8. *The Foreign Policy Concept of the Russian Federation (2000) Approved by the President of the Russian Federation V. Putin*, June 29, 2000, www.mid.ru/mid/eng/econcept .htm; also available in *Johnson's Russia List*, JRL 2000–4403, July 14, 2000, www.cdi .org/russia/johnson. See also "Kontseptsiia natsional'noi bezopasnosti Rossiiskoi Federatsii," *Nezavisimoe voennoe obozrenie* (Internet Version), July 11, 2000, http://nvo .ng.ru/concepts/2000–01–14/6_concept.html.

9. Central Bank of the Russian Federation, "Main Macroeconomic Indicators," 2001, www.cbr.ru/eng/statistics/credit_statistics/.

10. World Bank, *Russian Economic Report*, no. 16, June 2008, http://siteresources .worldbank.org/INTRUSSIANFEDERATION/Resources /rer16_Eng. pdf.

11. *Foreign Policy Concept of the Russian Federation.*

12. As many analysts have argued, the revived role of Russia as a regional and global political actor is based extensively on oil and gas production and exports, despite recent improvements in other aspects of the Russian economy. See, e.g., Kathleen J. Hancock, "Russia: Great Power Image versus Economic Reality," *Asian Perspective* 31, no. 4 (2007): 71–98; Michael McFaul and Kathryn Stoner-Weiss, "The Myth of Putin's Success," *Foreign Affairs* 87, no. 1 (2008): 68–84; and Rajan Menon and Alexander J. Motyl, "The Myth of Russian Resurgence," *The American Interest Online* 2, no. 4 (2007): 96–101, www.the-american-interest.com/ai2/article.cfm?Id =258&MId = 8. What the longer-term impact of the collapse of the global economy in the fall of 2008 and the dramatic drop in energy prices will have on the Russian economy and on Russia's ability to continue to pursue an assertive foreign policy is yet to be seen.

13. President's speech to the Federal Assembly, April 2005. BBC Monitoring, "Putin Focuses on Domestic Policy in State-of-Nation Address to Russian Parliament," RTR Russia TV, Moscow, April 25, 2005, trans. in *Johnson's Russia*, JRL 2005–9130, April 25, 2005, available at www.cdi.org/russia/johnson/. For recent discussions of the commitment of Russia's political elites to regaining great-power status, see Ingmar Oldberg, "Russia's Great Power Ambitions and Policy under Putin," in *Russia: Re-Emerging Great Power*, ed. Roger E. Kanet (Houndmills, U.K.: Palgrave Macmillan, 2007), 13–30; and Vladimir Rukavishnikov, "Choices for Russia: Preserving Inherited Geopolitics through Emergent Global and European Realities," in *Russia: Re-Emerging Great Power*, ed. Kanet, 54–78. Public opinion surveys in Russia indicate that a majority of Russians support the return of Russia to great-power status. Fifty-one percent of those surveyed in early 2008 expected Putin's successor to return Russia to a preeminent global role, while only 9 percent expect the next president to establish good relations with the West. See "Half of Russians Yearn for Super-Power Status," *Angus Reid Global Monitor*, February 4, 2008, reprinted in *Johnson's Russia List*, JRL 2008–208, February 4, 2008, available at www.cdi.org/russia/johnson/.

14. "Putin Slams US for Making World More Dangerous," *DW—World.DE Deutsche Welle*, February 10, 2007, www.dw-world.de/dw/article/0,2144,2343749,00.html. See also "Not a Cold War, but a Cold Tiff: Russia and America," *The Economist*, February 17, 2007, 60–61; and Stefan Wagstyl, "The Year Russia Flexed Its Diplomatic Muscle," *Financial Times*, December 17, 2007, reprinted in *Johnson's Russia List*, JRL 2007–257, December 17, www.cdi.org/russia/johnson/ What most Western commentators and analysts missed in Putin's remarks was his assertion that Russia was willing to work with the United States as an equal in areas related to the continued reduction of nuclear weapons and other arms control measures. See Vladimir Putin, "Putin's Prepared Remarks at 43rd Munich Conference on Security Policy," delivered February 10, 2007, www.washingtonpost.com/wp-dyn/content/article/2007/02/12/AR200702 1200555.html.

15. Mark R. Beissinger, "The Persistence of Empire in Eurasia," *NewsNet: News of the American Association for the Advancement of Slavic Studies* 48, no. 1 (2008): 1–8.

16. Clifford J. Levy, "Russia Adopts Blustery Tone," *New York Times*, August 28, 2008. See also President Medvedev's State of the Nation address in November 2008, "Russian President Medvedev's First Annual Address to Parliament," Rossiya TV, November 5, 2008, trans. in *Johnson's Russia List*, JRL 2008–292, November 6, 2008. From Moscow's perspective, however, its policy goals are not revisionist, but rather are intended to reestablish Russia's legitimate position in the aftermath of the West's having taken advantage of Russian decline in the immediate post–Cold War period.

17. Lilia Shevtsova makes this point. See Lilija Ševcova, "Ende einer Epoche: Russlands Bruch mit dem Westen," *Ostpolitik* 58, no. 11 (2008): 765–70.

18. For example, at the time of the January 2009 gas war between Russia and Ukraine, Alexander Medvedev, Gazprom's deputy chief executive, said, "It looks like . . . they [the Ukrainians] are dancing to the music which is being orchestrated not in Kiev but outside the country." Medvedev said he was referring to an unspecified agreement signed by the U.S. and Ukraine recently, an agreement he called "suspicious." Andrew Osborn and Marc Champion, "Ukraine Refuses to Open Pipeline, Halting Start of Gas Flows to Europe," *Wall Street Journal*, January 13, 2009, reprinted in *Johnson's Russia List*, JRL 2009–8, January 13, 2009, www.cdi.org/russia/johnson.

19. President's speech to the Federal Assembly, April 2005.

20. "Putin Slams US."

21. Medvedev of Gazprom cited by Osborn and Champion, "Ukraine Refuses to Open Pipeline."

22. Bertil Nygren, *The Rebuilding of Greater Russia: Putin's Foreign Policy toward the CIS Countries* (Abingdon, U.K.: Routledge, 2007).

23. Aybet, *European Security Architecture*; see also Yost, *NATO Transformed*.

24. For the development of this argument, see Christopher Layne, *The Peace of Illusions: American Grand Strategy from 1940 to the Present* (Ithaca, NY: Cornell University Press, 2006).

25. Evgenyi Primakov, "Rossiia ishchet novoe mesto v mire" (interview with E. Primkov), *Izvestiia*, March 6, 1996; Dmitrii Gornostaev, "Novoe v staroi kontseptsii Primakova," *Nezavisimaia Gazeta*, March 17, 1998.

26. In a nationally televised interview in August 2008, President Medvedev stated: "We do not need illusions of partnership. When we are being surrounded by bases on all sides, and a growing number of states are being drawn into the North Atlantic bloc and we are being told, 'Don't worry, everything is all right,' naturally we do not like it." Cited by Levy, "Russia Adopts Blustery Tone."

27. Berryman, "Russia, NATO Enlargement, and the Western Borderlands." See also Mark Webber, *The International Politics of Russia and the Successor States* (Manchester: Manchester University Press, 1996), 176; John Berryman, "Russian Security Policy and Northern Europe," in *Post-Communist States in the World Community*, ed. William E. Ferry and Roger E. Kanet (Basingstoke, U.K.: Macmillan, 1998), 108–16; and Aleksei Bogaturov, "An Inside Outsider," in *Is Russia a European Power? The Position of Russia in Europe*, ed. Tom Casier and Katlijn Malfliet (Leuven: Leuven University Press, 1998), 83; Leon Aron, "Russia's New Foreign Policy," *Russian Outlook*, May 1, 1998, 1, www.aei.org/include/pub_print.asp?pubID=8990.

28. Alexei Arbatov, "NATO and Russia," *Security Dialogue* 26, no. 2 (1995): 140.

29. Berryman, "Russia, NATO Enlargement, and the Western Borderlands," pp. 167–8. See also, Roland Dannreuther, "Escaping the Enlargement Trap in NATO–Russian Relations," *Survival* 41, no. 4 (Winter 1999–2000): 151–52. For an illuminating discussion of the U.S. objectives for retaining NATO in post–Cold War Europe, see Layne, *Peace of Illusions*, chap. 5.

30. E.g., the air strikes over Serbia during the Kosovo war—against the strong vocal opposition of Moscow—arguably made a mockery of the NATO–Russia Founding Act, which supposedly provided Russia with the ability to influence NATO decisions. However, Moscow's countermeasures were largely symbolic, and it very soon resumed its participation in the activities of the Permanent Joint Council. As one Russian analyst noted, although Russian concern about the welfare of fellow Slavs in Serbia was praiseworthy, it was important to recognize that NATO jets represented a market for Russian oil. See Egor Druzenki, "Ne dai Bog! Zashchishchaia Jugoslaviiu, Rossiia ne mozhet riskovat' svoim budushchim," *Neft' I Kapital*, no. 2 (1999): 78–81.

31. *The National Security Strategy of the United States of America* (Washington, DC: White House, 2002). Among the clearest summaries and trenchant critiques of the Bush Doctrine are Edward A. Kolodziej's chapters titled "American Power and Global Order" and "From Superpower to Besieged Global Power," in *From Superpower to Besieged Global Power: Restoring World Order after the Failure of the Bush Doctrine*, ed. Edward A. Kolodziej and Roger E. Kanet (Athens: University of Georgia

Press, 2008), 3–30, 299–337. See also Roger E. Kanet, "The Bush Revolution in U.S. Security Policy," in *The New Security Environment: The Impact on Russia, Central and Eastern Europe*, ed. Roger E. Kanet (Burlington, VT: Ashgate, 2005), 11–29.

32. Edward A. Kolodziej, "The Theory of Global Politics and Bargaining Strategies of the American Hegemon: Implications for Global Governance," unpublished paper presented at the CEEISA/ISA International Convention, Budapest, June 26–28, 2003, 6.

33. In January 1998, the Clinton administration's Baltic Partnership Charter promised to prepare the Baltic states for NATO membership. See Yaroslav Bilinsky, *Endgame in NATO's Enlargement: The Baltic States and Ukraine* (Westport, CT: Praeger, 1999), 12–13, 88.

34. For a fuller discussion of these developments, see Berryman, "Russia, NATO Enlargement and the Western Borderlands." This commitment was reaffirmed by the incoming Bush administration.

35. The final Polish decision to sign the agreement for the placement of radar and antimissile systems in their countries occurred soon after the Russian intervention in Georgia and was, no doubt, influenced by concerns about Russia's more assertive role in the region. Russian officials reacted immediately by noting that this decision would likely result in Poland and the Czech Republic being targeted by Russian missiles. See Thomas Shanker and Nicholas Kulish, "Russia Lashes Out on Missile Deal," *New York Times*, August 16, 2008; and Nicholas Kulish, "Georgian Crisis Brings Attitude Change to a Flush Poland," *New York Times*, August 21, 2008.

36. Dimitri Medvedev, "Russian President Medvedev's First Annual Address to Parliament," Rossiya TV, November 5, 2008, trans. in *Johnson's Russia List*, JRL 2008–202, November 6, 2008. In late January 2009, after the inauguration of President Barack Obama, the Russians announced that they were no longer planning to place missiles in Kaliningrad targeted at Poland and the Czech Republic. "Russia Ready Not to Aim Iskander Missile Systems against USA," *Pravda.ru*, January 28, 2009. http://english.pravda.ru/russia/politics/28–01–2009/107026-russia_iskander_eusa-0.

37. Joan DeBardeleben, "The Impact of EU Enlargement on the EU-Russian Relationship," in *Resurgent Russia and the European Union*, ed. Kanet.

38. See Roger E. Kanet, "Russia and the European Union: The U.S. Impact on the Relationship," *Jean Monnet/Robert Schuman Paper Series* (Miami European Union Center of Excellence) 9, no. 2 (January 2009), available at www.miami.edu/eucenter. Before the June 2008 EU–Russian Summit, two clear camps were emerging within the European Union on the issue of relations with Russia—the military incursion into Georgia in August 2008 reinforced those positions. On the one side were especially the new member states, led by Poland and Estonia. Allied with them at times and on some issues have been Sweden and the United Kingdom. For the Central European states recent Russian treatment of Georgia and Estonia, as well as continuing support for secessionist groups in post-Soviet countries, was viewed as reminiscent of almost half a century of Soviet domination throughout the region. Sweden has reacted especially to Russia's treatment of Georgia over the past several years, even before the military incursion, while the United Kingdom has been concerned with all of these issues, in addition to Russia's reported involvement in the 2006 murder of ex-Russian security officer Aleksandr Litvinenko in London. Conversely, important founding EU

members "are energetically making peace with Russia," according to Edward Lucas: "You've got France, Germany, and Italy, all in the Russian camp as far as energy is concerned." Quoted by Brian Whitmore, "Will Brussels Get Tough with Moscow?" *Radio Free Europe/Radio Liberty*, July 13, 2008, www.rferl.org/articleprintview/1183415.html. See also Brian Whitmore, "Russia Backed Litvinenko Murder, BBC Reports," *Radio Free Europe/Radio Liberty*, July 14, 2008, www.rferl.org/articleprintview/1182340.html

39. For a discussion of the divisions within NATO, see Roger E. Kanet, "A New U.S. Approach to Europe? The Transatlantic Relationship after Bush," *International Politics* 45, no. 3 (2008): 348–63.

40. See Bertil Nygren, "Putin's Attempts to Subjugate Georgia: From Sabre-Rattling to the Power of the Purse," in *Russia: Re-Emerging Great Power*, ed. Kanet, 107–23.

41. Luke Harding, "Bush Backs Ukraine and Georgia for NATO Membership," *Guardian.co.uk*, April 1, 2008, www.guardian.co.uk/world/2008/apr/01/nato.georgia.

42. Steven Erlanger and Steven Lee Myers, "NATO Allies Oppose Bush on Georgia and Ukraine," *New York Times*, April 3, 2008.

43. Steven Erlanger, "Georgia and Ukraine Split NATO Members," *International Herald Tribune*, November 30, 2008, www.iht.com/articles/2008/11/30/europe/nato.php.

44. This process is clearly traced in Nygren, *Rebuilding of Greater Russia*. See also Bertil Nygren, "Putin's Use of Natural Gas to Reintegrate the CIS Region," *Problems of Post-Communism* 55, no. 4 (2008): 3–15.

45. In early August 2008—after weeks of mutual verbal attacks between Moscow and Tbilisi and apparently with encouragement from political elements in the United States—President Saakashvili of Georgia, reportedly responding to rocket attacks from locations inside the breakaway region of South Ossetia, sent forces into the region to reincorporate the breakaway republic. (More recent evidence disputes the Georgian claims of the initial rocket attacks.) The Russians, who had apparently massed troops on the Russian–South Ossetian border in advance, almost immediately overwhelmed Georgian forces in the republic, as well as in a second breakaway region of Abkhazia, and advanced far into Georgia territory proper. The message to all—the Georgian government, Washington, and other former Soviet republics with grievances against Moscow—was quite clear. Russia is back, and Russia is willing to use its economic and military power to accomplish objectives that it views as important to its interests. Among the most salient analyses of the Russian intervention is that of George Friedman, who points to the importance in Russia's calculations of what Moscow perceived—not without reason—as a U.S. policy of containment in which Georgia and Ukraine were important elements. See George Friedman, "Georgia and the Balance of Power," *New York Review of Books*. 55, no. 14 (September 25, 2008).

46. For more detail on the areas of disagreement between Russia and Ukraine, see Berryman, "Russia, NATO Enlargement and the Western Borderlands."

47. Seventy-one percent of those who spoke Ukrainian at home supported expansion, while only about 35 percent of those who spoke Russian supported closer ties with or membership in NATO. See Igor Galin, "Mass Public Opinion in Ukraine about NATO and NATO–Ukraine Relationships: Analytical Report," www.nato.int/acad/fellow/96–98/galin.pdf.

48. See Paul Goble, "Russia's New Bases," *New York Times*, September 18, 2008, http://topics.blogs.nytimes.com/2008/09/18/; and RIA Novosti, "Russia to Open Military Bases in Abkhazia, South Ossetia in 2009," November 7, 2008, http://en.ria.ru/russia/20081107/118191240-print.html.

49. Berryman, "Russia, NATO Enlargement and the Western Borderlands."

50. Ian Traynor, "Obama Administration Offers Olive Branch to Russia and Iran," *Guardina.com.uk*, February 7, 2008, www.guardian.co.uk/world/2009/feb/07/us-russia-iran-biden-obama; and Yochi J. Dreazen and Alan Cullison, "Obama Administration Seeks to Reassure Russia," *Wall Street Journal*, February 8, 2008, http://online.wsj.com/article/SB123410795691660745.html.

51. See the summit press release, "Strasbourg/Kehl Summit Declaration," issued by the heads of state and government participating in the meeting of the North Atlantic Council in Strasbourg-Kehl, items 21, 29, 34, 35, and 54, April 4, 2009, www.nato.int/cps/en/natolive/news_52837.htm?mode=pressrelease. A generally negative, but quite comprehensive, assessment of the results of the Strasbourg-Kehl Summit can be found at the website of the Heritage Foundation, a very conservative U.S. think tank. See Sally McNamara, "NATO's 60th Anniversary Summit: Unfocused and Unsuccessful," *Heritage Foundation Issues*, April 8, 2009, www.heritage.org/research/europe/wm2388.cfm#_ftnref9.

52. Kanet, "New U.S. Approach to Europe?" See also Menon, *End of Alliance*, as well as the contributions to the symposium "Still Mars, Still Venus?"

CHAPTER 8

NATO Enlargement and the Western Balkans

Gabriele Cascone

ONE OF THE AREAS where a vision of NATO's transformation has been clearly articulated is its enlargement. Even if the initial phases of the enlargement debate showed some uncertainties and a number of differing views,[1] the initial tone had already been set by President George H. W. Bush's famous remark, in 1989, that the time had come for Europe to be "whole and free" and that this was "the new mission of NATO."[2] The vision underpinning enlargement was therefore quite clear: NATO was to extend its "security umbrella" to the rest of the continent, for the purpose of creating stability. This was also very much in tune with the aspirations of the Central and Eastern European states, which vocally demanded not to be left in a "gray zone" between NATO and Russia. A crucial role in articulating and advocating this position was played by the leaders of the "Visegrad Group" (or Visegrad Four),[3] which included the Czech Republic, Poland, Hungary, and Slovakia, and of which it can be said that their advocacy of enlargement was much stronger at the time than any similar voice originating from NATO or its members.

It was a tragic irony that Yugoslavia, considered until the late 1980s to be the most advanced and "liberal" communist country (and one that therefore could have been a prime candidate for enlargement), excluded itself from this process by taking the road to a tragic and bloody dissolution. As a result, NATO's first commitment to the Western Balkans was of an operational nature, which thus radically transformed its operations. Only after the situation created by the conflicts that had followed the disintegration of Yugoslavia had sufficiently stabilized was it possible for NATO to think realistically of enlarging its membership to include the Western Balkans. This development was, in a sense, fully natural, because integration was a logical successor

175

to stabilization as the best means to prevent further instability in the region. Also, in light of the "Europe whole and free" project, NATO's eventual inclusion of the Western Balkan countries as members constituted (and still constitutes) a logical continuation of the process started with its enlargement to include the Central and Eastern European states.

At the same time, however, the enlargement of NATO to the Western Balkans presented some new challenges and motives. For the countries in the region, in fact, the "gray zone" fear so acutely felt by the Central and Eastern European states was a much more distant prospect, in light of the physical and geopolitical distance of Russia. Conversely, the experience of having undergone actual conflicts, either with neighboring countries or within the countries themselves, gave a much more tangible meaning to the security guarantee offered by NATO. Finally, the experience of Central and Eastern Europe showed the Western Balkans states that a pattern had (de facto if not de jure) developed, whereby the European integration process of a country started with NATO membership and was followed by and concluded with EU membership.

My goal in this chapter is, therefore, to examine how the NATO enlargement process has so far unfolded in the Western Balkans. I thus look at the mechanics of the process, the requirements that it set for the countries in the region, their performance, and the results so far, as well as the perspectives for the future.

How Enlargement Works

As has been said above, none of the Western Balkan countries was ready to be considered for membership when NATO made its first post–Cold War (and fourth in its history) enlargement decision in 1997. The first involvement of the countries in the Western Balkans in the enlargement process came in April 1999, when the Alliance launched its Membership Action Plan (MAP), addressed to the nine European countries that had expressed an interest in joining it, among them Albania and the former Yugoslav Republic of Macedonia.[4] At NATO's Prague Summit in November 2002, the other seven "aspirants" (as the MAP termed the candidate countries for membership) were invited to join it. Albania and the former Yugoslav Republic of Macedonia were therefore left in the process, together with Croatia, which had been accepted into the MAP in May 2002. As a result, the NATO enlargement process after the Prague Summit only included the Western Balkan countries.

Therefore, the three Western Balkan aspirants were part of the MAP, which was actually started as a way to translate into practice the requirements laid out in the 1995 *Study on NATO Enlargement*.[5] This study, in fact, highlighted what was expected of prospective NATO members, but it did not deal with establishing a process to help interested countries to satisfy these requirements or monitor their progress. By the time the Czech Republic, Hungary, and Poland were invited to join NATO in 1997, there was a growing need to establish such a process. In fact, its three new members took at least a couple of years after accession to become fully involved in all areas of its work. This was because their integration had been "learned on the job" after accession, and because preaccession preparations had not been sufficient to inform them about many aspects of its work. And it also needed a more structured framework because of the growing list of European countries interested in joining it. This required more thorough preparations to allow it to better absorb new members, as well as a mechanism to assess the respective performance of aspirant countries and determine their suitability to join.

On this last point, however, it must be noted that NATO's requirements for joining it were quite generic and that its member states have always been wary, especially in the early MAP stages, of defining its requirements as specific "membership criteria." This is because it has always considered its enlargement decisions as political matters, in order to leave its members a certain discretional power in deciding which nations to admit (and when to admit them) rather than tying their hands because nations have met technical criteria. This reflected, in turn, the need for its members to reach a consensus on which nations to invite to become members given possibly diverging views on the pace and direction of enlargement.

Therefore, following NATO's 1997 accession round, its member states started to work on how to carry forward enlargement and ensure that it took place within a process that could provide the grounds for a safe assessment of aspirant countries and, once invited, for their seamless integration. This process was the MAP, whose documentation is divided into five chapters: political/economic, defense/military, resources, security, and legal. The first two chapters deal with substantive requirements, and the remaining three focus on procedural aspects, such as ensuring that the legal frameworks of new members do not contradict their membership obligations. The first chapter, on political/economic issues, largely focuses on the requirements generally associated with NATO's traditional values for its members, including a functioning democracy, a market economy, and some of the main transitional challenges of democracies in Central and Eastern Europe in the 1990s—the peaceful settlement of internal and external disputes, democratic control of the armed forces, and economic reform. The second chapter focuses on interoperability and on restructuring or establishing armed forces that can contribute to Alliance operations. When the *Study on NATO Enlargement* and the MAP were approved, it was already clear that the days of a possible massive military confrontation in Europe were gone. Therefore, contrary to a common misconception, the MAP's focus was not on building up new forces but on making whatever forces were available compatible and useful for the Alliance's possible future tasks—in essence, defense reform.

The MAP mechanism is an individually tailored iterative process between NATO and the aspirant country. It is structured in annual cycles (running broadly from September to May–June), which start every year with the submission of an Annual National Program (ANP) by each aspirant country, outlining its goals with respect to each of the MAP's five chapters. The ANP is then discussed between NATO's members and the aspirant state, which results in setting out specific goals toward membership. Progress in reaching the MAP goals is evaluated by a NATO Team, which drafts an Individual Progress Report, approved by the Allies and finally discussed with the aspirant at a "North Atlantic Council + 1" meeting, which is generally attended by the foreign and defense ministers of the aspirant country. At this meeting the Allies present their assessment of the aspirant and stress the areas where further efforts are needed. This is the mechanism in which the three Western Balkan aspirants have been involved from when they joined the MAP until now. The next section deals with the main challenges they have encountered in pursuing this process and how they have dealt with them.

The Western Balkan Aspirants and the MAP

As mentioned above, Albania and the former Yugoslav Republic of Macedonia were the first Western Balkan countries included in the MAP in 1999.[6] Already at the time, they appeared the weakest countries in the group, and there was a general recognition (both among the NATO member states and the Western Balkan countries) that the process toward their accession to full membership would require a significant amount of time, for four reasons.

First, the two countries were economically the weakest. Though economic issues do not play a major role per se in NATO's enlargement decisions, it was clear that reforms, on both the political and the military sides, would have put a tremendous strain on their fragile economies. Second, in addition to being fragile from an economic perspective, these countries were also politically fragile. Albania had narrowly avoided, in the spring of 1997, a

descent into civil war, but this had resulted in a collapse in its state administration and the powers of the state. At the time it was admitted to the MAP
process, its government still had work to do just to regain control in areas of
the country where state authority was all but gone. Conversely, the former
Yugoslav Republic of Macedonia was a country trying to affirm its national
and state identity in the face of neighbors that raised objections as to the
nature of this identity.[7] This soul-searching exercise had led to a defensive
and almost obsessive affirmation of a specific "Macedonian" identity and, as
a result, to the de facto disenfranchisement of the country's main ethnic
minority, the Albanians, who lived in its Western half and constituted
between 20 and 25 percent of its population. Third, there were issues regarding the rule of law in both countries. Although widespread corruption and
extensive organized crime networks plague the entire region, these were particularly visible in these two countries. This posed an additional challenge
for political stabilization and economic recovery.

Fourth and finally, there were substantial problems in both countries from
a purely military perspective. In Albania, notwithstanding its economic weakness, the Hoxhaist tradition of a huge militia army committed to static
defense of the national territory was far from gone in the senior cadres of the
Armed Forces, and it still affected some of their strategic thinking. In the
former Yugoslav Republic of Macedonia, the peaceful departure of the Yugoslav Army in 1992 (the only former Yugoslav republic where, at the time of
independence, the departure of the Jugoslavenska Narodna Armija, or Yugoslav People's Army, took place in such a peaceful way) was counterbalanced
by the virtual demilitarization of the country, because the departing Yugoslav
People's Army units took with them all the valuable military equipment.
Again, the economic situation of the country was not conducive to reestablishing a credible, albeit small, military force.

The political and economic weaknesses of the two countries also had an
effect on another related process. Albania and the former Yugoslav Republic
of Macedonia were the only two countries among the nine candidates for
NATO membership not to have signed a "Europe Agreement" with the
European Union by the time the MAP was launched. Although the EU's
and NATO's enlargements are independent, they are nevertheless considered
parallel processes. Therefore, the lack of the EU "safety net" further weak-
ened the negotiating positions of the two countries.[8] In fact, by April 1999,
the two aspirants had little more to offer to NATO than their enthusiasm
and desire to join it. The only other element in their favor (and one that may
have had a certain weight in the deliberations) was the role both countries
had played during NATO's air campaign in Kosovo from March to May

1999. Both had provided logistical support to the Allied presence in the region and had conducted a humanitarian relief effort in support of the Kosovar refugees who were flooding their territories.[9] It was therefore clear that a credible long-term effort was needed to make the two countries eligible for membership.

As mentioned above, a third country in the region, Croatia, also joined the MAP in May 2002. Croatia brought to the table a much stronger economy than the other two aspirants, even though it was still recovering from the 1991–95 period of conflict, and this was a significant asset when compared with its fellow aspirants' resources. However, Croatia was also bringing its own specific set of problems. These were, in particular, due to the regime led by President Franjo Tudjman (especially in the years just before his 1999 death), whose authoritarian tendencies had left their mark on Croatian society, for example, in the opaque and unaccountable intelligence structure and in the organization and powers of the judiciary.[10] NATO needed evidence that Croatia was moving toward becoming a stable and functioning democracy.

Another problem for Croatia's admission to the MAP was the issue of its cooperation with the International Criminal Tribunal for Yugoslavia (ICTY). Croatia's willingness to cooperate with the ICTY was viewed by NATO as major evidence of its readiness to turn the page on its sometimes controversial past and conform to the values and norms of Western democracies.[11] This was a specific challenge for the Croatian public, because the ICTY's indictments were of senior military officers, many of whom were still considered heroes of Croatia's war of liberation; in this sense, their indictment was seen as an indictment of the entire struggle to recover the Croatian territory occupied by the Serb breakaway "Krajina Republic."[12]

Finally, from a military perspective, the Croatian armed forces still comprised about 50,000 personnel and a huge paper reserve force of 150,000.[13] These were still very high numbers for a country of little more than 4 million inhabitants. The need for further restructuring and downsizing was therefore evident. But it was likely, coupled with the ICTY's indictments, to reinforce the feeling within the ranks of the armed forces of "being under attack."

It was therefore evident that all three countries faced a complex, although distinct, set of politico-military challenges in joining NATO. However, their geographical proximity, as well as the need to keep a "critical mass" of aspirants that could actively lobby for membership, pushed these countries toward a framework for cooperation in achieving the NATO membership goal.[14] This was established in May 2003 through the Adriatic Charter, which was modeled on the 1998 U.S.-Baltic Charter and, like this model, was established on two cornerstones: greater cooperation among the three aspirants, and assistance from the United States to all three countries to help them pursue their membership goal. At the same time the Adriatic Charter also took on the intrinsic ambivalence of the U.S.-Baltic Charter model—that is, encouragement by NATO of the countries to work together as a more effective way of lobbying for membership, while at the same time reaffirming the right of each country to be "assessed individually," specifically when its performance appeared superior to that of the others.

Notwithstanding this intrinsic tension, the Adriatic Charter proved to be a worthy initiative to keep NATO's focus on enlargement in the Western Balkans. Also, at a time when international attention in the Balkans was somewhat diminishing due to the emergence of a new crisis and challenges, the Adriatic Charter helped strengthen the theme of NATO membership as an element in the long-term stabilization of the region.

Apart from the Adriatic Charter, however, the bulk of the work lay with the progress of the reform efforts in each of the three aspirant countries for NATO membership. All of them planned to deliver a convincing performance to the Allies in a three- to four-year timeline after NATO's 2002 Prague Summit. This was based on observations of what could be seen by now as an emerging pattern in NATO's enlargement. After all, following NATO's 1997 Madrid Summit, when three invitations were issued for future membership, no invitations were issued at its 1999 Washington Summit. Similarly, the seven invitations issued at its 2002 Prague Summit were followed by no invitations for new members at its 2004 Istanbul Summit.

Therefore, the three aspirant Balkan countries expected the first summit after Istanbul, due sometime in 2006 and 2007, to reopen the enlargement door and consider countries for the next enlargement round. At the same time, in the period between the Prague and Istanbul summits, there had been significant progress among the Balkan aspirants, in particular Croatia and the former Yugoslav Republic of Macedonia (Albania had made some progress, but at a much less significant pace). In Croatia, the return to power of the Hrvatska Demokratska Zajednica (HDZ, or Croatian Democratic Union), the party founded by the late President Tudjman, following the national elections in the fall of 2003, had initially been met with some anxiety among observers. However, the new prime minister, Ivo Sanader, made it clear that the foremost priority for his country lay in European and Euro-Atlantic integration. And although concrete measures took some time, he signaled from the beginning his commitment to move forward on the more sensitive issues, such as cooperation with the ICTY and the return of Serb refugees who had left the country after the 1995 conflict.[15]

Progress in the former Yugoslav Republic of Macedonia was also impressive. In 2001 the country returned from the brink of civil war, between the Slav ethnic majority and the Albanian minority, due to international mediation. The solution to the conflict was embodied in the Ohrid Framework Agreement, which recognized a number of rights for the ethnic Albanian population (education, language, representation in public administration, etc.). After the 2002 elections, the victorious Social Democratic Union (Socijaldemokratski sojuz na Makedonija, SDSM) sealed a coalition agreement with the ethnic Albanian Democratic Union for Integration (Bashkimi Demokratik për Integrim, BDI), led by the ex-commanders of the National Liberation Army, the guerrilla organization that had taken up weapons against the government only one year before. This coalition moved forward quickly in implementing the main provisions of the Ohrid Framework Agreement and appeasing interethnic tensions in the country. At the same time, the former Yugoslav Republic of Macedonia embarked on a major defense reform process, which was assessed by NATO as highly successful.[16]

At this juncture, it is appropriate to discuss the kind of defense reform process that NATO generally considers successful. As mentioned earlier in this chapter, contrary to what is generally believed, the defense reform process supported by NATO is not based on building a large military or devoting major new resources to military expenses. Although it is true that there is a "magic figure" for defense expenditures, (i.e., 2 percent of gross domestic product), many NATO member states fall below this ideal figure, and therefore the essence of defense reform does not lie here. Instead, it involves putting in place a system that allows these resources to be spent in the most rational and effective way. This is achieved by starting with a Strategic Defense Review, whereby a country defines the tasks that it intends to assign to its armed forces. Matching its resources against these tasks and, in some cases, defining a specific expertise or role for its military, which may have emerged from its history and traditions, should provide a clear view of the ideal size and composition of its armed forces.

Although this Strategic Defense Review process may appear quite simple and straightforward, it is not always easy to impose it in the face of decisions based on prestige factors or, sometimes, outdated military doctrines. For example, it was important to convince countries that faced no immediate military threat to their territory (and, as part of NATO, would see such a threat as an even more distant possibility) to rid themselves of unrealistic reserve structures, which looked great on paper but had no real military value. Or, again, it was necessary to explain to small prospective members that keeping a modern air force would have drained a vast part of their defense budget and was therefore a waste of precious resources, when air defense could be easily provided by larger, neighboring NATO members. In most cases, and particularly for the countries of the Western Balkans, defense reform processes conducted in the framework of the Partnership for Peace or the MAP have invariably led to the downsizing of the existing armed forces and the destruction of large quantities of unneeded military equipment.

Despite the progress made by the three aspirants between NATO's Prague and Istanbul summits, they suffered a certain disappointment when, in September 2005, the United States first announced, and NATO subsequently confirmed, that NATO's next summit, scheduled for November 2006 in Riga, would not issue new invitations to join it.[17] Furthermore, NATO stated that no further decision on enlargement should be expected until a subsequent summit in 2008. The disappointment was particularly significant for the former Yugoslav Republic of Macedonia, because Albania was aware that several commitments still had to be met and Croatia was given an indication that no invitation would be issued until General Ante Gotovina (the last senior Croatian officer on the ICTY's most-wanted list) was arrested and transferred to the Hague. However, after the subsequent arrest of Gotovina in December 2005,[18] Croatia also felt that the postponement of a decision until 2008 did not reflect the progress it had made and the results achieved.[19]

The disappointment by the aspirants was probably due to the fact that, engrossed in their own membership aspirations, they had failed to notice how deeply NATO had changed since the September 11, 2001, terrorist attacks on the United States. The "peace-enforcing" NATO of the 1990s, which had itself succeeded "Cold War NATO," was no longer sufficient to tackle the challenges of possible military interventions aimed at the threats to member states that could appear anywhere on the globe. It was therefore necessary for NATO to find a moment for self-reflection devoted to the new challenges it now faced, and to then develop the means to respond to those challenges— and, in this context, enlargement had to take a back seat. The Allies realized, however, that, to keep aspirants committed to the MAP process and to continue the necessary reform processes, NATO had to provide some guarantee to the three countries that an enlargement decision would actually be made in 2008. This realization, coupled with some effective lobbying by the aspirants themselves (most notably, the visit by Croatian prime minister Ivo Sanader to Washington in October 2006[20]), led to the inclusion of this statement in the communiqué of the Riga Summit: "At our next summit in 2008, the Alliance intends to extend further invitations to those countries who meet

NATO's performance based standards and are able to contribute to Euro-Atlantic security and stability."[21] In this way, the partial reverse of the "two-summit strategy" was turned into a significant victory for the aspirants, which now had a clear deadline for which to prepare themselves. Without wanting to exaggerate the impact of the Riga Communiqué, it was evident that it played an important role in further accelerating the pace of reform in all the aspirant countries.

In this respect, the developments in Albania are of particular interest. Albania was in fact the only one of the three aspirants that even at a very late stage in the MAP had a missing EU "safety net." The EU had opened accession talks with Croatia in October 2005 and had declared the former Yugoslav Republic of Macedonia as an EU candidate (although without opening accession talks) in December 2005. These two countries were therefore well aware that reforms, especially in the political sphere, were serving a dual purpose, that is, NATO and EU enlargement, and this provided an increased incentive. Albania, conversely, only signed a Stabilization and Association Agreement (the first step toward EU integration of Western Balkan countries) in June 2007, and this agreement has not yet been ratified by all the EU member states. Therefore, for Albania, the mutually reinforcing goals of EU membership and NATO membership did not exist (although EU membership is clearly a long-term strategic goal of Albania). Nonetheless, the NATO membership magnet proved strong enough to move forward on key political reforms. Looking at all three aspirants in the period between the Riga and Bucharest summits, several main objectives were achieved in Albania, Croatia, and the former Yugoslav Republic of Macedonia. Let us briefly look at them.

In Albania, an overall understanding was reached between the ruling Democratic Party and the main opposition Socialist Party to work together for the approval and implementation of the reforms needed for NATO membership. This was a major achievement because, following the July 2005 national elections and until the February 2007 local elections, relations between these two main parties had been very tense, to the point that the date for the local elections had to be postponed because of the parties' inability to agree on the rules for the conduct of the elections. After this low point, the Democrats and the Socialists were able to agree on major electoral reforms for Albania (finally approved by the Albanian Parliament in November 2008), while the government started a major operation for the review of the civil registry (effectively, the voters lists), where duplicate registrations abounded, as well as the production of reliable identification documents (another major grievance at every election in Albania). At the same time, the main parties agreed on a "National Pact for Justice" aimed at approving new legislation to increase the independence, professionalism, and effectiveness of the judiciary. On the military and defense side, Albania approved a military strategy in early 2005 and reviewed it in December 2007, following its reorganization and streamlining of the structure of the armed forces.

In Croatia, additional measures were approved to facilitate the return of Serb minority refugees, which addressed the last outstanding questions related to this issue. More generally, laws were passed and administrative measures were taken to improve the rights of the minorities in the country. Measures were also taken to reform the judiciary and address some of the most evident signs of judicial dysfunction, such as the huge case backlog. NATO's member states had also expressed concerns about the level of public support for NATO in Croatia which, until the end of 2006, were about 32 or 33 percent. Doubts were expressed that a country with such low public support could stand the inevitable tests that membership in the Alliance carries with it, such as casualties in military operations. In response to this, the Croatian government launched a focused public communications campaign on NATO membership in 2007, which by the end of the year had raised the level of support for the Alliance to more than 50 percent.[22] On the defense and military side, Croatia approved in September 2005, after extensive wrangling among the main stakeholders (i.e., the president, Ministry of Defense, and the General Staff), a Strategic Defense Review and, in July 2007, a Long-Term Development Plan, which sets the goals for the structure and equipment of the Croatian armed forces until 2015.

In the former Yugoslav Republic of Macedonia, significant progress continued to be made in the implementation of the Ohrid Framework Agreement. Following the July 2005 elections, fears had been quickly dispelled that the return to power of the nationalist Vnatrešna makedonska revolucionerna organizacija–Demokratska partija za makedonsko nacionalno edinstvo (VMRO-DPMNE) party could lead to backtracking in the implementation of the Ohrid agreement. The new government quickly established a "Sector for the Implementation of the Ohrid Agreement" as a separate government department, with its own budget, and the approval and implementation of the remaining laws stemming from the Ohrid agreement, such as the police law, which established a more decentralized and ethnically balanced police force continued at a good pace. Efforts also continued to be made to improve representation of the Albanian community in the state institutions and in particular in the police and security apparatuses. The government was also able, with the mediation of the international community, to end a Parliament boycott by BDI, now in the opposition, through agreement on a list of laws that had to be approved by special interethnic quorums. Prime Minister-Nikola Gruevski also took a stronger stance on corruption and embarked on a number of fiscal measures to make his country an attractive place for foreign investors. Finally, on the defense and military side, the reforms launched with the approval of the Strategic Defense Review in 2004 were largely finished by the end of 2007.

The above summaries do not of course indicate that all problems and issues in relation to NATO accession have been addressed by the three aspirants. Electoral irregularities have continued to be reflected in the reports of international observers on elections in Albania and the former Yugoslav Republic of Macedonia. Another persistent problem has been the development of the judiciary's independence and professionalism, along with dealing with corruption and organized crime.

Despite these setbacks, throughout their period as aspirants, all three countries have done their best to prove that their participation in the NATO membership process is not only a political performance or an attempt to gain an easy security guarantee. Rather, they have all offered and deployed personnel to NATO operations in Afghanistan, and the current number of deployments—300 for Croatia, and about 150 each for Albania and the former Yugoslav Republic of Macedonia—are impressive when compared with countries of similar size and with comparable armed forces.

The efforts by all three countries prove that the magnet of Euro-Atlantic and European integration has remained one of the strongest incentives for reform. Issues raised in the NATO progress reports, and then discussed by the North Atlantic Council with the political leaderships of the aspirant countries, were immediately propelled to the top of the political agendas of the three countries and, though the measures adopted might have not always been the ones preferred by the Allies, they showed a real eagerness to address perceived shortcomings. At the same time, the prospects of NATO membership worked as a "force multiplier" for ongoing domestic reform efforts, providing decision makers and public opinion with an additional boost to continue on the path undertaken.[23]

As NATO's 2008 Bucharest Summit approached, discussions intensified among its member nations concerning an enlargement decision. In informal talks, the "1 or 3" options (which referred, respectively, to inviting only Croatia or all three aspirants) appeared the most probable, with a certain preference for the widest possible number of invitations. However, as the summit approached, the possibility of having only two countries invited to join looked increasing possible, as the issue of the name of the former Yugoslav Republic of Macedonia started to assume larger relevance. It was in fact increasingly evident that Greece would not consent to extending an invitation to Skopje unless the bilateral controversy on the name of the former Yugoslav Republic of Macedonia was resolved. Although the negotiating effort (which has been going on for the past fifteen years) intensified in the months leading up to the summit, no agreement could be reached. At that time, Macedonia had hoped that the other Allies (in particular, the United States, which had recognized the former Yugoslav Republic of Macedonia under its constitutional name in November 2004) would have put pressure on Athens to avoid the enlargement process being held hostage to a bilateral controversy.

However, even if opposition by Greece alone would have been enough to block an invitation to the former Yugoslav Republic of Macedonia, Athens was also able to gather support for its objections from other NATO member states, by appealing to the cornerstone of any alliance—the need for consensus and solidarity among the allies. There was also a growing frustration with the former Yugoslav Republic of Macedonia among some NATO member states for what was seen as its failure to make an effort to reach a compromise, as it was considered that, as the country demanding to join the Alliance, it was incumbent upon Skopje to make the greater effort.[24] It was therefore ultimately unavoidable that at the 2008 Bucharest Summit, NATO's heads of state and government issued an invitation to Albania and Croatia to join the Alliance, with an agreement "that an invitation to the former Yugoslav Republic of Macedonia will be extended as soon as a mutually acceptable solution to the name issue has been reached."[25]

Enlargement and the Western Balkans after the Bucharest Summit

The decisions of NATO's 2008 Bucharest Summit provoked understandably totally opposite reactions in the aspirant Balkan countries. The jubilation in Albania and Croatia was mirrored by strong disappointment in the former Yugoslav Republic of Macedonia. The Albanian and Croatian senior leaders, who were invited to address NATO's heads of state and government at the summit, appeared genuinely moved and convinced of being at a historic juncture for the country. Meanwhile, officials from the former Yugoslav Republic of Macedonia left the summit venue en masse, as did media representatives from Skopje.

The decision having been made, the roads of the three aspirants started to diverge. Albania and Croatia started and concluded accession talks with

NATO in the course of the spring of 2008. This in turn led to the signature of Accession Protocols by the Allies, which, once ratified, allowed Albania and Croatia to join NATO just before the April 2009 Strasbourg-Kehl Summit.[26]

Consequently, the former Yugoslav Republic of Macedonia is the only remaining aspirant from the original group. For the country, therefore, the MAP process continues, even though according to the decision made at the Bucharest Summit, the resolution of the name issue remains the only obstacle. If, however, no solution to the name dispute is found in the near future, there might be a problem in how the Alliance continues its accession process with the former Yugoslav Republic of Macedonia. The Bucharest Summit Declaration implies that, the name issue being the only remaining obstacle, Skopje has actually satisfied all the other performance standards to join the Alliance. How is it possible in this case to continue to exert leverage on reforms, if it has been determined that the requirements have been met?

The latest developments do not seem to suggest that a solution to the name issue will occur any time soon. Rather, the decision made by the former Yugoslav Republic of Macedonia in November 2008 to bring the issue to the International Court of Justice could change the timbre of current discussions, and either of the two sides might decide to wait until the court renders its verdict, which could take a few more years.[27] This could create a long-term deadlock, which could in turn have an impact on the vision of the entire Western Balkans with regard to integration with the Euro-Atlantic institutions. This would be particularly relevant if the remaining countries in the region were to start making decisive steps toward membership (e.g., joining the MAP).

The "Other Half" of the Western Balkans: Bosnia and Herzegovina, Montenegro, and Serbia

While the three aspirants were advancing through the MAP process, the nations forming the "other half" of the Western Balkans were on an entirely different track with regard to their relationship with NATO, for they were still struggling to get access to Partnership for Peace (PfP), the oldest (as it was established in 1994) cooperation program for non-NATO countries and the one seen by prospective members as the "entry level" for the membership path.[28] In this respect, NATO's Riga Summit established a sort of symmetry in the region by producing a concrete deadline for the invitation of the three aspirants and by admitting the remaining three countries from the region

(Bosnia and Herzegovina, Serbia, and newly independent—or again independent—Montenegro) to join the PfP. This was in no way an expected outcome, and it was actually only agreed on during the last few hours before the summit. Long discussions about Bosnia and Herzegovina and Serbia's PfP membership had been the result of NATO's conditionality over cooperation with the ICTY. When in fact, in about 2002–3, both Bosnia and Herzegovina and the then Federal Republic of Yugoslavia (subsequently Serbia and Montenegro) had requested to join the PfP, the Alliance had requested that these countries first cooperate in full with the ICTY.

As the issue of full cooperation became increasingly linked (as mentioned above with reference to Croatia) to the arrest of specific individuals indicted by the ICTY, it appeared that no progress might be possible until those arrests took place. At NATO's Riga Summit, however, the Allies decided that, without giving up on ICTY conditionality, stability and security in the region might better be served by embracing the three countries rather than keeping at least two of them (because Montenegro had no specific issue with the ICTY) at arm's reach. With this decision NATO therefore took, possibly for the first time, a holistic view of the region's long-term stabilization and integration. As the three aspirants pursued their road to membership, the rest of the region was put in the starting block to embark on the same journey as other aspirants. This opportunity was eagerly seized by Bosnia and Herzegovina and Montenegro (which immediately requested an intensified dialogue with NATO on membership issues—the first step in the membership process), while Serbia, the biggest nation in the group and, arguably, an unavoidable element for the stability of the region, took a more reserved position, welcoming the opportunity to cooperate with NATO but refraining from declaring an interest in joining it.

Serbia's unique position is due to the fact that, following the Kosovo air campaign of 1999, any reference to NATO in Serbia still has the potential for causing emotional public reaction and stirring nationalist feelings. Also, at the time of the Riga decision, negotiations on Kosovo's final status were in their final phase, with a clear possibility that this would result in Kosovo's declaration of independence. This created additional fuel for Serbia's existing anti-Western and anti-NATO resentment. To compound it all, the Serbian government of the time consisted of a fragile coalition between the pro-Western Democratic Party of President Boris Tadić and the nationalistic Serbian Democratic Party (Demokratska stranka Srbije, DSS) of Prime Minister Vojislav Kostunica. With parliamentary elections scheduled for January 2007, Tadic and the Democratic Party were of course wary of being portrayed as "anti-Serbian," if they showed too much enthusiasm for PfP admission or its follow-up. There was a subtle irony in this, because the PfP decision had been made by the Allies with a view to strengthening the reform forces in Serbia.

The PfP Presentation Document submitted by Serbia in September 2007 states in its opening paragraph: "The Republic of Serbia wishes to develop its relations with NATO member states and partners on the basis of direct, close and long-term cooperation and common action. It is considered that the implementation of this orientation is complementary to the Republic of Serbia's objective of joining the European Union."[29] It is easy to see how the "cooperation" with NATO is compared with the "objective of joining the European Union."

The group of three Western Balkan partners has therefore turned into another "2 + 1" group, with Bosnia and Herzegovina and Montenegro trying to move forward as soon as possible on the NATO membership road and Serbia starting very limited cooperation in the framework of the PfP. At the same time, NATO has repeatedly reaffirmed that, though all partnership tools were open to Serbia, it would be for Serbia to pick up the pace at which it wanted to progress in its cooperation with the Alliance. This was also in recognition of the difficulty for Serbia to balance its desire for cooperation with NATO with the expected emotional reaction following Kosovo's declaration of independence. This approach appears to have paid off, because the Democratic Party–led government that took office after new elections in July 2008 has shown a clear commitment to move forward in cooperating with NATO in the PfP framework.

However, both Bosnia and Herzegovina and Montenegro have tried, since joining the PfP, to move as quickly as possible through the various steps needed to be an effective partner and therefore be able to apply for the MAP. There was an increased attendance by military officers and civil servants at PfP events such as conferences, seminars, and exercises. They also signed an agreement on the protection of information with NATO, and they started work on the defense planning program devoted to partners, the Planning and Review Process. More important, they both started an Individual Partnership Action Plan (IPAP), which is a series of goals oriented toward domestic- and security-sector reforms that a partner sets with NATO, which provides assistance and assesses annually. Independent of the fundamental membership drive, the IPAP is nonetheless quite similar in process and structure to the MAP, and it is so far the most ambitious program for nonaspirant PfP countries. Involvement in the IPAP covers a much wider sphere of reforms than those in the defense and security sector. As such, this requires the involvement of a larger array of institutions and an understanding, on their side as well as on that of the general public, that interacting with NATO is not only a job for the Ministry of Defense and Foreign Ministry. Actually, as highlighted above, progress in political reforms makes or breaks an aspirant's chances to be invited to join NATO. Both Bosnia and Herzegovina and Montenegro thus can use the experience of the IPAP, with its more concerted effort to progress toward membership.

In addition to this common challenge, there are other, country-specific challenges. In Bosnia and Herzegovina, the inflamed nationalist rhetoric and the uneasy relation between the state and the entities pose the greatest problems.[30] In reality, both issues are indicators of a much wider issue, which is the degree of commitment of the local elites to Bosnia and Herzegovina as a state. In other words, when the war ended in 1995, two of the main ethnic groups in the country (Serbs and Croats) still thought (or had been led to believe) that their stronger ties were to, respectively, Serbia and Croatia and that at that point they had little to do with Bosnia and Herzegovina. The third group (the Bosniacs or Muslims), however, believed that the Dayton Peace Accords did not go far enough in establishing a proper state structure. For different reasons, therefore, most tended to see the constitutional framework reached during the Dayton negotiations as a provisional settlement to be renegotiated at a more favorable opportunity rather than as the starting point for recreating a genuine national community and a unified state. In parallel to this, the international community also sought institutional reform to develop state structures and consequently improve stability. The institutional and constitutional reform needed to permit Bosnia and Herzegovina to function more effectively as a state has been slowed by defined ethnic group interests. This leaves plenty of risks for a political crisis and makes politicians reluctant to reach compromise solutions.

One notable exception (and one that is very relevant for NATO) has been the defense reform process, which between 2003 and 2005 led to the merging of the two countries' armies—which had fought against each other only a decade before—into a single military force under a single, state-level Ministry of Defense. This process, which can rightly be considered the most significant reform process completed in the country since the signing of the Dayton Peace Accords, was only possible due to the sustained pressure and guidance of the international community. For Bosnia and Herzegovina to be able to pick up the challenges of NATO membership, more reforms will be needed, and they will require domestic agreements reached without outside pressure or support.

In Montenegro, so far, the main challenge has been in the size of the country, which limits its administrative capacity and the number of civil servants in key areas devoted to the integration effort. Also, the image of NATO and the issue of membership are still somewhat controversial, and opposition to joining the Alliance is quite strong.

Beyond the internal issues, several external ones could affect the chances of these countries eventually joining NATO. On the positive side, there is a consensus among NATO's member nations that the door to membership remains open and that the Western Balkan countries could join. On the negative side, applications to join the MAP at this stage (as with the one addressed to NATO by Montenegro in October 2008) risk falling victim to a divisive discussion among the Alliance's members about the enlargement process. The granting of MAP status, which previously had been a procedural step, has now become a political issue, following applications by Georgia and Ukraine. Of course the situations of the two groups of countries (Georgia and Ukraine on the one side, and the Western Balkans on the other) are completely different. However, any discussion on the MAP for the Western Balkan countries will unavoidably take place in the context of this wider discussion on the enlargement process, which also addresses Georgia and Ukraine. And though NATO does not yet suffer from "enlargement fatigue," it might be starting to suffer from fatigue over the "enlargement debate." In this respect it will be interesting to see the effects of the decision made at the NATO members' foreign ministers' meeting in December 2008 concerning Georgia and Ukraine. At this meeting, the foreign ministers decided "without prejudice to further decisions which must be taken about MAP" to start work with Georgia and Ukraine on reforms needed to support their progress toward membership within the framework of the two ad hoc bodies (NATO–Ukraine Commission and NATO–Georgia Commission).[31] This decision, which allows work related to membership to take place with Georgia and Ukraine without a decision on the MAP for these countries, might therefore create a different path for Kyiv and Tbilisi and make it easier for the Western Balkan countries to follow the standard course and move into the MAP, without conveying the impression that they are "moving in front of" Kyiv and Tbilisi.

However, as I have pointed out above, it has often been the case in NATO that the focus on enlargement becomes sharper when the list of potential candidates grows large enough to create a "critical mass," carrying enough weight to lobby the Allies more effectively for membership. This was the case with the Visegrad Four, the Vilnius Nine, and, although perhaps to a lesser extent, the Adriatic Charter Three. It may therefore be hard for Bosnia and Herzegovina and Montenegro alone (leaving out for the moment the issue of the former Yugoslav Republic of Macedonia) to create a "critical mass" that could effectively influence NATO's decision makers. The situation might of course change if Serbia were to abandon its position and declare itself interested in membership. But this is not yet an issue.

A final word should also be said about Kosovo, which is the youngest avatar in the Western Balkans geography. Any talk of Euro-Atlantic integration, or even cooperation in a framework like the PfP, is premature at this stage, for both legal and substantial reasons. From a legal perspective, NATO works by consensus and only accepts states as partners or prospective members. Therefore it will not be possible for Kosovo to enter any structured cooperative arrangement (as distinguished from possible ad hoc initiatives related to the NATO-led Kosovo Peacekeeping Force, or KFOR) until all NATO's members recognize it as a state. From a substantial perspective, it is fair to say that the fledgling institutions of Kosovo have more immediate priorities and needs on which to focus and that the KFOR's presence constitutes a security guarantee at least as strong as Article 5 of the Washington Treaty. However, once the necessary criteria are met, it is likely that Kosovo will also try to seek PfP membership. Only at that point will the issue become relevant for the Alliance, but such a request will clearly be consistent with the declared goal of bringing long-term stability to the entire region.

The EU's and NATO's Enlargements in the Western Balkans: Coordination, Cooperation, or Competition?

Before bringing this chapter to a conclusion, it is appropriate to consider one element that has often been raised above, which is the reciprocal impact of NATO's and the EU's enlargement processes. This is a vast subject, which would probably require a chapter of its own, but I will try here to highlight at least some of the main issues within this subject. The first element to underline is that NATO's decision to launch its enlargement process in the Western Balkans by admitting Albania and the former Yugoslav Republic of Macedonia to the MAP took place well before the EU decided to expand its membership to the region. The first structured EU approach to the integration of the Western Balkans came with the Stabilization and Association Process launched at the EU's November 2000 Zagreb Summit,[32] but even at that point no Western Balkan country was formally an EU candidate, and therefore the gap between NATO and EU integration was somewhat wider than in previous enlargement rounds.

This had several effects. First and foremost is the area of mutual incentives. Having been developed by two very similar groupings (or at least two groupings with very similar values), the standards required of new NATO and EU members are perfectly compatible where they overlap, such as the political criteria. As a result, a country embarked on both processes knows that certain reforms are good for NATO and good for the EU, which can be a powerful tool in overcoming domestic resistance and having these reforms passed. Second, the parallel process of enlargement brings with it an *exchange of expertise*. NATO has a distinct expertise in assisting countries in reforming the defense and security sector, and its specific presence on the ground in the Western Balkans has been related to these issues. In assessing progress in other areas, such as political criteria, the work done by the EU in its candidate countries, with its field missions and progress reports, constitutes a precious source for NATO's assessments. However, for those countries that remain only a part of the NATO enlargement process, this exchange of views, assessments, and expertise does not take place.

Also, the Stabilization and Accession Agreements, signed with the Western Balkan countries in the framework of the Stabilization and Association Process, were unavoidably focused in the beginning, in particular, on the "stabilization" aspect, with a wide range of EU assistance programs for the countries of the region. It might be argued that only following the EU's June 2003 Thessalonica Summit, with its clear call by EU leaders for membership to the Western Balkan countries,[33] the process of accession of the Western Balkan countries to the EU gained real momentum and the two processes started to be mutually reinforcing. This reinforcement took place, however, within the peculiarities and constraints of the NATO–EU relationship. Although the two organizations agreed, shortly after the Thessalonica Summit, on a "concerted approach to the Western Balkans," this was never translated into concrete mechanisms aimed at ensuring the coherence of NATO and EU efforts in the region.[34] This was largely left, on the one hand, to the countries that were members of both organizations (and could therefore strive for consistent positions in both parts of Brussels) and, on the other hand, to staff-level informal contacts on issues related to enlargement. Notwithstanding this, the core values to which both organizations adhere are largely the same, so the standards demanded of NATO aspirants and EU candidates are also very close, and no single instance could be found where NATO and EU membership forced Western Balkan countries to choose between their two paths. In this sense, the parallel enlargement processes are ultimately complementary and mutually beneficial.

Conclusion

As has been evident from the overview given in the previous pages, NATO's process of enlargement to the Western Balkan countries has been a uniquely complex one—and one that, like its operational counterpart, has shaped the identity of the Alliance, or at least its "updated" identity. For the first time, NATO's enlargement process has involved countries that are in many cases not only in a state of political transition but also of state reconstruction. Also for the first time, NATO's enlargement process has consciously comple-mented its earlier military stabilization efforts. The results achieved so far in this process, with the admission of Albania and Croatia to the Alliance, are but a good start, when compared with NATO's declared goal to consider Euro-Atlantic integration as the only recipe for the long-term stability of the Western Balkans.

The future remains as challenging as the past. NATO will need to ensure that the former Yugoslav Republic of Macedonia keeps to the course of reform and does not sink to a sort of lethargic state vis-à-vis the MAP, pend-ing resolution of the states's name issue. Also, although NATO has constantly declared that the issue of the states's name is a bilateral one where it has no role, it is not in its interest as a whole to see the process suffer long-term deadlock. With the states's accession to NATO (and the EU[35]) blocked, the country would be in a security "no man's land," and thus much weaker in facing internal or external turmoil.

Moving to the second tier of Western Balkan countries—the three new PfP members—NATO will need to make a careful decision about granting MAP status to Bosnia and to Herzegovina and Montenegro. It will then face a series of tough choices: Would it be better to move ahead only with these two countries or to wait for Serbia, if Serbia indicates interest in member-ship? And would moving ahead with Bosnia and Herzegovina help to stabilize the country, or rather import into the enlargement debate Sarajevo's institu-tional fragility and ethnic divisions? Turning to Montenegro, it is quite clear that NATO and EU membership perspectives have played so far the usual role of a strong magnet for reform, whose effect might be diminished or lost if Podgorica were to see itself put on a waiting list, notwithstanding its own progress, because of the lack of progress of its neighbors, coupled with NATO's possible preference for a "package deal." As newer and more imme-diate challenges seize NATO's attention, it is therefore fundamental that it does not forget its strategic goals in the Balkans and continues to pursue a course that offers a concrete perspective of integration to the remaining nonmember countries in the region.

Notes

1. A detailed reconstruction of the initial enlargement debate is given by Gerald B. Solomon, *The NATO Enlargement Debate 1990–1997: Blessings of Liberty* (Westport, CT: Praeger, 1998).

2. This is quoted from the text of the speech given by President Bush in Mainz in 1989, which is available at http://usa.usembassy.de/etexts/ga6-890531.htm. Quite ironically, President Bush had once famously stated his unease with "the vision thing" (the anecdote can be found at www.time.com/time/magazine/article/0,9171,963342 -2,00.html).

3. See Michael Žantovský, "Visegrad between the Past and the Future," Visegrad Group, www.visegradgroup.eu/main.php?folderID = 923&articleID = 4072&ctag = articlelist&iid = 1.

4. The other countries were Bulgaria, Estonia, Latvia, Lithuania, Romania, Slovakia, and Slovenia.

5. NATO, *Study on NATO Enlargement* (Brussels: NATO, 1995), www.nato.int/ cps/en/natolive/official_texts_24733.htm.

6. As I discuss in detail below in the text, the name "Yugoslav Republic of Macedonia" is highly sensitive. The country itself is called the "Republic of Macedonia" and is recognized as such by a number of countries (e.g., Turkey and the United States) but, due to the Greek objections to this name (which I explain in the text), the name I am using here is the denomination adopted in the interim agreement with Greece of 1995 to allow the country to join international organizations. As this denomination is lengthy and cumbersome, many instead use the acronym "FYROM"— which is, however, strongly refused by the country, because it would turn a temporary denomination into an official country name. To be as fair as possible, I have therefore decided to use "the former Yugoslav Republic of Macedonia" in full and consistently throughout the text.

7. This goes well beyond just the name issue. Greece, in fact, also objects to the use by the former Yugoslav Republic of Macedonia of state symbols that refer to the historical Macedonia of Alexander the Great (which Athens considers to be symbols belonging to Greek history and identity), whereas Bulgaria has raised objections for some time to the recognition of Macedonian as a separate language from Bulgarian. Finally, the Serbian Orthodox Patriarchate refuses to recognize the existence of an autocephalous (independent) Macedonian Orthodox Patriarchate. On all key aspects of identity, therefore—symbols, language, religion—the former Yugoslav Republic of Macedonia has had to face, at one or another point, objections or hostility.

8. See J. Simon, "The Need for a Post-Enlargement Strategy," in *The Challenge of NATO Enlargement*, ed. A. Bebler (Westport, CT: Praeger, 1999), 45.

9. According to available figures (see, e.g., http://migration.ucdavis.edu/mn/ more.php?id = 1801_0_4_0), Albania received about 375,000 refugees and Macedonia around 150,000.

10. A good portrait of the internal situation in Croatia can be found in the reports issued by the Organization for Security and Cooperation in Europe's Mission to Croatia. The report issued in September 1999 (available at www.osce.org/documents/mc/1999/09/1051_en.pdf), just months before President Tudjman's death, gives a good idea of the magnitude of the issues facing the new Croatian government, which took office in early 2000.

11. This was made clear at the Prague Summit in November 2002, just a few months after Croatia had become an Aspirant. In the Prague Summit Declaration (available at www.nato.int/docu/pr/2002/p02–127e.htm), the Allies underlined that "Croatia, which has made encouraging progress on reform, will also be under consideration for future membership. Progress in this regard will depend upon Croatia's further reform efforts and compliance with all of its international obligations, including to the International Criminal Tribunal for the former Yugoslavia (ICTY)."

12. This was, e.g., the feeling after the ICTY decided to refer to the operation "Storm" (the final Croatian military operation in August 1995, which led to the reconquest of the remaining Krajina territory) as a "joint criminal enterprise, the common purpose of which was the forcible and permanent removal of the Serb population from the Krajina region" (Ante Gotovina's amended indictment from 2004, available at www.icty.org/x/cases/gotovina/ind/en/got-ai040224e.htm). Though understandable as part of the ICTY Prosecution court tactics, the qualification of what Croats see as a war of national liberation as a mob activity unavoidably raises strong feelings in the country.

13. These data are available at www.nato-pa.int/default.Asp?SHORTCUT =326.

14. In reality, no definition for such a critical mass exists in NATO documents, and the Alliance has repeatedly and consistently stated that decisions on enlargement are based on "individual performance." Nonetheless, experience of the post–Cold War enlargement rounds proves that it is easier to focus the Allies on enlargement decisions when they are faced with the constant pressure of a plurality of aspirants and/or when the enlargement decision appears as beneficial for the stabilization and integration of a region (or part of it) rather than a single country.

15. Throughout the years, the Organization for Security and Cooperation in Europe's mission to Croatia and the EU, as part of Croatia's membership bid, published a number of reports on the issue of refugee return. These reports can be accessed at www.osce.org/zagreb/documents.html?lsi = true&limit = 10&grp = 270, and the latest progress report for Croatia by the European Commission at http://ec.europa.eu/enlargement/pdf/press_corner/key-documents/reports_nov_2008/croatia_progress_report_en.pdf. These reports show the clear progress made in the last years on this issue, although not all outstanding problems have been fully addressed.

16. Author's meetings in Skopje and Brussels in the framework of the MAP, 2005–8.

17. On the United States' announcement, see www.setimes.com/cocoon/setimes/xhtml/en_GB/features/setimes/features/2005/09 /09/feature-01.

18. Just as a reminder, Gotovina was arrested by the Spanish police in the Canary Islands. The cooperation provided by the Croatian authorities in the months preceding his arrest was, however, of crucial importance, as detailed, e.g., in the documentary *Carla's List* (www.youtube.com/watch?v = fj0b2Qk7w5s&feature = related).

19. The communiqué of the NATO Foreign Ministerial meeting on December 8, 2005 (www.nato.int/docu/pr/2005/p05–158e.htm) and issued almost at the same time as Gotovina's arrest in the Canary Islands, but reflecting an agreement reached before the news were broken), included this statement: "We note Croatia's improved level of cooperation with the ICTY as noted in the recent assessment by the Chief Prosecutor of the ICTY and urge Croatia to locate, apprehend and transfer to the ICTY in The Hague the fugitive Ante Gotovina." Similar sentences had been a standard issue in NATO's communiqués since the foreign ministers' meeting in December 2003 (www.nato.int/docu/pr/2003/p03–152e.htm), and mirrored similar requests issued to Serbia and Montenegro and Bosnia and Herzegovina concerning Ratko Mladić and Radovan Karadžić. However, in December 2005, the statement on Gotovina was moved from the usual paragraph devoted to the Western Balkan countries' obligations in respect of the ICTY to the portion of the communiqué related to the MAP and membership aspirations of the three aspirants. This established a very clear link between the two issues (membership for Croatia and Gotovina's arrest).

20. After meeting Sanader, President Bush declared: "I also believe it's in the world's interest that Croatia join NATO, as well as the European Union. To that end, when I go to Riga, I will make the case that Croatia should be admitted. It seems like a reasonable date would be 2008" (www.whitehouse.gov/news/releases/2006/10/20061017–5.html).

21. NATO, Riga Summit Declaration, www.nato.int/docu/pr/2006/p06–150e.htm.

22. A number of polls were conducted in Croatia in the past years on the issue of support for NATO and EU membership. Those that were generally considered more reliable (having had regard to the methodology used) were those carried out by the polling agencies GFK (which conducted quarterly polls on behalf of the government) and PULS. The PULS polls from, respectively, February 2006 and February 2008 showed an increase in support for NATO membership from 29 to 51 percent. Similar results were also shown by the GFK polls.

23. This is, of course, a very sketchy description of the mechanisms and influence of NATO conditionality. A much more detailed study of the NATO and EU conditionality is given by Frank Schimmelfenning, *The EU, NATO and the Integration of Europe* (Cambridge: Cambridge University Press, 2003).

24. A thoughtful analysis of the impact of the "name issue" on the latest enlargement round and of the strategies deployed by the main actors to achieve their goals, based on the "rhetorical entrapment" paradigm, is given by Lidija Levkovska, *The Limits of Rhetorical Entrapment: NATO Enlargement in Southeast Europe* (Saarbrücken: Verlag Dr. Müller, 2008).

25. NATO, "Bucharest Summit Declaration," www.nato.int/docu/pr/2008/p08–049e.html.

26. This process was marked by some final drama linked to a proposed referendum in Slovenia that, if successful, would have blocked Slovenia's ratification of the accession of Croatia (the proposal eventually failed, because it collected only a fraction of the number of signatures required to push the referendum forward).

27. The lawsuit by Skopje is based on the alleged violation, by Athens, of the provisions of the 1995 Interim Accord between the two countries. Article 11 of the Interim Accord (http://untreaty.un.org/unts/120001_144071/6/3/00004456.pdf)

states that "Upon entry into force of this Interim Accord, the Party of the First Part agrees not to object to the application by or the membership of the Party of the Second Part in international, multilateral and regional organizations and institutions of which the Party of the First Part is a member." In the elliptic formulation of the accord, devised to avoid using either "Macedonia" or "the former Yugoslav Republic of Macedonia," the "Party of the First Part" is Greece and the "Party of the Second Part" is the former Yugoslav Republic of Macedonia. Article 21.2 of the accord states that "Any difference or dispute that arises between the Parties concerning the inter-pretation or implementation of this Interim Accord may be submitted by either of them to the International Court of Justice." Greece's objection to the former Yugo-slav Republic of Macedonia's claim is that Skopje is the first one to have been in noncompliance with other provisions of the agreement.

28. It is probably important to stress that, though all the countries that joined after 1994 (the date the PfP was launched) have gone through the PfP before becom-ing new members, the PfP is not only about preparations for membership, but it is more generally a program of cooperation with NATO addressed to any non-NATO state belonging to the Organization for Security and Cooperation in Europe. As such, it also includes countries (e.g., the Central Asian states or the so-called Western Euro-pean Neutrals), that have no declared interest in membership.

29. For the text of the Presentation Document, see www.mfa.gov.yu/Policy/Priorities/srb_pfp_presentation_docum ent.pdf.

30. According to the Dayton Peace Accords of 1995, Bosnia and Herzegovina is a highly decentralized state, with minimal competences at the state level, and with two substate entities—Republika Sepska and the Federation of Bosnia and Herzego-vina—exerting most of the powers.

31. NATO, "Final Communiqué, Meeting of the North Atlantic Council at the Level of Foreign Ministers Held at NATO Headquarters, Brussels," NATO Press Release (2008) 0153, paragraph 19, www.nato.int/docu/pr/2008/p08–153e.html.

32. For a short summary of the Stabilization and Association Process, see http://europa.eu/scadplus/glossary/stabilisation_association_ process_en. htm.

33. "The EU reiterates its unequivocal support to the European perspective of the Western Balkan countries. The future of the Balkans is within the European Union." European Union, "EU–Western Balkans Summit: Declaration," EU Docu-ment 10229/03 (Press Release 163), Thessalonica, June 21, 2003, paragraph 2.

34. See www.nato.int/docu/pr/2003/p03–089e.htm.

35. The name issue is also delaying the opening of actual accession talks between the EU and the former Yugoslav Republic of Macedonia, which Skopje hoped to achieve in 2008.

CHAPTER 9

The Future of the Alliance

IS DEMOGRAPHY DESTINY?

Jeffrey Simon

A$_s$ NATO BEGINS THE PROCESS of drafting its new Strategic Concept, its members should consider that not only is their strategic environment changing dramatically but demographic factors in both the United States and Europe also have the potential to alter the shared identity that has underpinned the Alliance since its inception in 1949. These same factors are also likely to affect NATO's capacity to provide for the collective defense of its members. Indeed, the number of Europeans in the military—already diminished greatly since the end of the Cold War—will continue to shrink in future years because of social, economic, and especially demographic factors. This trend is likely to further constrain Europe's ability to deploy operational forces and strain the transatlantic relationship.

Will social, economic, and demographic forces pull the United States and Europe further apart, or will the increasing isolation of the Euro-Atlantic community based on common values and law from a wider, increasingly chaotic world draw the transatlantic relationship closer? To address the question of NATO's future, two social and economic factors that are likely to have an impact upon the transatlantic relationship will be examined—the shifting from large European conscript armed forces to smaller all-volunteer forces, and diverging transatlantic views on the military's role in providing defense and security. In addition, four aspects of demography will be examined as NATO advances toward the middle of the twenty-first century—increasing pressures on the age cohort available for European defense establishments, the United States' and Europe's diverging immigration patterns and changing social composition, diverging aging populations and its economic implications, and Europe's rapid demographic marginalization. In the end, these

202 ■ *Jeffrey Simon*

six diverging factors are likely to have a significant effect on Washington's and Brussels' future views of NATO's importance, its future role, and the transatlantic relationship.

Social and Economic Factors

First, it is important to recognize that NATO's trend in changing military forces—from maintaining large conscript forces, which were useful in the defense of European territory during the Cold War, toward smaller all-volunteer military establishments to carry out expeditionary operations—has had different political consequences in Europe and the United States. When the Cold War ended in 1989–90, the United States had an all-volunteer force of 2,181,000 troops while NATO's European members had 3,509,000 troops (roughly 60 percent more) under arms (see table 9.1). All these European members, with the sole exception of the United Kingdom, which had maintained an all-volunteer force since 1963, relied on largely conscript forces. During the Cold War, NATO's main role was the territorial defense of Europe; it never engaged in expeditionary operations. Such missions only began in December 1995, when the Dayton Peace Accords resulted in the deployment of a 60,000-troop Implementation Force and follow-on Stabilization Force to Bosnia and Herzegovina. After a seventy-eight-day bombing campaign against Serbia in 1998–99, NATO deployed its 50,000-troop Kosovo Force, which remains there today, with 16,000 troops. In August 2003, NATO also assumed command of the International Security Assistance Force, which, along with the United States–led Operation Enduring Freedom, had been deployed after the September 11, 2001, terrorist attacks on the United States.

During the post–Cold War period, when the former Soviet threat to Europe was diminishing and out-of-area risks were increasing, NATO's European armed forces declined by more than 1.5 million troops. When Europe was beginning to respond to new risks in 1995, it had already lost roughly half a million troops, then another 300,000 by 1999, and another 700,000 by 2004; by 2008 only 1,970,000 troops remained. At the same time, most of European NATO was abandoning conscription and moving toward smaller all-volunteer forces. By 2008, seven of NATO's military establishments had become professional; of the five military establishments retaining conscription (e.g., because of long-held threat perceptions in Turkey and Greece, territorial defense traditions in Norway and Denmark, and Germany's commitment to Innere Fuhrung—"citizens in uniform"), conscript

TABLE 9.1
Comparative Trends in the Defense Establishments of NATO's Cold War European Members[a]

Member	Strength of Defense Establishments (military force)					Conscription Term (months)			
	1990	1995	1999	2004	2008	1995	1999	2004	2008
United Kingdom	308,000	274,800	210,800	205,000	195,900	0	0	0	0
France[b]	550,000	502,000	421,000	347,000	301,000 (15)	12	12 (01)	0	0
Germany	545,000	352,000	322,000	258,000	245,000	15 (55,000)	12	10 (130,000)	9
Spain[b]	263,000	210,000	155,000	124,000	124,000	12	12 (01)	0	0
Italy[b]	493,000	435,000	391,000	315,000	298,000	12	12 (04)	0	0
Netherlands	104,000	67,000	55,000	51,000	51,000	12 (97)	0	0	0
Belgium	106,000	47,000	43,000	40,000	39,000	0 (94)	0	0	0
Denmark	31,000	27,000	25,000	20,000	18,000	9 (5,700)	9	9	4
Norway	51,000	38,000	33,000	22,000	20,000	8–9 (11,000)	8–9	8–9	8–9
Portugal	87,000	78,000	72,000	39,000	41,000	N.A.	7	0	0
Greece	201,000	213,000	205,000	132,000	142,000	12–36 (100,000)	12–36	12–36	12
Turkey	769,000	805,000	797,000	502,000	496,000	16–18	16–18	12–15	12–15 (391,000)
Total force	3,509,000	3,048,800	2,729,800	2,055,000	1,970,000				
Professional				1,407,300	1,408,200				

[a] The United States, Canada, Iceland, and Luxembourg are excluded.
[b] France = 100,000 Gendarmarie; Spain = 80,000 Civil Guards; Italy = 110,000 Carabinieri.

Sources: NATO, Financial and Economic Data Relating to NATO Defence, Press Release M-DPC-2 (1999) 152, December 2, 1999, table 6, p. 8; NATO International Staff, Defence Policy and Planning Division, NATO-Russia Compendium of Financial and Economic Data Relating to Defence, (Brussels: NATO, 2007), table 6, p. 10.

terms have shortened because of declining social support. In sum, in 2008 the twelve Cold War European NATO member countries have roughly the equivalent of the United States—about 1.4 million professional troops.

Also during the post–Cold War period, NATO has been enlarged by twelve new members, with some joining in 1999, in 2004, and in 2009. The military forces of ten of these new members (minus Croatia and Albania, which joined in 2009) have also experienced the same trend as that described above for NATO overall (see table 9.2). They have moved from largely conscript-based armed forces suitable for territorial defense to smaller all-volunteer forces for deployment in expeditionary operations. Because expeditionary operations had become the main focus of NATO's attention, the new members have focused on developing this capability and, before joining, participated in NATO operations to enhance their admission prospects.

In 1999, the ten military forces counted 230,000 professionals among their 618,000 troops. By 2004 their total force had declined to 409,000 troops, but their professional strength *increased* to 270,000. By 2008, eight of the ten new members had become totally professional, with only Lithuania and Estonia retaining conscription for a small part of their armed forces. As a result, 314,700 of their 317,000 troops were professional soldiers, who could be counted toward augmenting European NATO's potential deployable force.

But as European military forces shifted to smaller professional units concentrated in fewer caserns, there were significant social and political consequences. Because defense was no longer the priority that it had been during the Cold War and armed forces were becoming less visible to their publics, many European societies increasingly began to raise questions about their utility. This was particularly the case when forces were used in unpopular expeditionary operations in Afghanistan and Iraq. Additionally, because the armed forces no longer constituted the large voting blocs of earlier years, they were becoming less politically important to their national elites. This situation has already become acute in Bulgaria, Hungary, and the Czech Republic,[1] and it is becoming more so with the other new NATO members, with the notable exception of Poland.

A second factor likely to have a significant impact on NATO derives from the fact that the United States and NATO's European members are diverging in their views of the role of the military and how it contributes to security and defense. In the aftermath of September 11, although the United States did create a Department of Homeland Security, it substantially increased defense expenditures, consistently allocating 4 percent of its gross domestic product to defense since 2004.[2] The U.S. public and political elite have continued to see the military as providing a significant role in the defense of the

TABLE 9.2
Comparative Trends in the Defense Establishments of NATO's New Members

Member	Strength of Defense Establishments (military force)				Conscription Term (months)			
	1995	1999	2004	2008	1995	1999	2004	2008
Hungary	68,261	52,200	30,000	20,000	12	9	6	0 (05)
Poland	278,600	205,000	150,000	120,000(10)	18	12	12	0 (10)
Czech Republic	73,591	56,247	38,000	25,000	12	12	12	0 (05)
Slovakia	52,015	45,483	30,000	18,000	12	12	9	0 (05)
Romania	217,400	150,000	93,000	75,000	12	12	12	0 (07)
Bulgaria	118,000	82,000	40,000	34,000	18	12	6/9	0 (08)
Lithuania	8,000	9,850	11,450	10,000	12	12 (3,500)	12 (4,000)	12 (1,500)
Latvia	4,615	5,500	4,250	4,900	12	12 (1,500)	12 (300)	0 (07)
Estonia	3,270	3,800	3,800	3,800	12 (2,000)	12	8/11	8/11 (1,500)
Slovenia	N.A.	7,800	6,900	7,000	N.A.	7	0	0
Total force	820,000	618,000	409,000	317,000				
Professional	N.A.	230,000	270,000	314,700				

Sources: NATO, *NATO Expeditionary Operations: Impacts on New Members and Partners*, Occasional Paper 1 (Brussels: NATO, 2005), table 4, p. 23; NATO International Staff, Defence Policy and Planning Division, *NATO-Russia Compendium of Financial and Economic Data Relating to Defence, 20 December 2007* (Brussels: NATO, 2007).

Note: N.A. = not available.

country, which is reflected in defense budget allocations. In contrast most European NATO members are increasingly focusing on internal security, not defense, as a predominant concern. Not only do the recent white papers issued by the United Kingdom, Germany, and France reflect their growing internal security concerns, but their defense budgets, as well as those of other European NATO members, seem to correspond to those perceptions.[3] Though European interior ministries are growing and playing an increasingly important role in addressing security concerns, their defense budgets have been stagnating or decreasing.

This downward defense trend has been consistent among NATO's Cold War European members since the end of the Cold War (see table 9.3) and is unlikely to change anytime in the future. Only four of the twelve Allies maintain budgets meeting the generally accepted 2 percent threshold: the United Kingdom and France, with all-volunteer and expeditionary capabilities and experience; and Greece and Turkey, with large conscript forces and mutual defense concerns. France pledges to hold its defense budget constant at 2

TABLE 9.3
Comparative Trends in the Defense Budgets of NATO's Cold War European Members[a]

| Member | Defense Budget as Percentage of Gross Domestic Product (average current prices) | | | |
	1990–94	1995–99	2000–2004	2007
United Kingdom	3.7	2.7	2.4	2.3
France	3.3	2.9	2.5	2.0
Germany	2.1	1.6	1.4	1.3
Spain	1.6	1.3	1.2	1.2
Italy	2.0	1.9	2.0	1.8
Netherlands	2.3	1.8	1.5	1.5
Belgium	2.0	1.5	1.3	1.1
Denmark	1.9	1.7	1.5	1.3
Norway	2.8	2.2	1.9	1.4
Portugal	2.4	2.1	1.7	1.5
Greece	3.9	4.1	3.2	2.8
Turkey	3.8	4.4	4.2	2.7

[a]The United States, Canada, Iceland, and Luxembourg are excluded.
Source: NATO International Staff, Defence Policy and Planning Division, *NATO-Russia Compendium of Financial and Economic Data Relating to Defence, 20 December 2007* (Brussels: NATO, 2007), table 3, p. 7.

percent until 2012 but will reduce its defense establishment by 54,000 over the next seven years. Germany, Spain, Belgium, and Denmark have defense budgets that have declined to 1.3 percent or less.

When a terrorist train bombing killed 191 and wounded more than 1,400 in Madrid in 2004, Spain did *not* want NATO to invoke Article 5 of the Washington Treaty; it increased its Interior Ministry's budget and held defense expenditures steady at 1.2 percent. When NATO's other European members have faced similar challenges, they, too, have focused on internal security institutions, where NATO's defense instruments are less relevant. In sum, internal security challenges are becoming more relevant to European societies and political elites, an area where NATO's Article 5 has a *diminishing* role to play. Hence, many European NATO members apparently see defense allocations as *less* relevant to deal with their security challenges.

The same downward or static trend has been evident even among NATO's ten new members since their accession (see table 9.4). Only Bulgaria meets the 2 percent goal, and only Poland and Romania come close at 1.9 percent. Despite earlier promises, some members—Hungary, Lithuania, and the Czech Republic—have clearly returned disappointing defense results. And this trend is *not* likely to change among these new members in the near future.

TABLE 9.4
Comparative Trends in the Defense Budgets of NATO's New Members

Member	Defense Budget as Percentage of Gross Domestic Product (current prices)			
	1995	*1999*	*2004*	*2007*
Hungary	1.4	1.6	1.6	1.1
Poland	2.4	2.2	1.8	1.9
Czech Republic	2.6	1.9	2.0	1.6
Slovakia	2.6	1.7	1.7	1.7
Romania	N.A.	1.8	2.0	1.9
Bulgaria	2.6	2.1	2.5	2.0
Lithuania	0.5	1.5	1.4	1.2
Latvia	0.5	0.8	1.3	1.7
Estonia	1.1	N.A.	1.6	1.6
Slovenia	N.A.	1.5	1.7	1.7

Source: NATO International Staff, Defence Policy and Planning Division, *NATO-Russia Compendium of Financial and Economic Data Relating to Defence, 20 December 2007* (Brussels: NATO, 2007), table 3, p. 7.
Note: N.A. = not available.

In marked contrast to NATO's Cold War and new European members, the United States continues to see defense as the best instrument for dealing with threats. These diverging transatlantic views on how the military contributes to defense and security are likely to exert further pressure on European defense budgets and military forces, and on the transatlantic relationship.

Demographic Factors

The fact that the gap between the United States and European NATO members' age cohorts available for military service is widening is also likely to have implications for NATO's future. The U.S. population of 283,230,000 in 2000 is projected to grow to roughly 397,063,000 in 2050.[4] During this same period, the U.S. median age of 35.5 years is expected to increase only slightly, to 36.2 years.[5] Hence the United States should have an adequate cohort available for military service at current troop levels. In marked contrast NATO's European (both Cold War and new) members will not only experience population *declines*,[6] but the median age of 37.7 years in 2000 is also projected to increase to 47.0 years in 2050.[7] What this means is that Europe's shrinking cohort could affect NATO members' ability to meet planned force levels and make it more difficult to modernize their smaller, more expensive professional forces, in the face of mounting health and social costs for its aging population. Some European members may actually have to face the question of whether they will even be able to maintain a viable military.

Among NATO's Cold War European members (see table 9.5), the shrinking cohort and aging problem will be felt most acutely in Italy and Spain, where overall declines of 21 to 25 percent in population are projected. As a result, between 2005 and 2050 Italy's population of sixty years and older will increase substantially, from 25.5 to 41.6 percent, as will Spain's, from 21.4 to 39.7 percent. Although Greece, Portugal, and Germany have overall projected population declines of 10 to 15 percent, they also will experience an aging challenge. Between 2005 and 2050 the population of sixty and older will increase in Greece from 23 to 36.8 percent, in Portugal from 22.3 to 36.3 percent, and in Germany from 25.1 to 35 percent.[8] In all these cases, a shrinking fifteen-to-fifty-nine-year-old cohort will find it more difficult to fill out military billets to maintain existing force levels, while the need to subsidize the increasing health care and social welfare costs of an aging population will compete with efforts to maintain and modernize existing armed forces. Even France and Great Britain, which have favorable demographics,

TABLE 9.5
Cold War NATO European Members' Population between 2000 and 2050 (medium variant)[a]

Member	Population (thousands)		Difference	
	2000	2050	Absolute	Percent
United Kingdom	59,415	58,933	−482	−0.8
France	59,200	63,100	+3,900	+6.6
Germany	82,017	70,805	−11,212	−13.7
Spain	39,910	31,282	−8,629	−21.6
Italy	57,530	42,962	−14,568	−25.3
Netherlands	15,868	15,845	−18	−0.1
Belgium	10,249	9,583	−667	−6.5
Denmark	5,320	5,080	−240	−4.5
Portugal	10,016	9,006	−1,010	−10.1
Greece	10,610	8,983	−1,627	−15.3
Turkey	66,700	98,800	+32,100	+48.1
Totals				
Without France and Turkey	290,936	252,479	−38,453	−13.2
With France and Turkey	(416,836)	(414,379)	−2,457	−0.6

[a] Norway was not available.
Source: United Nations, *World Population Prospects*, Report E/CN.9/2001/4 (New York: United Nations, 2004), tables 4 and 6, pp. 17–20.

face challenges. In 2005 both had populations older than sixty of 21.1 percent; by 2050 France and Great Britain will have populations older than sixty of 33 and 29.4 percent, respectively.[9] In sum, NATO's European Cold War members will find it increasingly difficult to recruit, retain, and modernize their military establishments because of shrinking cohorts to fill necessary billets and to subsidize the increasing health and social welfare costs of an aging population.

If this situation appears challenging for NATO's European Cold War members, the situation by comparison is dire for its ten new members (see table 9.6), whose populations are projected to experience *substantial* decline. Between 2005 and 2050 Bulgaria and Estonia are projected to shrink to almost half their current size, facing declines of 43 to 46 percent, respectively. Bulgaria's population of sixty and older is projected to increase from 22.4 to 38 percent, and Estonia's from 21.6 to 33.6 percent. Latvia, Hungary, and Slovenia are projected to face population declines on the order of Spain and Italy, shrinking by 28, 24.9, and 23.2 percent, respectively. Although their actual projected decline is more moderate than that in Bulgaria and Estonia, they will face the burden of subsidizing an even *larger* aging population. Between 2005 and 2050 Latvia's population of sixty and older is projected to more than double, from 22.5 to 48 percent, and Slovenia's is expected to grow from 20.5 to 40.2 percent, and Hungary's from 20.8 to 36.2 percent. Although the Czech Republic and Lithuania face lower overall projected population declines, they will also share the burden of almost doubling populations of sixty and older, facing increases from 20 to 39.3 percent and 20.7 to 37.9 percent, respectively.[10] Hence, NATO's new European members will find it even more challenging than its Cold War members to retain modernized military establishments at their already significantly reduced troop levels.

In summary, the United States and European NATO members' age cohorts are moving in opposite directions. The Europeans' diminished age cohort and aging population will make it increasingly difficult for their military forces to meet existing, already much smaller, all-volunteer force recruitment goals. Mounting health and welfare costs for an aging population will also increasingly compete with resources necessary to modernize those smaller forces. Recruitment and retention pressures are already evident in Bulgaria, Hungary, the Czech Republic, and Romania. Shrinking European cohorts have resulted in lower intake standards and smaller forces and will further fuel the already strained transatlantic burden-sharing debate.

Additionally, the United States' and Europe's diverging immigration patterns and shifting internal demographics also seem likely to erode the common historical identity underpinning the transatlantic relationship. As

TABLE 9.6

NATO's New Members Whose Population Is Projected to Decrease between 2000 and 2050 (medium variant)

Member	Population (thousands)		Difference (thousands)	
	2000	2050	Absolute	Percentage
Hungary	9,968	7,486	−2,481	−24.9
Poland	38,605	33,370	−5,235	−13.6
Czech Republic	10,272	8,429	−1,842	−17.9
Slovakia	5,399	4,674	−724	−13.4
Romania	22,438	18,150	−4,288	−19.1
Bulgaria	7,949	4,531	−3,419	−43.0
Lithuania	3,696	2,989	−707	−19.1
Latvia	2,421	1,744	−677	−28.0
Estonia	1,393	752	−642	−46.1
Slovenia	1,988	1,527	−461	−23.2
Total	104,129	83,652	−20,476	−19.7

Source: United Nations, *World Population Prospects*, Report E/CN.9/2001/4 (New York: United Nations, 2004), table 6, p. 20.

European fertility declines, the contribution of international migration to population growth has increased in significance. Although immigration is one way to improve on the problem of the European cohorts available for military service, other demographic forces are pulling the United States and European NATO in different directions. The countries with the highest levels of net emigration are projected to be China (–329,000 annually), Mexico (–306,000), India (–241,000), the Philippines (–180,000), Pakistan (–167,000), and Indonesia (–164,000).[11] Though the United States and Europe will be net receivers of international migrants, their intake composition is increasingly different. The traditional U.S. immigration pattern has shifted more and more away from Europe, while Europe's pattern is increasingly Muslim immigration from Turkey, Asia, the Middle East, and North Africa. This could pull each side of the Atlantic in a different direction.

The United States faces very different immigration demographics from Europe; its birthrate is higher, and it can absorb many more immigrants. During the period 2005–50 the United States is projected to receive 1.1 million immigrants annually, many of whom are Hispanic (Spanish is rapidly becoming its second language) and Asian, whose populations will triple in size. The Hispanic population, 42 million in 2005, will rise to 128 million in 2050, constituting 29 percent of the U.S. population (compared with 14 percent in 2005 and 3.5 percent in 1960). The Asian population, 14 million in 2005, will grow to 41 million in 2050, constituting 9 percent of the U.S. population (compared with 5 percent in 2005 and 0.6 percent in 1960).[12] This means that 38 percent of the U.S. population will be either Hispanic or Asian in 2050, compared with only 4.1 percent in 1960.

During the same period, the internal demographics of NATO's European members will face dramatic changes as well. Germany is projected to receive 150,000 immigrants annually, along with Italy, 139,000; the United Kingdom, 130,000; and Spain, 123,000.[13] Immigration from Turkey, Asia, the Middle East, and North Africa to fill labor shortfalls already is having an impact on intercommunal relations and security concerns. Since September 11 concerns about Muslims in Europe have been on the increase, sparked in part by numerous outbreaks of violence. Security concerns have increased since the Madrid commuter train bombings in March 2004, the assassination of Theo Van Gogh because of a documentary on Muslim women in Amsterdam in November 2004, the terrorist bombings in London in July 2005, weeks of street violence and car bombings in France in October and November 2005, and the widespread riots following the publication of offending cartoons in a Danish newspaper in February 2006. Pew public opinion polls in Spain, Germany, Great Britain, France, and the Netherlands indicate that between 70 and 78 percent of respondents are either somewhat or very concerned about Islamic extremism.[14] Though Muslims make up relatively small percentages of the population in European countries—in the United Kingdom, roughly 3 percent (mostly Pakistanis and Bangladeshis); in Germany, 4 percent (mostly Turks); in France, 8 percent (mostly Algerians); in Spain, 2 percent (mostly Moroccans); and in the Netherlands, 6.6 percent (mostly Indonesians, Turks, and Moroccans)[15]—their fertility rates are three times higher than those of non-Muslims.[16] Muslim immigration has contributed to NATO's European members' increasing focus on internal security (i.e., vice defense) and will likely have an impact on Europe's political relations with the external Islamic world.

Although Muslim population growth resulting from immigration and higher fertility rates is clearly a factor for NATO's European members, it is also having an impact in wider Europe. During the same 2005–50 period, Russia is projected to decline from a population of 145.5 million to 104.3 million, with Muslims approaching the majority. Ukraine is expected to decline from 49.6 to 29.9 million, facing increasing pressures in South Crimea in the form of a higher birthrate among the Crimean Tatars.[17] Similarly, demographics in the Balkans will likely show some local Muslim populations (Albania, Kosovo, and Bosnia and Herzegovina) approaching majorities.

In summary, the United States and Europe's diverging and shifting internal demographics will likely continue to pull each side of the Atlantic in a different direction. The United States' reorientation from formerly predominantly European to increasingly Hispanic and Asian will likely pull diaspora attention toward these regions, while Europe's increasingly Muslim diaspora will likely draw attention in different directions.

Also of significance for NATO's future is the fact that the relatively young and growing U.S. population will contribute to its "slightly enhanced" global economic profile in 2050, while Europe's aging and shrinking productive population will contribute to its diminishing presence. NATO's European members face serious demographic challenges. Europe's fertility rates remain low (from 1.9 in the mid-1980s to 1.4 in 2008) and are projected to decline over the next decade;[18] and its active working population will decline from 331 to 243 million.[19] Hence, fewer productive people will need to devote more resources to provide health and social services to an aging European population. As a result, according to some estimates, Europe's (i.e., that of the fifteen EU members before the 2004 enlargement) share of the gross world product (GWP) will decline from roughly 22 percent in 2003 to 12 percent in 2050.[20] Europe's aging population will make up a shrinking portion of the global population, with economic, social, and security consequences.

During the same period the U.S. population, in marked contrast to Europe, will actually increase. Due to higher fertility rates of 2.1 and immigration flows, the United States' population, which had a median age of 35.5 years in 2003, will change only slightly, to 36.2 years in 2050,[21] and its active working population will actually *increase*, from 269 million in 2003 to 355 million in 2050. And according to some estimates, the U.S. share of GWP is projected to *increase*, from roughly 23 percent now to 26 percent in 2050.[22] In other words, the United States' experience will significantly diverge from that of Europe.

The United States' internal demographics could also have a dramatic effect on its identity and political orientation. Hence, while Europe will remain important to the United States, Asia and Latin America will be gaining in relative economic, social, and domestic political importance. These trends, too, are likely to have an impact on NATO and its future toward the middle of the twenty-first century.

The fact that the world's population will continue to reflect the inexorable shift away from the Eurocentric world that existed when NATO was created in 1949 to Europe's rapid demographic marginalization by 2050 constitutes a final trend with future implications for the Alliance. In 1950 the world population stood at 2.519 billion; shortly after NATO's fiftieth anniversary in 2000, it was 6.057 billion. Over these fifty years the Northern American (including Canada) share of world population of 172 million (or 6.8 percent share) grew to 314 million (or 5.2 percent), but it still declined as a percentage of the world population. During this same period, the population of the European Union's twenty-five members as of 2004 of 350 million (at 13.9 percent) had also grown to 452 million, but this represented an even greater decline than that experienced in North America, to 7.5 percent of the world population. In effect, Europe registered a significant demographic marginalization in relation to the rest of the world.[23]

In the coming decades, Europe's demographic marginalization will speed up. If NATO still exists in 2050, it will exist in a world with a population projected to be 9.322 billion. The North American population is projected at 438 million (or 4.7 percent of the world population), with a 26 percent share of GWP; the European Union's twenty-five members as of 2004 will decline from 452 million to 431 million (or 4.6 percent of the world population), and to only slightly more than 12 percent of the GWP. Significantly, the United States' political attention, thanks to an increasing non-European diaspora, will shift inexorably away from Europe and toward Latin America and Asia as these areas become more important. The population of Latin America and the Caribbean, which stood at 519 million in 2000 (up from 167 million in 1950), is projected to surpass Europe's by more than 30 percent in 2050, with a population of 806 million (or 8.6 percent of the world population). In Asia, China had 1.275 billion people in 2000 (up from 554.8 million in 1950), and it is projected to have 1.462 billion in 2050 (or 15.7 percent of the world population). During the same period India's 1 billion population in 2000 (up from 357.6 million in 1950) is projected to be 1.57 billion (or 16.8 percent of the world population) in 2050.[24] Both will make up 32.5 percent of the total world population and will play a larger role in the world economy. China's 25 percent share of GWP in 2050 will be roughly equal to that of the United States and twice that of the European Union's fifteen members before the 2004 enlargement. Internal demographic factors and external global shifts increasingly will draw U.S. attention away from its traditional European focus. Europe's rapid demographic marginalization and diminishing social, economic, and political weight will mean that it will no longer be the "center" of the world or of U.S. attention.

Is Demography Destiny?

NATO's future is increasingly challenged by social, economic, and demographic factors, although demography will further aggravate the economic and social conditions that will continue to divide the nations on both sides of the Atlantic. As noted above, the Alliance's future is being influenced by Europe's shifting from large conscript armed forces to smaller all-volunteer forces and diverging transatlantic views on the military's role in providing defense and security. In addition, as the Alliance advances toward the middle of the twenty-first century, increasing U.S.-European demographic divergences will likely emerge, adding pressures on the European cohort available for defense establishments: altering immigration patterns that further loosen traditional social ties, aging European populations competing with defense for ever-scarcer resources, and the changing global population mix reflecting Europe's demographic marginalization.

How will the diminishing overall "weight" of the West affect both Europe's and the United States' position and role *in* the world? Will these trends affect how the United States views the relevance of NATO in the decades ahead? Will these trends "loosen" further or actually undermine Article 5 of the Washington Treaty, the transatlantic foundation of the past half century, or will these trends actually foster a common sense of increasing Euro-Atlantic community and ignite the spark to seek a newly defined mutual security organization that could pull both sides of the Atlantic together to fend off the outside world?

As Europe's population of sixty years and older expands and NATO enters its seventh decade, these social, economic, and demographic factors are among the serious issues that should be on the Alliance's agenda as it looks ahead to writing a new Strategic Concept in 2010. Insofar as the trends described in this chapter have the potential to alter NATO's very identity and potentially its purpose, they highlight its need to find a new strategic vision—one designed for a dramatically altered strategic environment. The fact that NATO's member countries' percentage of the world population is shrinking, coupled with the rapidly growing political, economic, and military power of non-Western states such as China and India, should also prompt the Allies to devote further attention to NATO's relations with other international institutions and non-European partners.

Perhaps a reexamination of the 1949 Washington Treaty and an assessment of how NATO responded successfully to twentieth-century world challenges would be in order as the basis for exploring how the Washington Treaty might be refocused, updated, and/or recast to deal with the greatly transformed world of the middle of the twenty-first century. If NATO's Article 5 has less relevance in the twenty-first-century world, and if internal security concerns are becoming more relevant to Europe than defense, then NATO ought to examine whether any transatlantic security interests remain—whether transnational terrorism, the proliferation of weapons of mass destruction, regional conflicts and failed states, cybersecurity, illicit trafficking and criminal networks, energy, global warming, migration, or pandemics. Assuming that such mutual interests do remain, NATO's members must then discuss whether the Washington Treaty is an appropriate and/or relevant tool for addressing these challenges, and if so, how it would need to be revised.

In conclusion, demography need not be destiny, contra what Karl Marx predicted in relation to capitalism's demise. If, however, NATO's member countries take seriously the need to rethink its strategic vision in light of both changing demographic trends within the Alliance and a dramatically altered strategic environment since the end of the Cold War, demography could very well become the catalyst for the revitalization, if not rebirth, of the Euro-Atlantic Community.

Notes

Earlier versions of this chapter appeared as "NATO's Uncertain Future: Is Demography Destiny?" *Strategic Forum*, October 2008; and "NATO's Uncertain Future: Is Demography Destiny?" *Joint Force Quarterly*, April 2009. The views expressed in this chapter are those of the author and do not reflect the views of the Institute for National Strategic Studies at the National Defense University, the U.S. Department of Defense, or any other government agency.

1. Interviews with senior Bulgarian, Hungarian, and Czech defense officials in Sofia and Washington on April 26, 2007, June 3, 2008, and June 17, 2008.

2. Defence Policy and Planning Division, NATO International Staff, *NATO-Russia Compendium of Financial and Economic Data Relating to Defence* (Brussels: NATO, 2007), table 3, p. 7.

3. The U.K. White Paper sees "no major conventional threats . . . but the threat from proliferation and international terrorism remains very real. [Hence] defence forces must support Home defence and security in support of the Home Office and civil authorities . . . achieved though Joint Regional Liaison Officers to protect our citizens at home." U.K. Ministry of Defence, *Delivering Security in a Changing World: Defence White Paper* (London: Ministry of Defence, 2003), 3, 9. The German White Paper portrays internal and external security becoming increasingly interwoven arguing "the need for the protection of the population and of the infrastructure has increased in importance as a result of the growing threat that terrorist attacks pose to German territory" and calls for "expanding the Constitutional framework for the deployment of the armed forces." Federal Ministry of Defense, *White Paper 2006 on German Security Policy and the Future of the Bundeswehr* (Berlin: Federal Ministry of Defense, 2006), 9, 57. And the French White Paper claims that "the traditional distinction between internal and external security has lost its relevance," adding that uncertainty requires the ability to anticipate and take decisions autonomously. Hence, it calls for increased expenditures for intelligence and establishing a new Defense and National Security Council. President of the Republic, *The French White Paper on Defense and National Security* (Paris: President of the Republic, 2008), 5, 11, 16.

4. See United Nations, *World Population Prospects*, Report E/CN.9/2001/4 (New York: United Nations, 2004), "Table 4. Countries with a Population of 50 Million or More, 1950, 2000, and 2050 (Medium Variant)," 17. A recent Pew Research Center Report projects similar trends for the United States—showing an increase from 296 million in 2005 to 438 million in 2050. See Jeffrey S. Passel and D' Vera Cohn, *U.S. Population Projections: 2005–2050* (Washington, DC: Pew Research Center, 2008), 8.

5. These are from calculations by the University of Michigan demographer William Frey, cited in "Half a Billion Americans?—Demography and the West" (Special Report), *The Economist*, August 22, 2002, 22.

6. This is with the notable exceptions of Turkey and France, which project population increases, and the United Kingdom and Netherlands, which project populations that remain fundamentally unchanged.

7. United Nations, *World Population Prospects: The 2006 Revision*, Report ST/ESA/SER.A/261/ES (New York: United Nations, 2007), 9. These figures are similar to median age (e.g., the age that divides the older and younger halves of the population) calculations. In Europe in 2002, the median age was thirty-eight years; by 2050, it will be fifty-one. In Germany, it will be fifty-three; in Italy, fifty-seven. See Peter G. Peterson, *The Global Impact of a "Gray Dawn,"* Heritage Lecture 729 (Washington, DC: Heritage Foundation, 2002), 4.

8. Jack A. Goldstone, "Flash Points and Tipping Points: Security Implications of Global Population Changes, 2005–2025," paper presented to the Conference on Population Changes and Global Security, Berlin, November 13, 2006, table 5, 47.

9. Ibid.

10. Ibid.

11. United Nations, *World Population Prospects: The 2006 Revision*, 13.

12. See Passel and Cohn, *U.S. Population Projections*, "Figure 6. Population by Race and Ethnicity, Actual and Projected: 1960, 2005, and 2050," 9.

13. Ibid.

14. Pew Global Attitudes Project, *Islamic Extremism: Common Concern for Muslim and Western Publics* (Washington, DC: Pew Global Attitudes Project, 2005), 3. These figures also held in 2006; see Pew Global Attitudes Project, *Muslims in Europe: Economic Worries Top Concerns about Religious and Cultural Identity* (Washington, DC: Pew Global Attitudes Project, 2006), 5.

15. See Pew Forum, *An Uncertain Road: Muslims and the Future of Europe* (Washington, DC: Pew Forum, 2005), 3; and Maarten Alders, "Forecasting the Population with a Foreign Background in the Netherlands," paper prepared for the Joint Eurostat–UNECE Work Session on Demographic Projections, Vienna, September 21–23, 2005, 6.

16. Omer Taspinar argued in 2003 that the Muslim birthrate in Europe is three times higher than for non-Muslims, and that if current trends continue, the Muslim population in Europe will nearly double by 2015, while the non-Muslim population will shrink by 3.5 percent. Omer Taspinar, "Europe's Muslim Street," Brookings Institution, 2003, www.brookings.edu/opinions/2003/03middleeast_taspinar.aspx?p=1.

17. United Nations, *World Population Prospects*, 20.

18. "Half a Billion Americans?"

19. John Vinocur, "A Gloomy Scenario for Europe's Economy," *International Herald Tribune*, May 14, 2003.

20. Ibid.

21. "Half a Billion Americans?"

22. Ibid.

23. See Paul Demeny and Geoffrey McNicoll, *The Political Demography of the World System, 2000–2050*, Working Paper 213 (New York: Population Council, 2006), "Table 1. Population and Population Change by Major Country and Region, 1950–2050," 31.

24. See United Nations, *World Population Prospects*, "Table 1. Estimated and Projected Population of the World, Major Development Groups and Major Areas, 1950, 2000, and 2050," 9; and "Table 4. Countries with a Population of 50 Million or More, 1950, 2000, and 2050 (Medium Variant)," 17.

CHAPTER 10

Partnership Goes Global

THE ROLE OF NONMEMBER,
NON–EUROPEAN UNION STATES
IN THE EVOLUTION OF NATO

Rebecca R. Moore

DISCUSSIONS OF NATO's new global orientation often focus on its post–September 11, 2001, military missions in Afghanistan, Iraq, Darfur, the Mediterranean, and even Pakistan. Evidence of an increasingly global, less Eurocentric perspective, however, can also be found in the creation of NATO's new partnerships, which now extend well beyond the borders of Europe. These partnerships—including the Partnership for Peace, Euro-Atlantic Partnership Council, NATO–Russia Council, NATO–Ukraine Commission, NATO–Georgia Commission, Mediterranean Dialogue, and Istanbul Cooperation Initiative, along with less formal relationships with non-European allies or "global partners"—constitute one of the principal mechanisms through which NATO has sought to "project stability" through-out and beyond Europe. Indeed, though not all NATO's partners merit the label "liberal democracy," partnership has served as one of the principal means by which NATO's members have sought since the early 1990s to enlarge the pacific zone established in Western Europe during the Cold War years to include states outside NATO's traditional sphere of collective defense—largely by encouraging in Central and Eastern Europe the liberal democratic values central to NATO's post–Cold War vision of a Europe "whole and free."[1]

Although NATO has remained committed to its vision of a united and democratic Europe, after the September 11, 2001, terrorist attacks on the United States, its member states would also look to partnership as a means of improving its capacity to address a variety of increasingly global threats, including terrorism and weapons of mass destruction. This new emphasis overlapped with the earlier integrationist mission insofar as applicants for NATO membership were now informed that they would be evaluated in terms not only of their demonstrated commitment to liberal democratic principles but also their willingness or capacity to contribute to what the George W. Bush administration termed the "war on terror."[2] At the same time, however, a recognition that the threats confronting its members would increasingly come from beyond the Euro-Atlantic area prompted NATO to devote greater attention to its existing partners in the Mediterranean and Central Asian and Caucasus states, which did not necessarily aspire to NATO membership or demonstrate a commitment to liberal democratic principles but whose geostrategic significance had grown in the wake of September 11.

The desire to improve NATO's capacity to address global threats would ultimately also prompt its members to seek ways of enhancing cooperation with global partners, or what it now formally refers to as "other partners across the globe"—non-NATO, non-European states such as Australia, Japan, and South Korea, which emerged as key contributors to NATO's International Security Assistance Force mission in Afghanistan, even though they have not been incorporated into any of NATO's formal partnership structures.[3] These newest "partners" not only contribute significant military capabilities; many also share fully in the liberal democratic values common to all NATO's members. Yet they currently have no voice in its operational planning.

Indeed, as NATO's partnerships have multiplied, the growing diversity of their members has generated important questions regarding their structure and purpose—questions that NATO must consider in drafting its new Strategic Concept. Should, for example, the role of NATO's global partners be limited to contributions of troops or other military capabilities on an ad hoc basis? Or should NATO embrace through a more formal political framework those non-European partners that clearly share its values? Should NATO continue to structure partnerships along primarily regional lines, or should it adopt a more functionalist approach? To what extent does it jeopardize its own identity as a defender and promoter of liberal democratic values through cooperation with states that have not yet fully embraced these values, or whose practices stand in direct opposition to them? To date, NATO has not reached a consensus on these issues. The issue of global partners, in particular, has been a source of strong disagreement among its member states, some of which fear that its cultivation of global partners might constitute a first step toward a global Alliance. Ultimately, however, this is not simply a debate over the structure of NATO's partnerships. At a much more fundamental level, it is a debate over NATO's very purpose and identity.

Although NATO members have generally agreed that they must cooperate with non-European allies if the Alliance is to address the new, global threats they all now confront, its members remain divided as to just how global it should be. For some, NATO is and must remain an essentially Euro-Atlantic Alliance committed principally to the collective defense of its members and the civilizational identity with which it has historically been identified. Indeed, its identity is deeply rooted in the idea of the "West." As defined in the preamble to the original Washington Treaty, NATO's core function is to "safeguard the freedom, common heritage and civilisation of [its] peoples, founded on the principles of democracy, individual liberty and the rule of law." It was also to these values that NATO's leaders turned during the 1990s in making the case that the Alliance's cohesion no longer depended on the threat of a common enemy. In the words of its former secretary-general, Manfred Wörner, NATO did not need to invent a political role for itself in the post–Cold War order; it had "always been a community of values and destiny among free nations."[4]

The liberal democratic values with which NATO has long been identified, however, are no longer confined to the West.[5] As U.S. senator John McCain observed during the annual Munich Security Conference in February 2007, the "true legacy of [NATO's] victory in the Cold War" was the fact that "billions of people around the world now embrace the ideals of political, economic, and social liberty, conceived in the West, as their own." McCain, in fact, called for a "new global partnership" to defend these values now "under attack by the forces of violence, extremism and chaos."[6] Others have called even more explicitly for a more global NATO, thereby begging the question of whether the Alliance might someday be conceived as a growing, Kantian-like federation of liberal democracies, not confined to any particular geographic space. For some, however, NATO's identity is more fundamentally rooted in its historical, cultural, and geographical origins than in the values for which it stands. As these divergent perspectives suggest, reaching a consensus on the role and function of NATO's partners requires not only a new strategic vision that goes beyond the commitment its members embraced in the early 1990s on behalf of a Europe whole and free but also a willingness to grapple with the very identity of the Alliance, including its relationships with both those that do and those that do not share its values.

The Evolution of Partnership

If there is one common belief underpinning the entire spectrum of NATO's partnership efforts, it is the notion that NATO's own territory cannot truly be secure if instability reigns along its periphery. This conclusion prompted NATO as early as 1990 to seek dialogue and cooperation with its former Warsaw Pact adversaries in Central and Eastern Europe, first by inviting them to establish diplomatic liaisons to NATO, and later by establishing institutional frameworks for dialogue and military cooperation in the form of the Partnership for Peace (PfP) and the North Atlantic Cooperation Council—later renamed the Euro-Atlantic Partnership Council (EAPC). No longer would NATO be content to defend an existing security order. Rather, it embraced the mission of constructing a new one, grounded in liberal democratic values and encompassing areas outside its traditional sphere of collective defense.[7]

Reaching out to former adversaries constituted an essentially political means of encouraging the growth of liberal democratic values beyond NATO's borders and building a new, more unified and democratic Europe. Although NATO initially had no clear blueprint for such an ambitious new political mission, the partnership concept would ultimately play a central role in the construction of a new European security architecture, which by the late 1990s would comprise multiple overlapping institutions and partnerships, and encompass virtually the whole of Europe, including the traditionally nonaligned states Austria, Finland, Ireland, Sweden, and Switzerland. The PfP/EAPC framework, in particular, not only served to promote interoperability and training with NATO forces; it also permitted participation by nonmember states in NATO's post–Cold War peacekeeping and stabilization missions, including in Bosnia and Kosovo. Ultimately, the establishment of these new frameworks for cooperation constituted an important milestone in what came to be known as NATO's "out of area" debates. Yet NATO's partnership initiatives remained focused on the integration and stabilization of Europe.

The events of September 11, 2001, however, prompted a new phase in the out-of-area debates and NATO's thinking about the role of partnership. No longer could the Alliance afford the insular Eurocentric focus that had prevailed among its members during the 1990s. In a world that was ever more globalized, instability, even well beyond Europe's borders, was now understood to constitute a threat to the security of NATO's members, just as potential and realized instability in Central and Eastern Europe had threatened them during the 1990s. The presumption now was that the principal threats to the North Atlantic area would likely stem from areas to the south and east of NATO's territory, but its members also agreed that they would need to approach these likely threats from a functional rather than geographic perspective.[8] As the NATO foreign ministers agreed in Helsinki in

May 2002, the Alliance needed the capacity to mobilize forces "quickly to wherever they are needed" and "sustain operations over distance and time"[9]

This decision was affirmed in Prague in 2002,[10] and again during the Istanbul Summit in June 2004, when the NATO Allies declared that they were now "determined to address effectively the threats to our territor[ies], forces and populations from wherever they may come."[11] Accordingly, the role of NATO's partnerships also shifted. Although partnership remained an important tool for carrying out the unfinished business of integrating Europe, it also became an important vehicle through which to "project stability" beyond Europe, in part by encouraging partners—both those seeking NATO membership and those without such aspirations—to contribute in some capacity to NATO's military missions in Kosovo, Afghanistan, and even Iraq. Indeed, its prospective member states were put on notice that they were expected to behave as security producers and not simply consumers of its assistance.[12]

Partners beyond Europe

In seeking to increase its capacity to address new global threats, NATO would also increasingly look to partners outside Europe. In fact, NATO used its 2004 Istanbul Summit to focus attention on its partnerships with the states of the Caucasus and Central Asia, a region that had assumed far greater geostrategic significance after September 11, given both its proximity to Afghanistan and the fact that the Central Asian governments had offered the United States and NATO military assistance crucial to waging the war against the Taliban and al-Qaeda forces effectively, including the use of military bases.[13]

NATO's focus, however, was not limited to its existing partnerships. At the Istanbul Summit its members also declared their intention to transform the Mediterranean Dialogue (MD)—first established in 1994—into a genuine partnership.[14] The MD, which comprises seven states (Algeria, Egypt, Israel, Jordan, Morocco, Mauritania, and Tunisia) had originally been designed to promote mutual understanding with NATO's neighbors in the Mediterranean. The events of September 11 significantly heightened its importance, leading to various efforts aimed at enhancing political dialogue with the MD states and providing them with greater opportunities to participate in PfP activities and other training, as well as courses at NATO schools.[15]

The perceived success of the MD, coupled with the post–September 11 strategic environment, also led in 2004 to the unveiling of the Istanbul Cooperation Initiative (ICI)—a new program aimed at developing practical bilateral security cooperation between NATO and the states of the greater Middle

East. NATO identified particular issue areas for which it sought to offer tailored advice to participating states, "including defence reform, defence budgeting, defence planning and civil–military relations, promoting military-to-military cooperation to contribute to interoperability, fighting terrorism through information sharing and maritime cooperation, proliferation of weapons of mass destruction and their delivery means and fighting illegal trafficking."[16]

Both the enhancement of the MD and the creation of the ICI reflected a new commitment to projecting stability well beyond the borders of Europe as well as an understanding that security had become a cooperative endeavor, requiring dialogue and cooperation across geographic regions. These new initiatives not only created opportunities for cooperation with strategically important states; they also suggested the beginnings of a security community that was not confined to Europe but was potentially borderless. At the same time, however, these partnerships were fundamentally different from the partnerships that NATO had established with the states of Central and Eastern Europe. The vast majority of the MD and ICI partners were not liberal democracies, and although the Bush administration clearly did seek to enlist NATO assets in its efforts to democratize the Middle East, it would be difficult to argue that these partnerships had the same potential for integration or democracy promotion as had been demonstrated in Central and Eastern Europe through the PfP and the EAPC.[17] To the contrary, these relationships not only appeared to have been driven principally by strategic realities; they also generated questions about whether NATO, by cooperating with repressive, nondemocratic regimes, had put at risk its own identity as an Alliance increasingly grounded in a commitment to liberal democratic values. The fact that few of these states have aspired to NATO membership also meant that the Alliance was unlikely to enjoy the same degree of leverage with them that it did with the governments of Central and Eastern Europe, virtually all of which have sought full membership.

Riga and the Global Partners Initiative

During its 2006 Riga Summit, NATO would also utilize its now well-established partnership model to enhance relations with what have come to be known as global partners, although they were initially labeled "contact countries." These are non-NATO, non-European, nonpartner states that have sought dialogue or closer cooperation with NATO. In many cases these states, unlike some formal NATO partners, are already full-fledged liberal democracies. The impetus for this newest outreach effort, however, stemmed from the fact that a number of these non-European allies, including Australia, Japan, New Zealand, and South Korea, had emerged as key contributors to NATO's International Security Assistance Force (ISAF) mission in Afghanistan at a time when many NATO members had been slow to provide the troops and equipment deemed critical to the success of the ISAF mission by NATO commanders. In Riga, the Alliance's members agreed to "fully develop the political and practical potential of NATO's existing cooperation programmes" and "increase the operational relevance of relations with non-NATO countries" in two particular ways. First, it was decided that NATO should be able to "call ad hoc meetings as events arise" with contributors or potential contributors to NATO missions, including interested "contact countries," utilizing "flexible formats . . . based on the principles of inclusiveness, transparency and self-differentiation."[18] Second, the Allies agreed to make established partnership tools more widely available to interested Contact Countries and members of the MD and the ICI, on a case-by-case basis. This decision, which was characterized as a move to open up NATO's "toolbox," meant that states such as Australia, South Korea, New Zealand, and Japan would now have greater access to those partnership tools and activities already available to the members of NATO's PfP and EAPC, including training and other educational opportunities at NATO schools.[19]

By the time NATO's members met in Bucharest in 2008, they had negotiated Tailored Cooperation Packages (TCPs) with four of the "contact countries" or, as NATO now calls them, "other partners across the globe": Australia, New Zealand, Japan, and South Korea. Similar to the individual cooperation programs offered to the MD and ICI partners, the TCPs are essentially lists of cooperative activities—including military cooperation—that have been "tailored" to individual states based on NATO's priorities and the particular interests of its partner states.[20] During NATO's 2009 Strasbourg-Kehl Summit, its members reaffirmed their intent to enhance relations with global partners "on a case-by-case basis," noting their "increasing importance to the Alliance's goals in operations, security cooperation, and efforts, through political dialogue, to build common understanding of emerging issues that affect Euro-Atlantic security, notably Afghanistan."[21]

However, despite this strong consensus within NATO in favor of such cooperation, its members have been divided over the precise form of its cooperation with global partners. Indeed, a proposal advanced by the United States and Britain at the 2006 Riga Summit to create a new political framework, or "stability providers' forum," to draw allies such as Australia, Japan, and South Korea closer to NATO was greeted by many NATO members with considerable displeasure. Although the proposal did not specify those states that would make up such a forum or even use the term "global partnership," then–U.S. ambassador to NATO Nicholas Burns, in a press briefing just before the summit, gave the impression of a new, narrowly defined political framework on a par with NATO's existing partnerships in characterizing the Alliance "as 26 members and then a mosaic of partnerships in NATO," including the PfP, the MD, and "the global partners," which he explicitly identified as Japan, Australia, South Korea, Sweden, and Finland.[22]

According to one State Department official familiar with the proposal and the discussions surrounding it, while the Bush administration was indeed advocating a new political forum, the intent was not to promote dialogue as an end in itself but rather to focus on the need for practical cooperation and to recognize formally the extent of NATO's existing cooperation with its non-European partners.[23] The proposal also recognized that despite the meaningful contributions of these states to NATO's military missions—at a time when key NATO members had imposed significant caveats on where in Afghanistan their troops could be deployed—they had not been offered an opportunity to participate fully in the PfP's activities and training. Nor did they have a voice at NATO in operational planning, which, as Ronald Asmus observes, was at odds with a "long-standing rule in NATO" that "the more troops a country is prepared to put on the ground, the greater its voice should be in Alliance decision making about such future operations."[24]

The new partnership initiative was also designed to enhance NATO's ability to operate effectively in contexts other than Afghanistan. Indeed, the notion of global partners was consistent with the Comprehensive Political Guidance that NATO adopted in Riga in anticipation of the need for a new Strategic Concept. Over the course of the next ten to fifteen years, they agreed, the principal threats and challenges to the Alliance would stem from terrorism; the proliferation of weapons of mass destruction; "instability due to failed or failing states; regional crises and conflicts, and their causes and effects; the growing availability of sophisticated conventional weaponry; the misuse of emerging technologies; and the disruption of the flow of vital resources." Given this new security environment, the NATO Allies further agreed that NATO must develop the "agility and flexibility to respond to complex and unpredictable challenges, which may emanate far from member states' borders and arise at short notice."[25] The focus on global partners was therefore also a reflection of a less geographical and more functional approach to partnership and security generally. As the new NATO secretary-general, Jaap de Hoop Scheffer, explained, in an age of "globalised insecurity," geography matters less than a country's "willingness to engage."[26]

However, as evidenced in part by the secretary-general's repeated assertions that NATO is not becoming a "global alliance" but rather an "alliance with global partners," many of NATO's members were and remain uneasy with the prospect of deepening political ties between the Alliance and states well beyond the transatlantic region. Although the Bush administration had stressed repeatedly during the preparation for the Riga Summit that its global partnership initiative should not be construed as a push for global members, some NATO members, including both France and Germany, objected strenuously to the creation of a new political framework or "stability providers' forum."

The fact that the Bush administration had identified as part of the proposed new consultative framework two states (i.e., Sweden and Finland) that were already members of the EAPC also generated concern among some NATO members that the United States, by appearing to extend preferences to some NATO partners but not others, was undermining the EAPC in favor of a more functional partnership structure. In fact, then–U.S. ambassador to NATO Victoria Nuland had floated the idea of a new political framework for global partners during NATO's annual partnership conference in Oberammergau in January 2006, while calling for the reform of NATO's existing partnerships, including potentially the dissolution of the EAPC.[27] Underpinning her call for reform was a widely shared recognition that the three rounds of NATO enlargement since the mid-1990s have had significant implications for the EAPC. Many of its original members have acceded to the Alliance, leaving behind two diverse groups of nonmembers: the neutral European states, Austria, Finland, Ireland, Sweden, and Switzerland, all well-established democracies; and the Central Asian and Caucasus states, all significantly less advanced in terms of their political and economic development.[28] The EAPC has also long been perceived as a forum for dialogue that has little capacity for action. NATO's challenge, therefore, has been to identify an agenda for action that serves the needs of these two very diverse groups and keeps the non-NATO EU partners on board.[29] Despite recognition of the challenges confronting the EAPC, however, some NATO members resented what they perceived as a unilateral effort on the part of the Bush administration to restructure NATO's existing partnerships.[30]

"Global Alliance" or "Alliance with Global Partners"?

In part, the idea of a global partnership was controversial because of a fear on the part of some NATO member countries that global partners might simply be a first step toward a global NATO or a NATO with global membership and therefore broader political influence. Indeed, several commentators—including Ivo Daalder and James Goldgeier, and former Spanish prime minister José Maria Aznar—have explicitly called for opening NATO's door to any liberal democratic state willing to contribute to its responsibilities and to what Aznar has called an "open and liberal way of life."[31] Advocacy of a more global NATO has also been linked to calls for a Concert of Democracies, an idea first proposed in 2004 by Daalder and James Lindsay.[32]

Although controversial, the proposed Concert of Democracies has attracted a substantial following, including the support of U.S. senator John McCain, who, while speaking favorably of NATO's promotion of "global partnerships" during a speech at the Hoover Institution in May 2007, urged that the United States "go further and start bringing democratic peoples and nations from around the world into one common organization, a worldwide League of Democracies" that would "form the core of an international order of peace based on freedom."[33] This idea was also endorsed in the 2006 report of the Princeton Project on National Security, a bipartisan initiative aimed at developing a "sustainable and effective" U.S. national security strategy for the United States of America."[34] Although the report advocates reforming the United Nations, it also proposes as an interim step establishing a "Concert of Democracies," both to encourage U.N. reform and to serve as "an alternative forum for liberal democracies to authorize collective action, including the use of force."[35]

Support for this Concert of Democracies presumes that an institution comprised exclusively of liberal democracies would not suffer from the paralysis that has prevented the United Nations Security Council from responding to a series of humanitarian crises dating back to the early 1990s, including those in Somalia, Bosnia, Rwanda, Kosovo, and Darfur. Indeed, despite then–UN secretary-general Kofi Annan's repeated appeals to the Security Council to reach a consensus on the question of humanitarian interventions, the council still appears as divided as ever, with Russia and China firmly committed to an understanding of state sovereignty that precludes these interventions. NATO's appeal as the core of a potential global democratic alliance thus derives in large part from its established record of acting in at least some of the humanitarian situations where the UN has been ill prepared or divided.

Some of NATO's key members, however, while expressing support for developing closer cooperation with global partners, have also raised red flags over the prospect of establishing more formal political ties with NATO's non-European allies on the grounds that such a change would undermine its political cohesion and transform its very nature. Thus, voicing long-standing French opposition to a more global NATO, former French foreign minister Michele Alliot-Marie argued in late 2006 that, whereas the Alliance should try "to improve the practical modalities" of its relationships with nonmember states such as Australia and Japan, "the development of a global partnership" could potentially "dilute the natural solidarity between Europeans and North Americans in a vague ensemble." Then–French president Jacques Chirac also argued that cooperation with global partners should be "confined to practical matters and focused on situations that may require military intervention by the alliance and its partners" so as not to distract it from its central mission as a "guarantor" of members' collective security. "The UN," he insisted, "must remain the sole political forum with universal authority."[36] France's opposition to a proposed global political framework for NATO was consistent with its long-standing objection to any initiative with the potential to heighten the Alliance's stature as a political actor on the world stage and thereby reduce the role of the European Union.[37]

Indeed, concern arose among Europeans that a global partnership could distract the United States from the Alliance's collective defense mission and enable it to circumvent the task of developing an internal NATO consensus by instead forming bilateral coalitions with like-minded external partners.[38] Like France, Germany also favored greater cooperation with these NATO global partners, but with the shared caveat that this cooperation should occur on a "case-by-case" basis and should be driven by expressions of interest from the global partners themselves. "The core of the Alliance," Germany's ambassador to NATO insisted in late 2006, "remains transatlantic."[39]

Both France and Germany also expressed concern that a more formal consultative framework would, in the words of Alliot-Marie, "send a bad political message: that of a campaign launched by the West against those who don't share their ideas."[40] The French scholar and foreign policy adviser Francois Heisbourg made essentially the same point, suggesting that a partnership between NATO and "like-minded states in the Asia-Pacific region" could potentially lead to needless friction with a rising China."[41] Similarly, Germany presented its opposition as deriving from a fear that transforming NATO into a bloc of "like-minded countries" had the potential to "set a 'global NATO' against the rest of the world."[42]

Europeans, however, were not alone in resisting the creation of a new political forum for global partners. In fact, interest in greater cooperation with NATO has not necessarily generated support for a more formal political framework, even among those considered most likely to be included. Rather, for a variety of reasons, NATO's global partners have generally expressed a preference for continuing their cooperation with the Alliance through more informal mechanisms, which they consider to be adequate for the purpose of coordinating their participation in its military missions. In the words of one Australian scholar, "the notion of an expanded NATO to include Australia in some form of membership is probably optimistic because there seems little need for it and because even at the governmental level in Canberra, the emphasis currently remains on cooperation albeit in a heightened form."[43]

The Australian foreign minister, Alexander Downer, also remarked in early 2007 that the emerging consensus that NATO will not be a "global alliance" but rather "an alliance with global partners" would be the "right outcome." He added, however, that "new threats that respect no borders have to be . . . tackled globally." Referencing new threats in Asia, including North Korea's development of weapons of mass destruction, he welcomed NATO's "initiatives to strengthen cooperation with countries outside of the trans-Atlantic base," noting that Australia would "see value in NATO expanding informal linkages to some parts of South East Asia," including Singapore, Malaysia, and Indonesia.[44]

To some degree, the fear that a more formal political framework for NATO's global partners might prompt a "clash of civilizations" also reso- nated with states such as Australia and Japan, which worried that such an entity might have negative implications for their relations with China. For Japan, this worry extended to Russia as well. Indeed, the concern existed that closer cooperation between NATO and the Pacific Rim states might push Russia and China toward the creation of a counteralliance. For example, Masashi Nishihara, a Japanese commentator on international security affairs and president of the Research Institute for Peace and Security, observes that China's fears of "being sandwiched in by Europe and the Pacific" are already evidenced by its decision to join with Russia, Kazakhstan, Uzbekistan, Kyr- gyzstan, and Tajikistan in forming the Shanghai Cooperation Organization, an antiterrorism alliance, which is also likely intended to limit U.S. influence in Central Asia.[45]

Yet despite these concerns, it is clear that NATO's members recognize the need for increased, albeit less formal, cooperation between NATO and global partners, including in contexts outside Afghanistan, and that its global part- ners are eager to cooperate.[46] Indeed, NATO's then–secretary-general, Jaap de Hoop Scheffer, spoke in mid-2008 of cooperation with global partners in Afghanistan as a "model for the future."[47] And at their meeting in December 2008, the foreign ministers of NATO's member states also stressed that the Alliance was already engaged with global partners in practical cooperation and political dialogue on issues such as terrorism and weapons of mass destruction and now sought to develop further political dialogue and practical cooperation with them in areas of common interest.[48]

The Purpose of Partners

It thus seems inevitable that the debate over the form of NATO's relations with global partners will continue. Resolving this issue, however, will require first reaching a consensus on the purpose of these partners. As Ronald Asmus has noted, NATO's members have yet to clarify whether relations with global partners are simply about lining up contributors for NATO's ongoing military missions or whether they have a broader role to play in shaping a global order more favorable to its interests and values. In Asmus's words, NATO members must ask whether partnerships with Australia or Japan are "really just about squeezing more troops and money out of them for NATO-led missions" or whether they should "be about building strategic relationships in new and important regions."[49] These are questions that must be considered in drafting a new Strategic Concept. They cannot, however, be addressed apart from a much larger question: What is now the purpose of NATO? Indeed, the debate over the Alliance's global partners is in many respects a reflection of differing viewpoints about its very identity. Perhaps it is not even too much to suggest that this is a struggle for the soul of NATO. Unless its members reach a consensus on a new strategic vision for NATO, disagreements over the structure and function of all its partnerships will continue.

To date, however, these questions have largely been avoided by NATO. Indeed, the stability providers' forum proposed at the Alliance's 2006 Riga Summit came about largely because the Bush administration had sought to push it in an increasingly global direction by focusing on opportunities for practical cooperation rather than encouraging intra-Alliance discussion regarding the development of a new strategic vision for NATO. The reluctance to engage in such a conversation was driven in part by a belief that practical cooperation and initiatives among NATO's members had outpaced theoretical understandings of its role.[50] In fact, just before the Riga Summit, U.S. deputy secretary of state for European affairs Daniel Fried asserted that "what NATO is becoming in practice—although not yet in theory—is an organization, an alliance which does not have geographic limits on its operations. It is potentially worldwide in its missions."[51]

Similarly, deputy U.S. ambassador to NATO Richard G. Olson suggested in November 2007 that the global partnership effort begun at Riga "reflects what in reality was already taking place on the ground in our various operations, especially in Afghanistan and the Balkans."[52] From the Bush administration's perspective, the actual experience of conducting a stabilization mission in Afghanistan was a transformative one. As Fried put it in testimony before the House Foreign Affairs Committee in June 2007: "The tools that NATO needs to succeed in Afghanistan—from combat forces, to peacekeeping, to global partners, to coordination with civilian donors and institutions largely define the directions in which NATO must grow in the future."[53] U.S. ambassador to NATO Victoria Nuland had also made this point just before the Riga Summit. In her words:

> When Allied Heads of State meet in Riga they will contemplate an Alliance that has grown stronger both politically and operationally because, in large measure, of NATO's commitment in Afghanistan. This has resulted in a powerful irony. While the North Atlantic Council documents reflect continuing disagreement over the nature and extent of the Alliance's power, the demands of everyday operations have forced NATO to blow past the theoretical limitations on its missions. For example, the concept of NATO global partnerships—indeed, the very term—has long been controversial. The practice of global partnerships, however, is a reality today on the ground.[54]

Indeed, NATO's experience in Afghanistan, in addition to its peacekeeping and stabilization missions in the Balkans, has also been instrumental to the evolution of its Comprehensive Approach, which is discussed in chapter 4 of this volume. Like NATO's early partnership initiatives, it recognizes the deficiencies of a purely military approach to dealing with twenty-first-century threats. In some respects it is itself a partnership initiative, insofar as it involves expanding and deepening NATO's relations with a variety of other organizations, such as the United Nations, the European Union, the African Union, the Arab League, and nongovernmental groups.[55]

A Functional versus Regional Approach to Partnership?

Adding to NATO's partners, however, will not necessarily address the continuing lack of clarity regarding the fundamental purpose of partnership. As suggested above, NATO's partnerships have over time served multiple functions. Initially, partnership constituted an essentially political means of integrating and democratizing Europe. It represented one means by which NATO could shape or construct a new European security order, grounded in the liberal democratic values enshrined in the preamble to the original North Atlantic Treaty: democracy, individual liberty, and the rule of law. The advancement of liberal democratic values has, in fact, been a stated goal of all NATO's partnerships. In the context of Europe, partnership constituted not only a proving ground for NATO membership but also an opportunity for a prospective member to assert its identity as a member of the Euro-Atlantic community. Although Europe is today more united and democratic than ever before, the project of creating a Europe whole, free, and at peace remains unfinished, and NATO appears committed to the continued use of partnerships to realize this vision. In 2006, for example, NATO continued its efforts to stabilize the Balkans by inviting Bosnia-Herzegovina, Serbia, and Montenegro to join the PfP and the EAPC. NATO's members also agreed in late 2008 to establish a NATO–Georgia Commission, designed to assist Georgia in preparing for full membership.

As noted above, however, the EAPC is not without its problems. One of the most significant is the fact that, following three rounds of post–Cold War NATO enlargement, few of the remaining EAPC members have demonstrated any interest in NATO membership, and many would not qualify because of their lack of democratic credentials. Given that preparing aspirants for NATO membership has served as a principal focus of the PfP and the EAPC, the Alliance must now confront the reality that these institutions might no longer serve as the democracy promotion vehicles that they once did.

NATO's vision of partnership as a tool for creating a borderless democratic security community in Europe was also challenged by Russia's military intervention in Georgia in 2008. As U.S. senators Lindsey Graham and Joseph Lieberman wrote in a *Wall Street Journal* op-ed article: "Russia's invasion of Georgia represents the most serious challenge to this political order since Slobodan Milošević unleashed the demons of ethnic nationalism in the Balkans. What is happening in Georgia today, therefore, is not simply a territorial dispute. It is a struggle about whether a new dividing line is drawn across Europe: between nations that are free to determine their own destinies, and nations that are consigned to the Kremlin's autocratic orbit."[56]

Thus far, NATO has failed to articulate a unified coherent response to this challenge. In fact, despite a statement in its 2008 Bucharest Summit communiqué declaring that Ukraine and Georgia will become members, its current member states were deeply divided in Bucharest on the question of whether the two aspirants should receive invitations to join its Membership

Action Plan. Although the United States strongly supported extending these invitations, the action was opposed by France and Germany, among others.

Since the September 11, 2001, terrorist attacks, however, partnership has also become an increasingly important means for equipping NATO to address new, global threats through both political and military cooperation. Although the military assets that many of its partners bring are limited, the events of September 11 served to generate new expectations of them. The Alliance now expected all its partners to act not simply as consumers of its assistance but rather as security producers, in part by supporting its military missions. This new partnership function overlapped with the early integrative mission insofar as NATO's prospective members were put on notice that their membership applications would now be evaluated partly on the basis of their willingness to act as security producers.

NATO's focus on security producers also led it to look beyond Europe for partners that are well positioned geographically or militarily to help it address global threats. NATO's efforts to reach out to partners in Central Asia as well as the Mediterranean and greater Middle East, however, were less about integration than they were about capabilities, even if the partnerships were regionally based. Its efforts to enhance cooperation with its global partners, including the stability providers' framework proposed at Riga, suggested an even stronger shift in the direction of a more functional and less regional approach to partnerships. Although the PfP and the EAPC were designed to serve purposes that were largely political rather than military, NATO's desire to facilitate greater cooperation with non-European allies stems principally from a belief that these states have the capacity not only to make significant military contributions to NATO's ongoing military missions in Kosovo, Afghanistan, and Iraq but also to cooperate with it in responding to a broad range of global threats.

However, despite a broad consensus regarding the need for all of NATO's partnerships to become more functional, many of its members did not support the Bush administration's efforts to emphasize the functional attributes of partnership at the expense of a regional focus. Indeed, Trine Flockhart and Kristian Søby Kristensen have suggested that "the overall geo-strategic reason for the European panic in relation to global partnerships is that the ideas behind it break with everything regional. NATO's other partnerships have all been argued from a regional or geographical logic. . . . Going global introduces another logic which is restructuring partnerships. Instead of geographical location, now functionality becomes the underlying logic, not 'where are

they?'"[57] Viewed from this perspective, the debate over the form and function of NATO's partnerships is really a debate over the importance of a common regional and cultural identity to the partnerships' continuing cohesion
and appeal.[58]

Ultimately, however, this debate extends to the very purpose and identity
of NATO itself. Is the Alliance's identity today more fundamentally rooted
in its historical, cultural, and geographical origins or in the values for which
it stands? As one member of NATO's International Staff put it, the ongoing
debate about NATO's partners—its global partners, in particular—is in effect
a "proxy war" over its nature and direction.[59] Ronald Asmus also emphasized
this question of identity in a series of questions he asked at the time of the
2006 Riga Summit: "Will NATO . . . continue to see itself as an exclusively
American-European alliance that increasingly works closely with non-European partners? Or should NATO define itself as the military arm of the Western democratic world and therefore be open to close partnerships with other
non-European democracies that could eventually become strategic in nature
and even grow into membership at some point in the future?"[60] As NATO
begins work on the new Strategic Concept launched at its 2009 Strasbourg-
Kehl Summit, it must finally begin to address these matters of identity,
including its relationships with different types of partners.

NATO: An Exclusively Euro-Atlantic Alliance?

Given the Barack Obama administration's stated goal of improving the
United States' relations with its European Allies, the new administration
might be tempted to avoid, as did the Bush administration, the identity issue
that ultimately underpins questions about NATO's purpose and the role of
global partners in realizing it. If, conversely, the Obama administration welcomes the debate—as it should—the United States and its NATO Allies
would do well to reflect on several lessons of the immediate post–Cold War
era. The first point stems from that fact that one of NATO's principal
strengths is that it has always had a political as well as military function. As
then–secretary-general de Hoop Scheffer observed just before the Bucharest
Summit in 2008, looking at NATO from a historical perspective suggests
that it "must be an Alliance that provides us with both immediate protection
against immediate threats, and with an instrument to shape the strategic environment in a way that is conducive to our interests and values. NATO has
always been able to do both."[61]

Indeed, NATO's successful adaptation to become a post–Cold War Alliance in the early 1990s did not occur simply because it retained secondary functions that were not specific to the Soviet threat. Rather, NATO survived due to a concerted effort to shape, rather than simply respond to, the emerging security order. It did so by embracing what was an essentially *political* rather than military mission: the construction of Europe, whole and free. Moreover, this was not the first time that NATO had actively embraced a political function. From the beginning, its members had committed themselves to safeguarding and promoting their shared values within the transatlantic region borders. Of course, in committing NATO in 1990 to enlarging the democratic space in Europe, the Allies appreciably enlarged this mission. The tools with which NATO ultimately sought to build this new European security order—including new partnerships, new institutions, and even the Alliance's enlargement—were essentially political, but so too was the mission for which they were established. As they have in adopting the Comprehensive Approach, NATO's member states must continue to recognize partnership as a vital political tool if they are to continue to shape a strategic environment that favors their values.

It is also worth remembering that NATO's identity has not only served as a source of considerable strength over the years; it also continues to evolve in ways that could eventually lead the Allies to reconceive the nature of the NATO community and its principal functions. Indeed, NATO's identity as a "pacific federation"—a community of states that have established peace with one another—was not only central to its choice of mission in the early 1990s; it also became a tool for encouraging the implementation of liberal democratic values in Central and Eastern Europe. Recognizing that many of these states looked to both NATO and EU membership for confirmation of their place in Western civilization, NATO consistently advised its prospective members that to be identified as a member of the Western world, they would be required to implement Western values in clearly specified ways. NATO's identification with the West remains an important tool for shaping the strategic context in which it must operate. Indeed, Georgian president Mikheil Saakashvili, speaking at the annual Munich Security Conference in 2008, invoked the concept of identity as a factor shaping Georgia's interest in NATO. It made sense for Georgia to "look West" and seek "integration into the Euro-Atlantic Alliance," he explained, because "we are joined by a common and unbreakable bond—one based on culture—on our shared history and identity—and a common set of values."[62]

Yet, although NATO's identity remains deeply rooted in the concept of the "West," it has evolved since the end of the Cold War and will continue to do so. As Alexandra Gheciu has observed, "The meaning of Western liberal democratic identity," with which NATO prospective members were expected to align, changed during the 1990s, shifting "away from the pre-given, fixed civilizational essences, and toward greater attention to specifying the political implications of liberal democratic values," including proper legislative and institutional frameworks. This shift in the meaning of what it means to be a member of the West, Gheciu says, has also meant that, in the post–Cold War world, there are in principle "no rigid, impossible-to-transcend dividing lines between members of the Euro-Atlantic community and those who have not yet been included. There are no fixed adversaries, no predefined civilizational otherness within Europe, and all states, regardless of their 'civilizational history' are potential members of the community of values embodied in NATO."[63]

The fact that NATO now confronts a strategic environment that differs dramatically from the one it confronted immediately after the Cold War will undoubtedly continue to have significant implications for its identity. Its growing network of security relationships is increasingly blurring the lines between its members, and in some quarters is contributing to changing perceptions of which states properly belong to the NATO community. If identities derive in part from social interaction, as constructivists argue, it is certainly conceivable that NATO's experience of working with non-European states that share its core values, and have demonstrated a willingness to defend them, might over the long term alter its identity as an exclusively Euro-Atlantic community. At a minimum, the Alliance will need to consider seriously how the fact that its values have now been embraced well beyond the borders of Europe should affect its sense of self and purpose.

This is not to suggest that NATO should become a global Alliance or a Concert of Democracies. Nor does it suggest that NATO should not count among its partners states such as Pakistan and China that are not liberal democracies. To the contrary, it makes good sense for NATO to establish functional relationships with partners that do not necessarily share its values—as it has already done with the MD, the ICI, and the Central Asian states. Indeed, such relationships are vital, not only to NATO's ability to wage the war in Afghanistan successfully but also to its ability to address a wide range of global threats. As interest-based rather than values-based partnerships, however, these arrangements will not serve the same functions as NATO's original partnerships in Central and Eastern Europe, and they may be short term or tied to a fairly narrow set of shared goals. As such, they might work better as bilateral rather than multilateral relationships. Such partnerships will still play a role in NATO's efforts to "project stability," and they may even suggest that its appeal as a political actor and facilitator of cooperation extends well beyond Europe, but any such appeal is less likely to be identity based and less likely to assist the Allies in enlarging a zone of security grounded in shared values.

As NATO's members formulate a new Strategic Concept, they will therefore need to consider ways of promoting greater interoperability and dialogue with their global partners across a wide range of areas of mutual interest and geographic space. At the same time, however, NATO will almost certainly need to recognize different categories of partners, think seriously about the purposes these various partners might serve, and then consider what sort of structures best facilitate these goals. In some cases, bilateral frameworks will likely make more sense than multilateral frameworks, although the utility of the latter should not be dismissed simply because of the divisions within some current NATO partnerships. Indeed, NATO's experience with partnerships during the 1990s suggests that a common identity can serve as a powerful source of both cohesion and attraction.

This also suggests that NATO should very seriously consider a role for some of its global partners in enlarging even further the liberal security order that it has sought to construct since the early 1990s. Although much of the interest in these global partners stems from their capacity to contribute to its military missions, unlike many current members of the EAPC, non-European allies such as Australia, New Zealand, and Japan are full-fledged liberal democracies well positioned to cooperate with NATO in shaping a global security order that is conducive to the flourishing of their shared values. In this sense, the partnership concept still has the potential to play an integrative role, albeit a very different one from the Central and Eastern Europe model, in which partnership constituted a vehicle for the democratization of the partners themselves.

Ultimately, NATO's ongoing debate over its relationships with both its regional and global partners contributes to the imperative of developing a new grand strategy. This strategy must define the larger political purposes to which NATO's capabilities and partnerships should be devoted.[64] Until NATO reaches a consensus on this larger vision, its internal tensions over the form and function of partnerships will surely continue.

Notes

1. George H. W. Bush first articulated this vision in May 1989 during a speech in what was then West Germany. See George H. W. Bush, "Proposals for a Free and Peaceful Europe," Speech at Mainz, Federal Republic of Germany, May 31, 1989 (Current Policy no. 1179).

2. For a discussion of the various changes in the way prospective members were evaluated in the aftermath of September 11, see Rebecca R. Moore, *NATO's New Mission: Projecting Stability in a Post–Cold War World* (Santa Barbara, CA: Praeger Security International, 2007), 83–91.

3. Although a commonly used term, "global partners" is not a concept agreed on by NATO. Rather, NATO documents refer to "other partners across the globe."

4. Manfred Wörner, "The Atlantic Alliance and European Security in the 1990s, Address by the Secretary General to the Bremer Tabaks Collegium," May 17, 1990, www.nato.int/docu/speech/1990/s9000517a_e.htm.

5. On this point, see, e.g., Timothy Garton Ash, *Free World: America, Europe and the Surprising Future of the West* (New York: Random House, 2004), 176–77.

6. John McCain, Speech at the 43rd Munich Conference on Security Policy, February 10, 2007, available at www.securityconference.de.

7. Declaration on a Transformed North Atlantic Alliance (The London Declaration), July 6, 1990, www.nato.int/docu/basictext/b900706a.htm.

8. Lord Robertson, "NATO: A Vision for 2012," speech at a conference sponsored by the German Marshall Fund of the United States, Brussels, October 3, 2002.

9. NATO, "Final Communiqué, Ministers' Meeting of the North Atlantic Council held in Reykjavik," Press Release M-NAC-1 (2002) 59, May 14, 2002, www.nato .int/docu/pr2002/p02–059e.htm.

10. NATO, "Prague Summit Declaration," Press Communiqué PR/CP (2002) 127, issued by the heads of state and government participating in the meeting of the North Atlantic Council in Prague, November 21, 2002.

11. NATO, "The Istanbul Declaration: Our Security in a New Era," Press Release (2004) 097, June 28, 2004, www.nato.int/docu/pr/2004/p04097e.htm.

12. For further discussion of the evolution of NATO's expectations for partners, see Moore, *NATO's New Mission*, 83–86.

13. See NATO, "Istanbul Summit Communiqué," PR/CP (2004) 096, June 28, 2004, www.nato.into/docu/pr/2004/po4–096e.htm; and B. Lynn Pascoe, "Uzbekistan: The Key to Success in Central Asia?" Testimony before the Subcommittee on Central Asia, House International Relations Committee, Washington, DC, June 15, 2004, www.state.gove/p/eur/rls/rm/33579.htm. See also Jim Garamone, "Central Asia: Crucial to War on Terror," American Forces Information Service, June 27, 2002.

14. NATO, "Istanbul Summit Communiqué."

15. Ibid. See also "Fact Sheet on Mediterranean Dialogue, Ministerial Meeting, December 8, 2004," www.nato.int/med-dial/2004/041208e.pdf.

16. "NATO Elevates Mediterranean Dialogue to a Genuine Partnership, Launches Istanbul Cooperation Initiative," *NATO Update*, June 29, 2004, www .nato.int/docu/update/2004/06-june/e0629d.htm.

17. For examples of the Bush administration's efforts to characterize partnership in the Middle East and Central Asia as having the potential to assist in the democratization of the region, see Lorne Cook, "U.S. Plans for NATO Meet Resistance of France, Germany," Agence France-Presse, February 8, 2004; and R. Nicholas Burns, "NATO and the Greater Middle East," Brussels, May 18, 2004, www.nato.usmission .gov/ambassador/2004/20040518_Brussels.htm.

18. NATO, "Riga Summit Declaration," Press Release (2006) 150, November 29, 2006.

19. See ibid.; NATO, *NATO after Riga: Prevailing in Afghanistan, Improving Capabilities, Enhancing Cooperation*, February 14, 2007, www.nato.int/docu/nato_after_riga/nato_after_riga_en.ht m; and the author's telephone interview with a U.S. Department of State official, January 2006. See also "The PfP Planning Symposium," interview with Martin Erdmann, assistant secretary-general for political affairs and security policy, January 16, 2007, www.nato.int/docu/speech/2007/s070116a.html.

20. NATO, "Bucharest Summit Declaration," Press Release (2008) 049, April 3, 2008; author's e-mail interview with a NATO International Staff member, January 20, 2009.

21. NATO, "Strasbourg/Kehl Summit Declaration," Press Release (2009) 044, April 4, 2009, www.nato.int/cps/en/natolive/news_52837.htm?mode = press release.

22. R. Nicholas Burns, "Briefing on NATO Issues Prior to Riga Summit," Washington, November 21, 2006.

23. Author's telephone interview with Department of State official, January 2007. On this point, see also David T. Johnson, minister, "The New NATO: World Class Capabilities in Global Partnership Remarks," at the U.K. Defence Forum, December 2006, http://london.usembassy.gov/ukdcm12dec06.html.

24. Ronald D. Asmus, "Introduction," in *NATO and Global Partners: Views from the Outside*, ed. Ronald D. Asmus (Washington, DC: German Marshall Fund of the United States, 2006), 1.

25. NATO, "Comprehensive Political Guidance Endorsed by NATO Heads of State and Government," November 29, 2006, Riga, www.nato.int/docu/basictxt/b061129e.htm.

26. Jaap de Hoop Scheffer, "Global NATO: Overdue or Overstretch?" Brussels, November 6, 2006. On the notion that geography matters far less than it once did in determining shared interests, see also Jaap de Hoop Scheffer, speech in Tokyo, April 4, 2005.

27. Author's interview with Department of State official, January 2007. On Nuland's speech, see also Karl-Heinz Kamp, "'Global Partnership': A New Conflict within NATO?" *Analysen und Argumente der Konrad-Adenauer-Stiftung*, 29 (2006): 3.

28. The EAPC members Albania and Croatia have begun the process of acceding to NATO. Macedonia's membership has been delayed due to a dispute with Greece over the name under which the country would accede to the Alliance.

29. See, e.g., Robert Weaver, "Continuing to Build Security through Partnership," *NATO Review*, no. 1 (Spring 2004), www.nato.int/docu/review/2004/issue1/english/art/_pr.htm and Jeffrey Simon, "NATO's Partnership for Peace: Charting a Course for a New Era," *RFE/RL East European Perspectives* 6, no. 16 (August 7, 2004), www.rferl.org/reports.

30. Author's e-mail interview with a NATO International Staff member, January 2007.

31. See Ivo Daalder and James Goldgeier, "Global NATO," *Foreign Affairs* 85, no. 5 (September–October 2006): 106; and José Maria Aznar, *NATO: An Alliance for Freedom: How to Transform the Atlantic Alliance to Effectively Defend Our Freedom and Democracies* (Madrid: Fundacion para el Analisis y los Estudios Sociales, 2005), 40.

32. Daalder and Lindsay's original proposal called for an "Alliance of Democratic States" that would address challenges ranging from terrorism to weapons proliferation to global warming, in addition to working to advance liberal democratic values.

They later adopted the term "Concert of Democracy" to describe the proposed institution. See Ivo H. Daalder and James M. Lindsay, "An Alliance of Democracies," *Washington Post*, May 23, 2004; and Ivo Daalder and James Lindsay, "Democracies of the World Unite," *The American Interest Online*, Winter 2006–7, www.the-american-interest.com/aiz/article.cfm?ID + 219&MId = 6.

33. John McCain, "An Enduring Peace Built on Freedom," Speech at the Hoover Institution, Stanford University, May 1, 2007.

34. G. John Ikenberry and Anne-Marie Slaughter, codirectors, *Forging a World of Liberty under Law: U.S. National Security in the 21st Century: Final Report of the Princeton Project on National Security*, Princeton Project Paper (Princeton NJ: Woodrow Wilson School of Public and International Affairs, Princeton University, 2006).

35. Ibid., 7.

36. Jacques Chirac, "France's Vision for NATO," *Christian Science Monitor*, November 28, 2006.

37. On this point, see Karl Heinz-Kamp, "NATO Summit 2006: The Alliance in Search of Topics," *Konrad Adenauer Stiftung* (Berlin), no. 156/2006, February 2006; John R. Schmidt "Last Alliance Standing? NATO after 9/11," *Washington Quarterly* 30, no. 1 (Winter 2006–7), 99–100; and "Predictions of Its Death Were Premature," *The Economist*, November 25, 2006.

38. Henning Riecke and Simon Koschut, "NATO's Global Aspirations," *Internationale Politik*, Summer 2008.

39. Ambassador Edmund Duckwitz, "NATO after the Riga Summit," speech at the Konrad Adenauer Foundation European Affairs Office, December 6, 2006.

40. Michele Alliot-Marie, *Washington Times*, October 20, 2006.

41. François Heisbourg, "Why NATO Needs to Be Less Ambitious," *Financial Times*, November 22, 2006.

42. Duckwitz, "NATO after the Riga Summit."

43. Jeffrey Grey, "Future Directions for NATO: An Australian Perspective," in *NATO and Global Partners: Views from the Outside*, ed. Asmus, 33.

44. Alexander Downer, "NATO in the Age of Global Challenges," speech, February 10, 2007, www.foreignminister.gov.au/speeches/2007/070121O_nato.html.

45. Masashi Nishihara, "Can Japan Be a Global Partner for NATO," in *NATO and Global Partners: Views from the Outside*, ed. Asmus, 39. For more on the possible anti-U.S. role of the Shanghai Cooperation Organization, see Geoff Dyer and Richard McGregor, "Opposition to U.S. Inspires 'NATO of the East,'" *Financial Times*, June 22, 2006.

46. Simon Koschut and Henning Riecke, "NATO's Global Aspirations: The Dispute over Enlargement Reflects Uncertainties about NATO's function," *Internationale Politik*, Summer 2008.

47. Jaap de Hoop Scheffer, "NATO: The Next Decade," speech at the Security and Defense Agenda, Brussels, June 3, 2008, www.nato.int/docu/speech/2008/s080 603a.html.

48. NATO, "Final Communiqué, Meeting of the North Atlantic Council at the Level of Foreign Ministers Held at NATO Headquarters," Brussels, Press Release (2008) 153, December 3, 2008, www.nato.int/docu/pr2008/p08–153e.html.

49. Ron Asmus, "Bucharest: The Place Where Answers Take Place?" *NATO Review*, March 2003, www.nato.int/docu/review/2008/03/ART4/EN/index.htm

50. See, e.g., Victoria Nuland, "NATO's Mission in Afghanistan: Putting Theory into Practice," *NATO Review*, Winter 2006, www.nato.int/docu/review/2006/issue4/english/art3.html; and Daniel Fried, "NATO/Riga Summit Issues," Roundtable with European Journalists, Washington, DC, October 4, 2006.

51. Fried, "NATO/Riga Summit Issues."

52. Richard G. Olson, "Next Steps: NATO's Partnerships in a Globalized Era," Brussels, November 19, 2007.

53. Daniel Fried, "The Future of NATO: How Valuable an Asset?" Testimony before the House Committee on Foreign Affairs, U.S. Congress, June 22, 2007.

54. Victoria Nuland, "NATO's Mission in Afghanistan: Putting Theory into Practice," *NATO Review*, Winter 2006, www.nato.int/docu/review/2006/issue4/english/art3.html.

55. NATO, "Final Communiqué, Meeting of the North Atlantic Council at the Level of Foreign Ministers Held at NATO Headquarters."

56. Lindsey Graham and Joe Lieberman, "Russia's Aggression Is a Challenge to World Order," *Wall Street Journal*, August 26, 2008.

57. Trine Flockhart and Kristian Søby Kristensen, *NATO and Global Partnerships: To Be Global or to Act Globally?* DIIS Report 7 (Copenhagen: Danish Institute for International Studies: 2008), 12.

58. Author's telephone interview with a NATO International Staff member, January 2009.

59. Ibid.

60. Asmus, "Introduction," 2.

61. Jaap de Hoop Scheffer, "Beyond the Bucharest Summit," speech at the Brussels Forum, March 15, 2008, www.nato.int/docu/speech/2008/s080315a.html.

62. Mikheil Saakashvili, speech at the forty-fourth Munich Conference on Security Policy, February 9, 2008, at available at www.securityconference.de.

63. Alexandra Gheciu, *NATO in the "New Europe": The Politics of International Socialization after the Cold War* (Stanford, CA: Stanford University Press, 2005), 238.

64. Four think tanks participating in the Washington NATO Project—the Atlantic Council of the United States, the Center for Strategic and International Studies, the Center for Technology and National Security Policy at the National Defense University, and the Center for Transatlantic Relations at the Paul H. Nitze School of Advanced International Studies of Johns Hopkins University—have called in their final report for the adoption of a new Atlantic Compact that would go beyond providing guidance for a new Strategic Concept. Its purpose would also be to renew a "covenant" or sense of partnership among the Allies. See Daniel Hamilton, Charles Barry, Hans Binnendijk, Stephen Flanagan, Julianne Smith, and James Townsend, *Alliance Reborn: An Atlantic Compact for the 21st Century* (Washington, DC: Atlantic Council of the United States, Center for Strategic and International Studies, Center for Technology and National Security Policy at the National Defense University, and Center for Transatlantic Relations at the Paul H. Nitze School of Advanced International Studies of Johns Hopkins University, 2009), www.acus.org/files/publication_pdfs.

CONCLUSION

Looking Forward

Gülnur Aybet and Rebecca R. Moore

In its seventh decade, NATO is faced with a plethora of challenges and the need to forge a common vision to tackle them. As Jamie Shea points out in chapter 1, however, it has been the crises in NATO's history that have led its members to forge consensuses. Perhaps the challenges that have been explored in this book, from managing relations with Russia to succeeding in Afghanistan, can assist NATO's member states in forging a much-needed new consensus. Such a consensus must encompass not only a grand strategic vision but also a common threat assessment that goes beyond a lowest common denominator among the twenty eight member states. As noted by Shea and also by Gülnur Aybet in chapter 2, achieving such a consensus will require a careful balancing between Article 4 and Article 5 of the Washington Treaty or, in other words, what NATO ought to do both in and beyond the territories of its member states to safeguard their security. It is also increasingly clear that NATO cannot face these challenges by itself. It will need to reinforce its working relationships with other institutions, most notably the European Union, build new global partnerships, and establish its Comprehensive Approach to civil–military cooperation, encompassing close cooperation with international institutions, including the United Nations, and nongovernmental organizations in postconflict stabilization operations.

Even during the Cold War, when NATO's core mission was to provide a static, territorially based collective defense for its member states, with little need for global partners or a comprehensive approach to fulfill that mission, the Alliance did not act alone. In fact NATO was at the heart of a "Western security community," constructed around the norms and values of a liberal order based on democratic governance and free market economies. In this normative sense, NATO has never stood distinctly apart from other Euro-Atlantic institutions such as the European Union, the Organization for Security and Cooperation in Europe, and the Council of Europe.

However, new challenges require new working relationships. Global security issues such as nuclear nonproliferation, stability in the Middle East and the Caucasus, the security of energy supply routes, and regional geopolitics require a far more intensive working relationship between the EU and NATO to discuss the wider strategic issues that affect the interests of both organizations. NATO's experiences in Kosovo and Afghanistan have also forced its members to recognize that success in conflict resolution and stabilization missions requires improved civil–military cooperation, including closer relationships with other institutions and civilian agencies working in the field. Indeed, as Friis Arne Petersen, Hans Binnendijk, Charles Barry, and Peter Nielsen argue in chapter 4, NATO's Comprehensive Approach seeks to make civil–military cooperation an integral part of its activities and must therefore serve as one of the principal building blocks for its new Strategic Concept. Such cooperation, they argue, is no longer sustainable on a purely ad hoc basis. Rather, NATO must begin to develop systemic, institutionalized procedures that will enable it to cooperate more effectively with other national and international actors that are in a position to contribute the nonmilitary resources so essential to meeting the conflict resolution and reconstruction challenges posed by situations like Afghanistan. Although Afghanistan has provided the learning curve for creating this new Comprehensive Approach, as Shea points out, it will take time to implement, and it remains "a work in progress as far as the [International Security Assistance Force] mission in Afghanistan is concerned."

In the short run, the fact that NATO has yet to implement the proposed Comprehensive Approach is not the only problem it faces in Afghanistan. National caveats that prevent some nations' troops from being deployed in areas where they are likely to engage in combat produces a "two-tier NATO," whereby some members provide deployments in combat areas and other do not. The "two-tier Alliance" concept is also reinforced by the fact that some Alliance members are committed to rapidly deployable expeditionary capabilities and others to a Cold War–style static territorial defense. This creates the danger of a "bifurcated Alliance," which can only be addressed by a new common threat assessment. Finding a balance between Articles 4 and 5 that reassures Allies that want more tangible "in area" Article 5 commitments without detracting resources from "out of area" Article 4 missions such as Afghanistan will thus be a key point of consideration in drafting any new Strategic Concept.

In striking this balance, NATO's member states would do well to recognize that territorial defense and the maintenance of competent expeditionary capabilities are hardly mutually exclusive or contradictory. Indeed, NATO's first out-of-area missions—which should be understood to include its enlargement and partnership initiatives, in addition to its new military missions in Bosnia, Kosovo, and Afghanistan—have all been driven by the realization that, in an increasingly globalized world, instability along its periphery is not without implications for the security of its members' own territories.

That said, the Baltic states and Poland, in particular, desire a clearer NATO visibility in their territories as an assurance of Article 5 guarantees against a resurgent Russia. Missile defense systems based on the territories of NATO's new Eastern European members—Poland and the Czech Republic—are therefore viewed by these new NATO members as a bargaining chip for securing more U.S. assistance to their armed forces and their defense. Yet, as Sean Kay observes in chapter 6, NATO's endorsement of ballistic missile defense in the region has also contributed to a deterioration of its relations with Russia. Although Kay recognizes that missile defense came to be understood as an important instrument for fulfilling NATO's collective defense responsibilities, he also argues that the effective management of new threats posed by the proliferation of weapons of mass destruction—particularly the threat posed by Iran—will ultimately require Russia's full cooperation. He therefore suggests that NATO needs to reevaluate its missile defense policy and formulate a more comprehensive strategy for dealing with nuclear weapons and missile technology proliferation that includes a more cooperative and transparent relationship with Russia based on common interests.

Ultimately, as Shea points out, reaching a consensus on a new Strategic Concept will require NATO to address three issues. First, NATO must preserve the "acquis atlantique," the sense of common purpose that has been forged over decades of cooperation. Maintaining this "acquis" will necessitate a wider debate on the Middle East, Iran, and the future of the Non-Proliferation Treaty and nuclear arms control. Second, NATO's members must resolve its "two-tier Alliance" approach to Afghanistan. And third, the Allies must reach a consensus on how to deal with Russia. On the first of these challenges, Aybet observes in chapter 2 that in the past, NATO has dealt with many successful "twin-track" approaches involving a resolute preparedness for defense on the one hand and dialogue and arms control with adversaries on the other. The combination of military hardware and diplomacy is not a new task for NATO. In fact, some of its members, such as Germany, would like to see its diplomatic forte in arms control come back to center stage.

On the third point of relations with Russia, Shea asserts that NATO needs to forge a common approach toward Russia that is based on a more realistic, functional relationship of common interests rather than the seemingly empty rhetoric of common values and partnership. At the same time, he urges the Alliance to draw some "red lines" that would prevent Russia from playing one ally against the other, thus requiring more Alliance solidarity against Russia. In chapter 7 Roger Kanet explains that many of the ills present in NATO–Russia relations today were also to be found in the political and security developments of Russian–U.S. relations in the 1990s. During that period, the United States, and the West more generally, "benefited geopolitically" from a weak Russia and, from a Russian perspective, were seen to be encroaching on Russia's legitimate spheres of influence. The Western policy of containing Russian influence in the 1990s was partially responsible for the deterioration of Russia's relations with the West.

However, as Kanet further explains, the unilateralist policies of the George W. Bush administration exacerbated the souring Russian–U.S. relationship by further undermining Russia as a regional power, especially at a time when Russia, under Vladimir Putin, was on the rise as a significant international player bolstered by its emerging power as an energy supplier. The widening differentiation in Russian and American perspectives on the world is highlighted by Kanet in his comparison of the Bush administration's *National Security Strategy* on the one hand and Russia's *Foreign Policy Concept* on the other. These two documents, approved within two years of each other, respectively signify the objectives of the United States' unchallenged rise to global hegemony through unilateralism and preemptive strikes, and Russia's challenge to U.S. unipolar dominance through its rise as a regional center of influence in a multipolar world. In hindsight, Kanet concludes that a "less triumphalist and more cooperative U.S." approach toward Russia during the early 1990s could perhaps have created an environment for Russian–U.S. relations in later decades in which Russia would have felt less of a need to pursue aggressive and revisionist policies.

Yet as Martin Smith observes in chapter 5, it is also true that personalities played important roles during the 1990s in preventing the further exacerbation of NATO–Russia tensions. For example, the good working relationship between then–NATO secretary-general Javier Solana and the Russian foreign minister, Yevgeni Primakov, should not be underestimated. Smith also notes that NATO's solidarity during its 1997 Madrid Summit, when invitations were extended for its first post–Cold War expansion, was significant in curtailing possible bilateral deals between its individual members and Russia.

A decade later, during the Georgian crisis, Alliance solidarity vis-à-vis Russia appears to have been much harder to muster.

Exploring the structural aspect of the NATO–Russia relationship, Smith concludes that both the Permanent Joint Council of 1997 (PJC) and the NATO–Russia Council (NRC) of 2002 suffered equally from the lack of an "agreed-on conceptual basis for the relationship." This would prove to be an enduring weakness in NATO–Russia relations. Although the PJC had completely failed as an early-warning consultative mechanism in the period preceding NATO's 1999 military action in Yugoslavia, the NRC saw little evidence of a spillover from low to high politics and hence did not become the forum for a wider strategic and political debate between NATO and Russia. Rather, the Kosovo crisis proved the need for more significant cooperation between NATO and Russia, especially given Russia's diplomatic efforts to persuade the government of the Federal Republic of Yugoslavia to accept the terms to end the bombing.

Yet, as Smith explains, the same imperative to work together or even restore relations to the status quo ante bellum was not evident in the immediate aftermath of the Georgian crisis. Indeed, it was the lingering impact of NATO's 1999 war in Kosovo, which subsequently led to the unilateral declaration of independence by the Albanian authorities in Kosovo in February 2008, that paved the way for Russia's recognition of the breakaway territories of South Ossetia and Abkhazia. Tensions between NATO and Russia were therefore not just a consequence of the enlargement issue but also of the recognition issue. Hence, the Georgian crisis can be seen as a catalyst for the breakdown in NATO–Russia relations from both angles. As Smith points out, in this context, both the enlargement and recognition issues have their roots in the impasse between Russia and NATO over the Conventional Armed Forces in Europe Treaty, which is linked in large part to "frozen conflicts" in the Caucasus. Thus Russia's announcement that it would suspend the implementation of the treaty can be traced back to its dissatisfaction with developments in the Euro-Atlantic area since the 1990s.

Both Kanet and Smith observe, however, that the deteriorating relations between NATO and Russia can also be understood partly as a function of Russia's recent domestic politics. Although many of the current tensions in the NATO–Russia relationship date back to the 1990s, Putin's success in reestablishing Russia as a preeminent regional power, at "great cost to political liberty and democracy," in Kanet's words, has meant that Russia now confronts the NATO member states from a considerably stronger position. At the same time, however, Russia's maintenance of a strong degree of central control over its domestic politics benefits from the existence of external enemies. As Smith points out, an enlarging NATO was an "obvious candidate."

In fact, the issue of NATO's enlargement is another area that looms high in NATO–Russia relations and is also central to the future shape of the Alliance. It is no coincidence, as Smith points out, that Russia's intervention in Georgia was timed between NATO's Bucharest Summit in April 2008, when the United States indicated its desire to extend NATO's Membership Action Plan to both Ukraine and Georgia, and NATO's December 2008 foreign ministerial meeting, where the issue would be raised once again.

Perhaps for all these reasons, the limits to NATO's enlargement for now lie in the Western Balkans. As Gabriele Cascone points out in chapter 8, the integration of the Western Balkan states into Euro-Atlantic structures was a logical continuation of the process started with the enlargements of the EU and of NATO to the Central and Eastern European countries as part of the "Europe whole and free" project. NATO's second round of enlargement, which included three Western Balkan states, also highlighted the need for a more structured approach to preparing its aspirant countries for full membership in the form of the Membership Action Plan. Conversely, due to its success in implementing defense reform in Bosnia and Herzegovina, it has been able to link conditionality through enlargement to state building. The Balkans therefore constitute a test case for NATO insofar as they involve enlargement to countries experiencing not only a political transition but also reconstruction. The process of completing the "Europe whole and free" project by integrating the Western Balkans into Euro-Atlantic structures also creates its own package of unique challenges, such as the issue of Kosovo, Serbia's deferment of NATO membership in the short run, and the unresolved issue between Greece and the former Yugoslav Republic of Macedonia over the latter's name.

NATO's continued enlargement will no doubt continue to influence its regional policies and, even more significantly, NATO–Russia relations. Indeed, as Kanet points out, the accession of the three Baltic states of Latvia, Estonia, and Lithuania to NATO in 2004—itself a highly controversial step in terms of Russia–NATO relations—led Russia to draw a red line after the 2004 enlargements that NATO should go no further. NATO's pledges to admit Ukraine and Georgia—albeit in the indefinite long term—seriously overstep this red line.

What prospects remain for the future of NATO–Russia relations? Here we can reiterate Shea's suggestion that recent tensions in the relationship, including the temporary suspension of consultations between NATO and Russia in the NRC after the Georgian crisis, constitute an opportunity for the Alliance to develop a more realistic, functional relationship with Russia that is not embedded in the rhetoric of "common values" and partnership. As Smith points out, in fact, the NATO–Russia relationship has never been a partnership based on common values. A recognition of this reality may also put a stop to the West's erroneous and patronizing suggestions that all troubles in the relationship can be attributed to Russia's insufficient respect for Western "norms." Indeed, Smith concludes that despite ongoing NATO–Russia tensions, a structured NATO–Russia relationship has become a permanent feature of the European security architecture and there is little will on both sides to entirely dismantle it.

In this context, it is also important to note the impact of NATO's new members on its policies. Kanet reminds us that the speed with which Poland and the Czech Republic ratified their agreements with the United States to establish missile defense systems on their territories, after long periods of waiting and debating, illustrates the impact of Russian intervention in Georgia in August 2008. How NATO's new members perceive their security vis-à-vis a reemergent Russia and the return of geopolitics to the region will therefore also have deep repercussions for the current debate among NATO's members concerning the Alliance's priorities for territorial Article 5 defense versus expeditionary deployments to out-of-area missions like Afghanistan.

Given the need to take a hard look at the three pressing issues of Russia, Afghanistan, and finding the balance between Articles 4 and 5, as outlined above, NATO's next Strategic Concept must not be a merely "reactive" document in relation to the challenges it faces today. As Aybet points out, its new Strategic Concept must be more than a simple update of the 1999 Strategic Concept if it is to account for new challenges. In fact such an update has already been done in a series of communiqués since its 1999 Washington Summit, but these are largely reactive documents, designed to address the changing security issues of the moment. NATO's new Strategic Concept cannot be, in Shea's words, a "shopping list" for all the challenges now facing the Alliance today and how to tackle them. Too often, in fact, NATO gets involved in an issue or a region only after its troops are deployed there. Its perpetuation on such a "reactive" basis is not viable, however, when the security challenges of the twenty-first century are so multiple and interconnected.

NATO's new Strategic Concept must therefore constitute a new grand strategy. As Aybet points out, a grand strategy is a mixture of military and nonmilitary means to pursue security and nonsecurity goals. NATO in this sense has been part of a wider "Western" grand strategy in the post–Cold

War era, which had as an ultimate goal the preservation and promotion of a liberal international order based on the norms of democratic governance and free markets. She suggests that mixing an appropriate preparedness for defense while engaging in dialogue or even arms control is not a new mission for NATO but one that it has done several times before, most notably in its dual adoption of flexible response as a military strategy and the 1967 Harmel Report as a basis for a wider political engagement and dialogue. Yet NATO's current challenges are far more complex than those it faced in 1967. A new Strategic Concept must not only serve as political-military guidance for how it should meet these new challenges—that would be nothing more than another in a series of reactive documents. Instead, a document that embodies NATO's long-term strategic vision is necessary because, too frequently, its European members imply that their presence in Afghanistan is aimed principally at demonstrating their loyalty to the Alliance. As Shea notes, if NATO's missions are based on a sense of mutual obligation rather than a shared threat perception and common security interests, they will not succeed.

In sum, NATO needs an overarching vision, one that gives substance to its members' solidarity in establishing a balance of priorities between Articles 4 and 5, asserting a common threat perception, and preventing its members from making separate bilateral deals with Russia to the detriment of its unity. This vision must also encompass the completion of NATO's unfinished business of integrating the Balkan states into Euro-Atlantic structures, upholding the rights of states that wish to join NATO while engaging in a realistic dialogue with Russia grounded in areas of common interest and cooperation, and enabling NATO to achieve its goals in Afghanistan through global partnerships and the development of the Comprehensive Approach. Finally, NATO must become the transatlantic forum for discussing wider strategic global issues, ranging from the spread of weapons of mass destruction to stability in the Middle East, including Iran's nuclear ambitions.

This is not the first time that NATO has found itself in need of a new direction in changing times. It would be wrong to deduce from NATO's mission-driven evolution in the post–Cold War era, however, that if it works in practice, it does not need to work in theory. There is still a need for NATO's leaders today, as in the past, to shape its vision and to decide the direction in which it should proceed when, as Shea says, it reaches that "fork in the road." As Ryan Hendrickson observes in chapter 3, at pivotal points in NATO's evolution, its secretary-general has played a key role in shaping its strategic vision and building a consensus in favor of new roles. Although some secretaries-general have been more inclined than others to view their office as an independent agent within NATO or as a catalyst for promoting a new direction, Hendrickson concludes that the secretary-general has played an increasingly expansive institutional role since the end of the Cold War. Indeed, he makes the case that NATO's secretaries-general have been critically important in making many key decisions in its post–Cold War transformation, including the extension of opportunities for partnership to its former rivals in Central and Eastern Europe, its enlargement, and its adoption of new out-of-area military missions in Europe and beyond.

The process of defining a new strategic vision for NATO and determining just what NATO should *do*, however, will require its member states to first come to terms with what NATO *is*. From NATO's inception in 1949, its members have attributed to it a core identity that has informed its choice of missions in significant and far-reaching ways. Indeed, its identity as a "pacific federation" or community of states that had established peace with one another during the Cold War years was clearly central to its decision in the early 1990s to reach out to the states of Central and Eastern Europe and to encourage the implementation throughout the region of the liberal democratic values deemed so essential to the pacification of Western Europe.

NATO's identity no doubt remains deeply rooted in the concept of the "West." Yet it has also evolved significantly since the end of the Cold War and will continue to do so. As Jeffrey Simon observes in chapter 9, changing demographics on both sides of the Atlantic now have the potential to alter the shared sense of a common identity that has underpinned NATO from the beginning. Simon points, in particular, to divergent immigration patterns in the United States and Europe, which he suggests could pull the states on the Atlantic's two sides in very different directions. Although immigrants to Europe are increasingly Muslim, the United States increasingly draws its immigrant population not from Europe, as was once the case, but rather from Asia and Latin America. At the same time, the United States' population will continue to grow, while Europe will be forced to confront a population that is both shrinking and aging in ways likely to contribute to a diminishing global economic presence. At the same time, however, Simon notes that the "weight" of the West is diminishing as its proportion of the world's population decreases. This trend, he suggests, could conceivably foster a stronger sense of Euro-Atlantic community among NATO's member countries, grounded in their common values and a growing sense of isolation in the larger international community. However, Kanet points out that NATO's cohesion could also be diminished as its new Central and Eastern European and Baltic member states form closer ties with the United States and distance themselves from the policy positions of its older European member states, because of their security concerns over Russia after the Georgian crisis and the energy dispute with Ukraine.

Yet, as Rebecca Moore observes in chapter 10, NATO's values have now been embraced well beyond the borders of Europe and the West, as traditionally conceived. Indeed, NATO's members have increasingly looked to "global partners" that share their values to assist them in addressing new global threats, including contributions to NATO's military missions in the Balkans and the Middle East. As Moore also notes, however, the precise relationship of these new global partners with NATO has been the subject of significant controversy among its members. Although some members have expressed concern that global partnerships constitute a step toward a "global NATO"—a development they fear would profoundly alter the very nature of the Alliance—others, including the United States, have been more inclined to see in global partners an opportunity to direct NATO's attention beyond Europe to those regions where threats to the Allies are now most likely to originate.

Indeed, the ongoing debate over NATO's global partners is ultimately a debate over NATO's very purpose and identity. Since the end of the Cold War, NATO has increasingly portrayed itself as a community of like-minded states whose cohesion depends not on the existence of a common enemy but rather on a common commitment to the preservation and promotion of liberal democratic values. Yet recent debates over NATO's relationships with other global actors suggests that, for at least some of its member states, NATO's cohesion and its identity are fundamentally more rooted in its historical, cultural, and geographic origins than in the values for which its stands. This debate goes beyond the desire for NATO to focus more narrowly on its collective defense mission. Rather, it extends to the question of just what it is that NATO should be defending. Is it defending merely territory or rather a set of values, now embraced well beyond the Euro-Atlantic area, as reflected in its increasingly close relations with global partners in Asia? These competing conceptions of what NATO *is* and what it *could be* will undoubtedly continue to challenge the process of identifying a new strategic vision to which all NATO's members can subscribe.

CONTRIBUTORS

Gülnur Aybet is a lecturer in international relations at the University of Kent at Canterbury. She is a senior associate member of Saint Antony's College, Oxford, and was previously visiting scholar at the Woodrow Wilson International Center for Scholars and at the Center for Transatlantic Relations at the Paul H. Nitze School of Advanced International Studies of Johns Hopkins University. She is principal investigator for a British Academy–funded project on NATO and EU Conditionality in Peace to State Building in Bosnia. She is the author of *The Dynamics of European Security Cooperation 1945–1991* (Palgrave, 2001) and *A European Security Architecture after the Cold War: Questions of Legitimacy* (Macmillan, 2000). Her book titled *NATO's Developing Role in Collective Security* was commissioned by the Center for Strategic Research in Ankara for distribution at NATO's 1999 Washington Summit. She has published widely on European security issues in journals such as *Security Dialogue, International Journal*, and *Journal of South East Europe and the Balkans*, as well as various op-ed articles in daily newspapers and for *NATO Review*.

Charles Barry is a senior fellow at the Center for Technology and National Security Policy at the National Defense University researching NATO and EU capabilities and transatlantic relations. As a retired combat soldier with operational experience in Asia, Europe, Africa, and Central America, he also studies joint and multinational network integration, counterinsurgency and stability operations, military strategy, and the U.S. Army's force structure. He writes, teaches, and speaks on political-military topics, U.S.–European affairs, and operational strategic concepts across the spectrum of conflict. He received a PhD in public administration from the University of Baltimore.

Hans Binnendijk is currently the vice president for research and Theodore Roosevelt Chair in National Security Policy at the National Defense University. He is also the founding director of the Center for Technology and

National Security Policy at the National Defense University. From 1999 to 2001, he served on the National Security Council as special assistant to the president and as senior director for defense policy and arms control.

Gabriele Cascone works in the Political Affairs and Security Policy Division of the NATO International Staff, where he holds the desk for most of the Western Balkan countries. From 2005 to 2008 he coordinated NATO's Membership Action Plan for aspiring members. His connections with the Balkans and experience in the region date back to the 1990s, when he served as an officer in the Headquarters of NATO's Stabilization Force. He has published a number of essays on NATO in the Balkans, including a chapter on the NATO–EU relationship in the Balkans in the book *European Security and Defence Policy: An Implementation Perspective* (Routledge, 2007), and he is currently conducting doctoral research at the University of Leuven, focusing on postconflict state building in Bosnia and Herzegovina.

Ryan C. Hendrickson is professor of political science at Eastern Illinois University. He is author of *Diplomacy and War at NATO: The Secretary-General and Military Action after the Cold War* (University of Missouri Press, 2006) and *The Clinton Wars: Congress, the Constitution, and War Powers* (Vanderbilt University Press, 2002), as well as journal articles that have been published in *Armed Forces & Society, European Security, Journal of International Relations and Development, Journal of Strategic Studies, Political Science Quarterly*, and *Security Dialogue*.

Roger E. Kanet is professor in the Department of International Studies at the University of Miami, where he served as dean of the School of International Studies from 1997 to 2000. He previously taught in the Department of Political Science at the University of Illinois at Urbana-Champaign, where he served as head of the department from 1984 to 1987 and as associate vice chancellor for academic affairs and director of international programs and studies from 1989 to 1997. His research and teaching focus on democratization in postcommunist Europe and on the foreign and security policies of postcommunist states. He has published more than 225 scholarly articles and edited more than 25 books. His publications include a number of edited volumes—*The European Union and the United States in a Changing World* (Republic of Letters Publishing, 2009); *A Resurgent Russia and the West: The European Union, NATO, and Beyond* (Republic of Letters Publishing, 2009), and, with Edward A. Kolodziej, *From Superpower to Besieged Global Power: Implications for American Foreign Policy and Global Order* (University of Georgia Press,

2008), and *Russia: Re-Emerging Great Power* (Palgrave Macmillan, 2007). He is a member of the Council on Foreign Relations.

Sean Kay is professor of politics and government and chair of international studies at the Ohio Wesleyan University. He is also a Mershon Associate at the Mershon Center for International Security Studies at Ohio State University. He is the author of *NATO and the Future of European Security* (Rowman & Littlefield, 1998) and *Global Security in the Twenty-First Century: The Quest for Power and the Search for Peace* (Rowman & Littlefield, 2006). He is the coeditor of *Security Governance in Eurasia* (Manchester University Press, 2003) and *NATO after 50* (Scholarly Resources, 2001). He has also published extensively on NATO in journals such as *Contemporary Security Policy*, *Current History*, *Cambridge Review of International Affairs*, and *Security Dialogue*.

Rebecca R. Moore is professor of political science at Concordia College in Moorhead, Minnesota. She held a NATO–Euro-Atlantic Partnership Council Fellowship from 2001 to 2003 and is the author of *NATO's New Mission: Projecting Stability in a Post–Cold War World* (Praeger, 2007). She has published on NATO and other topics in both peer-reviewed and policy journals, including *Contemporary Security Policy*, *World Policy Journal*, and *The Washington Quarterly*. Her publications also include a chapter on NATO's role in democracy promotion in a volume on humanitarian intervention, *International Intervention in the Post–Cold War World: Moral Responsibility and Power Politics*, edited by Michael Davis (M. E. Sharpe, 2004).

Peter Lehmann Nielsen is an officer in the Danish Foreign Service. During his posting to the Danish Embassy in Washington, DC, from 2006 to 2009, he was actively involved in promoting Denmark's approach to NATO's Comprehensive Approach and civil–military cooperation in crisis operations, particularly through cooperation with the National Defense University on workshops and various publications. Before his posting to Washington he worked in the Danish Ministry of Foreign Affairs' Security Policy Department and at the United Nations Secretariat in New York. He is currently serving in the Danish Prime Minister's Office.

Friis Arne Petersen is currently Denmark's ambassador to the United States. In recent years one of his key priorities in Washington has been promoting NATO's Comprehensive Approach and civil–military cooperation in crisis operations. Earlier in his career with the Danish Foreign Service, he served in various senior positions, including head of the Foreign Ministry (permanent secretary of state) and undersecretary for foreign and security policy. He has written on NATO's Comprehensive Approach and civil–military cooperation as a coauthor with Hans Binnendijk in *NATO Review*, *Defense Horizons*, and the *Washington Times*.

Jamie Shea is director of policy planning in the Private Office of NATO's Secretary-General. He was director of NATO's Office of Information and Press from 2000 to 2003, and in 2003 was appointed to the position of deputy assistant secretary-general for external relations in NATO's new Public Diplomacy Division. He was NATO spokesman from 1993 to 2000. In addition to his NATO responsibilities, he holds a number of academic positions, most notably with the Collège d'Europe, Bruges, and the Brussels School of International Studies of the University of Kent at Canterbury. He received his PhD in philosophy from Oxford University in 1981.

Jeffrey Simon is adjunct senior research fellow in the Institute for National Strategic Studies at the National Defense University. Previously he was chief of the National Military Strategy Branch of the Strategic Studies Institute at the U.S. Army War College. He has taught at Georgetown University and has held research positions at System Planning Corporation and the RAND Corporation. His publications include numerous articles and thirteen books, including *NATO Enlargement: Opinions and Options* (National Defense University Press, 1995), *NATO Enlargement and Central Europe: A Study in Civil–Military Relations* (National Defense University Press, 1996), *Hungary and NATO: Problems in Civil–Military Relations* (Rowman & Littlefield, 2003), *NATO and the Czech and Slovak Republics: A Comparative Study in Civil–Military Relations* (Rowman & Littlefield, 2004), and *Poland and NATO: A Study in Civil–Military Relations* (Rowman & Littlefield, 2004). He holds a PhD from the University of Washington and an MA from the University of Chicago, and he has been awarded the Knight Cross of the Order of Merit with Star by the Republic of Poland.

Martin A. Smith is senior lecturer in defense and international affairs at the Royal Military Academy Sandhurst. His main research interests are in the areas of international and European security, with a particular focus on the post–Cold War evolution of NATO. He is the author or editor of eight books, including *Russia and NATO since 1991: From Cold War through Cold Peace to Partnership?* (Routledge, 2006); *The Kosovo Crisis and the Evolution of Post–Cold War European Security*, with Paul Latawski (Manchester University

Press, 2003); and *Building a Bigger Europe: EU and NATO Enlargement in Comparative Perspective*, with Graham Timmins (Ashgate, 2000). His work has also appeared in such journals as the *Journal of Strategic Studies*, *West European Politics*, *Contemporary Security Policy*, *European Security*, and *International Peacekeeping*.

INDEX

Pickering, Thomas, 103
piracy, actions against, 29, 32
PJC. *See* NATO-Russia Permanent Joint
   Council
Planning and Review Process, 190
Poland
   advocacy of NATO enlargement by,
      175
   EU-Russia relations, impact on,
      163–64
   joining NATO, 65
   logistical support for in Iraq, 3
   missile defense deployment in, 133,
      135–42, 144–45, 147, 163, 172n.35
Ponsard, Lionel, 47
population trends. *See* demography
Prague Capabilities Commitment, 3, 66,
   71
Prague Summit of 2002
   defense reform, pledges of, 66
   enlargement of NATO at, 61, 67, 110,
      176, 197n.11
   new focus in response to terrorist
      attacks, 3, 223
Primakov, Yevgeny, 100, 107, 123, 159,
   246
Princeton Project on National Security,
   228
Provincial Reconstruction Teams, 92–93,
   95
Putin, Vladimir
   CFE participation, suspension of,
      114–15
   foreign policy conduct by, 99
   missile defense diplomacy by, 116, 137
   NATO-Russia relations, actions
      regarding, 107–10, 166
   reestablishment of Russia as a major
      power, commitment to, 121,
      155–58, 165, 246–47
   as Yeltsin's successor, 154, 161

Reagan, Ronald, 15, 132
Reagan administration, actions in Libya,
   58

Rice, Condoleeza, 18, 137
Riga Summit of 2006
   "Comprehensive Political Guidance"
      adopted at, 44
   future invitations to new member
      countries, statement regarding,
      183–84, 188–89
   global partners, initiation of, 224–25
   initiative for the Comprehensive
      Approach at, 79
   new Strategic Concept, guidance
      adopted for development of a, 226
   "stability providers' forum" proposed
      at, 225–27
Robertson, George, Baron Robertson of
   Port Ellen, 3, 65–68, 71, 107–9, 111,
   119
Robin, Gabriel, 60–61
Romania, 65
Rome Summit principles, 59–60, 62
Rumsfeld, Donald, 162
Russia
   challenge posed by, 4, 25–27
   demographic trends in, 213
   energy production and exports,
      renewed status as world power based
      on, 169n.12
   European Union, relations with,
      163–64
   Georgia, intervention in, 4, 113–14,
      117, 165, 173n.45
   internal divisions within NATO
      revealed by, 4–5, 168
   Iranian nuclear intentions, as diplo-
      matic player in addressing, 146
   missile defense, relations with the U.S.
      and, 115–16, 137, 144–45, 148 (*see
      also* missile defense)
   missile deployment plans by, 137,
      172n.36
   NATO, relations with (*see* NATO-
      Russia relations)
   public opinion supporting return to
      great-power status by, 170n.13

United States (*continued*)
  defense and military spending as continued focus for, 204, 206, 208
  demographic factors and the future of the transatlantic relationship (*see* demography)
  enlargement of NATO, support for, 154
  European Defense Community, promotion of, 13
  formation of NATO, hesitance regarding, 12
  France, relations with, 54–55
  France and, divides between, 69
  Hurricane Katrina, NATO relief operations in response to, 91
  immigration dynamics in, 212
  internal demographics and external global shifts in, 213–15
  Iraq, invasion of (*see* Iraq War)
  military forces in Europe and, diverging trends in, 202–8
  missile defense, limitations placed on, 142
  missile defense, relations with Russia and, 115–16, 137, 144–45, 148, 163
  missile defense initiatives by, 132–41, 163
  new members of NATO, support of policies by, 164
  population trends in, 208
  post-Cold War retention of NATO, reasons for, 158–59
  Prague Summit of 2002, position at, 3
  Russia, relations with, 155–57, 159–68
  secretaries-general, relations with, 55–56, 58
  See also Bush administration, George W.; State Department, U.S.
U.S.-Baltic Charter, 181
U.S. Civilian Stabilization Initiative, 94
Utgoff, Victor, 134
Üzümcü, Ahmet, 67

Van Gogh, Theo, 212
Vondra, Alexander, 139

Washington NATO Project, report of, 2–3, 242n.64
Washington Summit of 1999, invitations for future membership not issued at, 181
Washington Treaty. *See* North Atlantic Treaty
Western Balkans
  Bucharest Summit decisions on NATO entry, reactions to, 187–88
  countries not part of the original MAP group, question of NATO membership for, 188–93
  enlargement of NATO to the, 175–76, 195–96, 248
  MAP for three countries of, 176–87
  Stabilization and Association Process of the European Union for countries of the, 193–94
"Western security community," 48n.1, 243
Wörner, Manfred, 60–62, 71, 221
Wright, David, 66

Yeltsin, Boris, 101–2, 104, 107–8, 120, 154, 159, 161
Yost, David, 47
Yugoslavia
  disintegration of, NATO enlargement and the, 175–76
  International Criminal Tribunal for Yugoslavia (ICTY), 180, 182, 189, 197n.11–12, 198n.19
  Russian support for, 159–60
  1990s crisis in the former (*see* Balkans crisis of the 1990s; Kosovo crisis)
  See also Western Balkans
Yugoslav People's Army, 179